D0041101

Praise for *Dear William*

"It's been decades since I've read a literary offering like *Dear William*. Through inventive storytelling and heart bursting revelations, David Magee welcomes us into the making and near breaking of an American family. Tone is one of the hardest narrative tools to responsibly wield. The tone here is breathtakingly brilliant, carrying us into unexpected depths of despair and concentrated layers of joy. Walk with this book, consider new beginnings and ends of loss, and be forever changed."

—Kiese Laymon, author of *Heavy* and Carnegie Medal winner

"David Magee passionately brings to life a story of joy and devastation—one that invites the reader into a world of boundless love and sacrifice. I feel so lucky to bear witness to this vital recollection. This powerful and revelatory memoir plants seeds for a future in which his son's legacy becomes synonymous with the word *love*."

—Aimee Nezhukumatathil, *New York Times*
bestselling author of *World of Wonders*

"*Dear William* is a staggering and generous gift. Here, David Magee documents and illuminates an epic American family saga. In the writing, he translates pain into revelation, loss into propulsion, tortured despair into buoyant hope."

—John T. Edge, author of *The Potlikker Papers* and host of True South

"*Dear William* educated me as a parent, dazzled me as a writer, and moved me as a human. This book is a big, soulful account, told with fearless honesty and insight. David Magee's ardent-hearted journey will inspire all."

—Tom Franklin, *New York Times* bestselling author
of *Crooked Letter, Crooked Letter*

"*Dear William* is big and bold. It is heartbreaking and unflinching, a story of loss and grief and pain that knocks us to the floor yet lifts us back up to somehow face the world. A remarkable story."

—John Archibald, Pulitzer Prize–winning columnist
and author of *Shaking the Gates of Hell*

"David Magee connects with parents and students on the topic of substance misuse and personal responsibility like few people I have witnessed. He started a movement . . . and he hasn't let up since—inspiring students and parents as a speaker and starting a university wellness center. His voice resonates with vulnerability and common sense, with a story every parent and every student can benefit from."

—Dr. Brandi Hephner LaBanc, Vice Chancellor for
Student Affairs, University of Massachusetts

Dear William

Also by David Magee

How Toyota Became #1

MoonPie: Biography of an Out-of-This-World Snack

The John Deere Way

The Education of Mr. Mayfield

Endurance: Winning Life's Majors the Phil Mickelson Way

Ford Tough: Bill Ford and the Battle to Rebuild America's Automaker

Playing to Win: Jerry Jones and the Dallas Cowboys

Turnaround: How Carlos Ghosn Rescued Nissan

Dear William

A Father's Memoir of Addiction,
Recovery, Love, and Loss

DAVID MAGEE

Matt Holt Books
An Imprint of BenBella Books, Inc.
Dallas, TX

BenBella Books, Inc.
10440 N. Central Expressway
Suite 800
Dallas, TX 75231
benbellabooks.com
Send feedback to feedback@benbellabooks.com

BenBella is a federally registered trademark.
Matt Holt and logo are trademarks of BenBella Books.

Printed in the United States of America
10 9 8 7 6 5 4 3 2 1

Library of Congress Control Number: 2021020358
ISBN 9781953295682
eISBN 9781637740026

Copyediting by Lyric Dodson
Proofreading by Michael Fedison and Greg Teague
Text design and composition by PerfecType, Nashville, TN
Cover design by Brigid Pearson
Cover image © Shutterstock / Lunatictm
Author photo by Lo Magee
Printed by Lake Book Manufacturing

Special discounts for bulk sales are available.
Please contact bulkorders@benbellabooks.com.

For every child who is lost
and every parent who has lost a child.

Contents

This story is true, according to my memory and interpretation.
Others may recollect differently. Also, some names
and characteristics are changed.

Introduction

The officer standing in the doorway raised his arm when I stepped forward, blocking my entrance to my son's apartment. I tried to peer over his blue-uniformed shoulder to gaze around the corner to where the body of my son sat on the couch. My precious William—I saw him take his first breaths at birth, and I'd cried as I looked down at him and pledged to keep him safe forever. Now, within a day of his final breath, I wanted to see him again.

"Please," I said to the officer.

"Listen," he said, and I dragged my eyes from straining to see William to the officer's face. His brown eyes were stern but not unkind. "You don't want to see this."

"I do," I said. "It's my son."

He glanced over his shoulder, then back at me. "Death isn't pretty," he said. "He's bloated. His bowels turned loose. That's what happens when people die and are left alone for a day or more."

I didn't say anything. I couldn't.

"And there's something else," he said.

"What?"

"He's still got a $20 bill rolled up in his hand used for whatever he was snorting."

1

I felt the pavement beneath my feet seem to tilt. I reached to steady myself on the splintered doorjamb one of the officers had forced open with a crowbar just minutes before.

At his hip, the officer's radio squawked. I knew the ambulance would be here soon. "Your son—we found him with his iPad in his lap. It looks like he was checking his email to see what time he was due at work in the morning."

Yes, William was proud of holding down that job at the Apple Store. He was trying to turn things around.

"It's typical, really," the officer continued. "That's how addicts are. Snorting a fix while hoping to do right and get to work the next day. It's always about the moment."

This past year, William had been the chief trainer at the Apple Store, and he'd been talking again about heading to law school, the old dream seeming possible once more now that he was sober. He seemed to have put the troubles of the previous year, with his fits and starts in treatment, behind him. They'd kicked William out of one center in Colorado because he drank a bottle of cough syrup. Another center tossed him out because he and a fellow rehabber successfully schemed over two weeks to purchase one fentanyl pill each from someone in the community with a dental appointment. They swallowed their pills in secret, but glassy eyes ratted them out to other patients, who alerted counselors. When asked, William confessed, hoping the admission might move the counselors to give him a second chance. But they sent him packing back to Nashville, where his rehab treatment had begun. One counselor advised us to let William go homeless. "We'll drop him off at the Salvation Army with his clothing and $10," he said. "Often, that's what it takes."

We knew that kind of tough-love, hit-rock-bottom stance might be right, but our parental training couldn't stomach abandoning our son to sleep at the Salvation Army. Instead, my wife and I drove five hours from our home in Mississippi to Nashville to pick him up. He was fidgety but he hugged us firmly, looking into our eyes. We took him to dinner at Ruth's Chris Steak House, and, Lord, it felt good to see his broad smile, our twenty-two-year-old son adoring us with warm, brown eyes. We told stories and laughed and smiled and swore the bites of rib eye drenched in hot butter were the best we'd ever had.

The next morning, after deep sleep at a Hampton Inn under a thick white comforter with the air conditioner turned down so low William chuckled that he could see his breath, we found a substance treatment program willing to give him another chance.

"This dance from one treatment center to another isn't unusual," a counselor explained at intake. "Parents drop their child off for a thirty-day treatment and assume it's going to be thirty days. But that's just the tip of the iceberg." My wife and I exchanged a look; that's exactly what we'd thought the first time we got William treatment. Thirty days and we'd have our boy home, safe and healthy.

The counselor continued, "If opiates and benzos are involved, it often takes eight or nine thirty-day stays before they find the rhythm of sobriety and self-assuredness. The hard part for them is staying alive that long."

When we left William in Nashville for that first thirty-day treatment, weeks before Thanksgiving, we imagined we'd have him home for Christmas. In early December, we bought presents that we expected to share, sitting around the tree with our family of five blissfully together. But William needed more treatment. Thanksgiving turned into Christmas, and Christmas turned into the new year, and the new year turned into spring. We missed William so much, but finally, the treatment was beginning to stick. We saw progress in William's eyes during rare visits, the hollowness carved by substances slowly refilling with remnants of his soul.

Now, when parents ask me how they can tell if their kid is on drugs, I say, "Look into their eyes." Eyes reveal the truth, and eyes cannot hide lies and pain. In William's eyes, we saw hopeful glimmers that matched improved posture and demeanor. Progress, however, can become the addict's worst enemy since renewed strength signals opportunity. Addicts go to rehab because substances knocked them down, yet once they are out of treatment and are feeling more confident, they forget just how quickly they can be knocked down again.

Yet we, too, were feeling confident about William's prospects. He'd always been scrappy, a hard worker. In college, he ran the four-hundred-meter hurdles in the Southeastern Conference Outdoor Track and Field Championships, despite the fact that he had short legs for a college hurdler. He overcame that by being determined, confident, and quick. And all the time he was competing at the Division 1 level, he was an A student in the Honors College. He'd set his mind on law school and people had told us that with his resumé he could get into most any law school in America.

During that year after his graduation, in 2012, when William was in and out of treatment, I decided to quit my job as a newspaper editor to spend more time with him. I wanted to keep an eye on his progress and be there if he started to slide, so I visited him in Nashville every other week. He worried I was throwing my career away, but I would throw away anything to help him. Also, I had a plan. Instead of the daily grind of editing a newspaper, I thought quitting might provide the opportunity to return to a book project I'd abandoned. *The Greatest Fight Ever* was my take on the John L. Sullivan versus Jake Kilrain bare-knuckle boxing match of the late 1800s. The Sullivan-Kilrain fight was an epic heavyweight championship held in South Mississippi, lasting seventy-five rounds in sultry July heat, part showmanship theater and part brute brawl. I had researched the story for years and was once excited about explaining its role in the playing—and hyping—of sports today. I enjoyed sharing anecdotes over the years, like how the mayor of New Orleans served as a referee. Or that the notorious Midwestern gunslinger Bat Masterson took bets ringside on the fight, which set the standard for sports' bigger-than-life culture that continues today.

I had written other books by then, including some that found commercial success, but looking back at them from a distance, I judged none to be as excellent and useful as they could have been. I wanted the Sullivan-Kilrain fight story to change that. But William noticed as we visited that my enthusiasm for the story had evaporated. I wasn't spending time crafting the manuscript.

"You need to finish your book," William said that April when I visited him in Nashville. We were eating breakfast at a café known for pancakes, but I was devouring bacon and eggs as William wrestled with a waffle doused with jelly.

"I'm trying," I said between sips of coffee. "It's easy to tell a story, but it's more difficult to tell a good story. That's what I'm working at."

"You are a good writer. You can do it if you get focused."

"It's hard to immerse yourself in a championship boxing match from the 1800s when you and your family are in the fight of a lifetime," I said.

William looked at me over his jelly-slathered waffle. He knew I wasn't just referring to his struggles. I was referring to my own as well. Two years earlier, I'd almost destroyed our family completely through a string of spectacularly bad decisions, and we, individually and collectively, were fragile.

"William," I said. "I'm worried about you. I'm worried about me. I'm worried about all of us."

We hadn't talked so much about my own self-immolation. But now William turned to me. "I'm sorry if the mistakes I've made were what made it worse for you. I mean—" he looked off and took a breath. "For so long, I thought drugs were for fun, and I didn't realize how deep I was in. And then it was too late. I needed them. I'm sorry for making it harder on you and Mom."

"No, William, don't put that on yourself. I caused my own problems. And I want to apologize to you too. I'm sorry for when you struggled in college and I was so caught up in my own life or career that I wasn't there when you needed me. I failed you."

We went on that way for a while, saying the things that had burdened us, the things we'd needed to say for a long time. That weekend was our best, most direct connection in years. I was glad to sit beside my son over coffee and a breakfast we could live without for conversation we'd been dying for, glad I'd quit a decent editing job, glad even to stop pretending I was writing a book that no longer held my interest.

"Maybe there's another book you should be writing, Dad," he said.

"About sports?"

"About us."

I looked at his plate, the waffle barely eaten. I looked at his eyes, shining with encouragement.

"Do you ever think maybe other people could learn something from hearing about our story? I mean, when we were growing up, no one would have looked at our family, this all-American family that pretty much lacked for nothing, and predict how bad we'd crash. But maybe hearing what happened to us could help people. Maybe that's the story you should tell."

"Maybe we should tell it together," I said after a bite.

"I'm not ready yet," he said. "But one day, we'll do it."

"Yes," I said, clutching his hand in mine. "One day, we'll do it."

We said goodbye then and told each other we loved each other, and I walked to my car.

"Dad," William called out.

"Yeah?" I turned over my shoulder.

"Make sure you finish that book," he said.

I stopped. "What book? *The Greatest Fight Ever*?"

He smiled and waved goodbye.

I wiped tears away, then drove home.

That was the last time I ever saw my firstborn child.

Five sleeps later, William died. He didn't plan on dying. But the early days of sobriety can be the loneliest days. And it's never hard for an addict to find an excuse.

William's excuse was a concert that warm spring Friday when he got off from the computer store after a long week. He met up with a fraternity brother from college, who'd also moved to Nashville, for a Widespread Panic show at the amphitheater. William had seen the southern rock jam band several times in college, always getting messed up along with the rest of the crowd, the "anything goes" mood at these shows bolstered with a smorgasbord of substances. This time, however, William had planned to go easy, utilizing some of the skills he'd learned in rehab. He'd drink one beer, maybe two—that's it.

But he was out with an old friend, tapping his feet to the old jams, and the old cravings came roaring back. He drank a beer, then another. After a few beers, William wanted vodka. After some vodka, he wanted marijuana. After marijuana, he wanted cocaine. After cocaine, he wanted opiates, the one that most controlled him. By the time the concert ended, William had ingested alcohol and drugs for hours, consumption on par with his peak days of use before rehab. It's not what he set out to do that evening, but after that first beer, the night was beyond his control.

When William's friend drove them home, he noticed William's clenched jaw from too much stimulant. "Dude," he said, dropping William off at his apartment. "Go to bed, OK?"

William nodded.

"That's enough," he said. "I mean it. No more. Do you hear me?"

William waved over his shoulder and let himself into his apartment.

Once inside, William texted a dealer, buying more cocaine.

The body can only take so much, after all. Eventually, it shuts down. That's what happened to William's body—the body I used to watch soar over hurdles as he raced around the track, the body that seemed to defy gravity—as he snorted the last of the cocaine through that twenty-dollar bill.

While my son sat on his couch, dying alone, I was at our condo in Chattanooga, two hours away. I called him that night to check on him, as I did every night. When he didn't answer, I knew. I knew, though I hoped and prayed. Surely there was an explanation. He took a spur-of-the-moment trip. Something. Anything. When I called the computer store in the morning, William would be there.

But when I called the computer store, he wasn't there.

"It's not like William to miss work," his coworker said.

No, not like him at all.

I rushed to my car and sped to Nashville, praying the whole time, *Let him be alive, just let him be alive. Let him be scared or messed up or even hurt, but let him be alive.*

When I reached his apartment, I found his car parked in front, with the apartment shades drawn. *Dear Lord*, I prayed, *let him be asleep inside.*

I pounded on the door. "William," I yelled. "William!"

I called the Nashville police, then leaned against William's slate-colored Toyota 4Runner, rehearsing the lecture I planned to deliver if he was alive, if this were merely a mix-up. Thirty minutes later, the police arrived, forced the door with a crowbar, and found William inside.

I let out a muffled cry and fell to my knees on the pavement.

Two officers stayed inside and another moved to the doorway. "I'm sorry," he said quietly.

I stood up and made a move toward the door, but that's when the officer stretched his arm out, holding me back. "You don't want to remember him that way."

The officer was right. That's not what I wanted.

I preferred instead to remember the sweet toddler who curled into my lap to cuddle as if I was a giant safety blanket.

I preferred to remember that shy little boy who sang in the church choir, wearing his red robe with a white collar, belting out words to "This Little Light of Mine," slightly off key but sounding just right. "Don't let Satan (blow) it out! I'm gonna let it shine. Don't let Satan (blow) it out! I'm gonna let it shine."

I preferred instead to remember that middle schooler who collected Beanie Babies, collapsing in a faux faint when he received the most-desired Diana Bear for Christmas.

I preferred instead to remember that teenager who realized he'd never be great at football and instead turned his passion to track and field, who stood on the winners' podium at the state meet and dipped his head with a modest grin as the officials draped a medal around his sweaty neck.

I preferred instead to remember that college man who endured a two-hour track practice and a two-hour study session for Spanish, then had so much energy to laugh and spend time with family and friends.

Yet, less than one year after graduating from college with so much promise, William was hauled away on a gurney with a sheet covering his head. I stayed outside, watching with a hand over my mouth muffling sobs. Two days later, we had him cremated, and I didn't ask to see his body before they reduced it to ashes. At the memorial service, I declined to speak, crippled by pain and a sense of responsibility. Besides, I did not understand what happened to William, what happened to me, what happened to our family, so how could I use words to put his life in perspective?

But I was wrong about all of it. I shouldn't have listened to that police officer. I should have fought my way to William's side, wept beside his body. I should have stroked his wavy brown hair back from his forehead and kissed his cheeks. I should have found words to tell him the love in my heart. I should have held his hand, and I should have closed his eyelids on the world.

Now, I'm ready to tell our story, the story of the greatest fight. It is for you, my dear William, the book you told me to write. I hope and pray it makes a difference for someone, somewhere.

Chapter One

Beneath the Surface

I grew up in a big, old house with tall oak trees in the front yard and a dachshund called Happy. And happy is what we might have been called by others who peered through the window of that big, old house and saw our family of four: a daughter, a son, and two parents with college degrees and jobs.

But inside the house, where Dad makes our dog live in the basement, where the fleas are so bad we can hardly approach, we're not so happy. None of the four of us are blood related. My sister and I have both been adopted. And my sister isn't happy about it, erupting into nighttime rages that distract me from homework and sleep. Also, my dad is, well, odd. Old and odd. He buys expired food from the discount bin, which I have to serve my friends when they come over. He works hard at his hobbies—beekeeping, landscaping, cake baking—but his wacky attempts at mastery usually end in failure, his depression, and my shame.

His newest obsession is me. My skin, to be exact. He wants a clear-skinned boy. I'm twelve, and my nascent puberty is more substantial than his will.

"You're too handsome to have these marks on your face," Dad says, running his fingers across my forehead. I fidget at his touch. I just want Clearasil, I tell him, like everyone else in junior high. My father, a professor at Ole Miss down the street, has a PhD in microbiology; he will solve this microbial problem and save precious money at the same time.

"Clearasil is inherently flawed," he replies, his breath hitting my face. "It's a solution used after the fact. The whole point is to prevent the oil from gathering in your pores and becoming infected, causing bacterial eruptions, in the first place."

His eyes peer through glasses perched on the tip of his nose, and I turn my gaze away. He wants me to look like a clean-cut boy with silky smooth skin he can pose in photos.

I want him to look like something besides an embarrassment. He wears decades-old suits that he preserves in mothballs. He smells like a grandpa, and he looks like one too. His head is bald, with only a gray fringe.

"If I can solve your face, we might even get rich!" he adds, dreaming of his long-awaited recognition. He also thinks he's going to cure cancer. I hope he does, if only because he could buy a new car and stop driving his old Dodge Dart.

Days later, I find a plastic container on the shelf of my bathroom sink. It has instructions typed on white paper strips, taped to the side.

Swab affected areas with a cotton ball and solution in the morning after the shower. Swab affected areas with a cotton ball and solution at night.

So, I do it because it'll be the first thing he asks me. The thick pink concoction doesn't absorb into the cotton ball. It lays on top like a layer of goo, and when I swipe it on my face, it does the same thing.

I don't see how it can work if it doesn't soak in. I know pimples start way underneath. I can feel them before they erupt, red and volcanic, making me want to squeeze them into submission. But if I don't comply, Dad will withhold my weekly allowance, and I need the eight dollars to get into the skating rink or the movie theater on Fridays and buy a drink and a snack. I wonder if my real dad, my birth dad, would keep me hostage by withholding my allowance.

I'm desperate to flee the terminal loneliness of my house and go roving in Oxford, a town in which I know who lives in the houses in every direction, and I know the store owners, the schoolteachers, the preachers, and the professors on campus. Our town, with about eight thousand students and eight thousand residents, is a kind of town-and-gown Mayberry, nestled into the gentle, rolling hills of North Mississippi. We're big enough for a five-day-a-week newspaper, even if it has only eight pages a day. But we're small enough that you have to drive to Memphis for a commercial airline flight, and Mom has to drive me to Tupelo to buy cleats. We have one two-screen movie theater, a skating rink with disco lights, and a new McDonald's that's such a big deal our elementary school practically dismissed for several consecutive afternoons as we all got hamburgers, fries, shakes, and smiles. Yet the university keeps things from feeling too cloistered and precious and excels in developing All-American quarterbacks, Rhodes Scholars, and Miss Americas—Mississippi had back-to-back crowns in 1959 and '60, in fact.

My parents aim to make our patchwork family of four fit picture-perfectly into the quaint community. We take an annual Christmas card photo, posed in bulky sweaters we rarely ever wear otherwise, with me holding a ball and my older sister, Eunice, holding a clarinet she doesn't much play. They named us from the Bible, and I'm OK with David, but she hates Eunice, visibly withdrawing each time Dad says her name.

Our family home is among the most picturesque in the town, one that visitors who come for football games, university symposiums, or campus visits take one look at before proclaiming, "I want to live there." Constructed in the late 1800s, painted a Williamsburg yellow, its big wraparound front porch has swings just perfect for reading or watching folks on a stroll. You can walk for five minutes in one direction and land on campus, or walk five minutes in the other direction to arrive at the town square.

We have a big front yard, which Dad manages with hours of Saturday morning yard work. He is clumsy with pruning, hacking away to achieve symmetry but failing, much the same way he gives me haircuts in the kitchen. At least, that is, until Mom sneaks me off to a salon on a Saturday morning while he relocates the azaleas.

I think nothing can be worse than his yard work, until the hot morning he skips the yard work, deciding it's time we bond over father-and-son activities. First up: golf. I know he knows I love all kinds of sports, though neither of us has ever golfed before. We walk the university course since he won't pay for a cart, his face growing redder and redder as the temperature climbs. After the first nine holes, we pass the clubhouse, where he insists on stopping. Inside, he slumps into a chair and vomits on the floor, splashing his unfashionable plaid trousers. I hand him a towel, looking around to see who might be watching.

Dad has just enough energy to raise his head. "Call the ambulance."

I ride in the back of the ambulance with him on the way to the hospital, growing scared as he vomits up the salt tablets the medical technician gave him. It occurs to me he might be dying; these might be our last moments together. I hold an ice pack on his forehead and see my tears are splashing on it. "Dad," I say, "I'm so sorry. I'm so sorry you felt we needed an athletic father-and-son activity . . ."

"I'm sorry I got sick," he says, barely lifting his head.

"No," I say, as more tears drip, "I'm sorry."

In the end, we learn he had heat stroke, caught just in time since we'd reached the clubhouse before the back nine. So there are no repercussions, except for the fact that everybody has heard. When I bicycle to the ballpark for baseball, my friend's father approaches. "I heard Lyman had a heart attack," he says. "Is he gonna be all right?"

Only grandfathers had heart attacks, and I'm embarrassed by my father's age: forty years older than me. I wonder how old my birth father is. I wonder if he could throw me a football or take me hunting or walk a golf course without puking.

Dad can't catch a ball, even when I throw it underhand. He didn't play sports in high school because boys teased him, calling him a sissy. In college, during the war, the football coach encouraged him to fill a needed position on the offensive line because of his girth but ran him off after the first week because he "moved like a girl."

He fits in better in our university town than he ever did in the army, his awkwardness less of a spectacle. And some trappings of his job seem cool to my friends, like the human skull he keeps in his study at home and the slice of a human lung from a lifetime cigarette smoker framed on the wall. The lung is black, with holes bored out from years of tar, and Dad brings students back to see it, hoping they'll avoid cigarettes. I bring friends to see it, too, simply because I want to impress them. The only time I feel terrible is when I show my friend Jon. We are eight or nine years old, and Jon's mother, Dean, smokes several packs of cigarettes a day. He looks up at the pockmarked lung for the longest time.

"That's what my mother's lungs look like," he finally says.

The best thing about Dad's job is the mice he brings home from the biology lab. I keep them as pets and name them all Stuart after my favorite book, *Stuart Little*. Eunice doesn't like the mice; she keeps a hamster named Mabel. But one afternoon, Mabel seems sick. She's dragging her rear end around.

"Her rectum has prolapsed," exclaims Dad, bending close, who always claims he should have gone to medical school. He fetches some dissecting tools from the biology department, threads his arms through his white lab coat, and tries to surgically repair Mabel's prolapsed rectum with a clumsy incision and stitches. Mabel dies two days later, and we bury her in a shoebox in the backyard while Eunice sobs, hysterical, "Dad killed Mabel!"

I silently pray that Dad will never play doctor on me.

Yet here I am, waiting for his pink goo to dry on my face. I've been ordered not to squeeze my pimples, not even to touch my face beyond applying his miracle serum. But my fingers feel itchy. To avoid the mirror, I walk up and down the stairs, passing the closed door of Eunice's room where I can hear her cursing, screaming into her pillow. Eventually, I can't stand the urge. I return to the bathroom and squeeze the most massive red and swollen bumps so they erupt, splashing pus into the mirror, leaving my face bruised and throbbing.

Luckily, Dad is distracted. He's in the kitchen, making a special dinner. He's not hard at work cooking for Eunice or me, and certainly not for Mom—he'll get her a card for Valentine's, a blender for Christmas, but I've never seen them kiss without pursed lips or hug with torsos touching. He's not making *her* a four-course meal, that's for sure. So who will be the recipient of these hours of labor, this gravy over which Dad stops humming in order to lean in and taste it? His students. His good-looking male students.

When Dad cooks for these young men, he aims for fancy gourmet, though he buys from the bargain bin at Kroger and uses older items from the refrigerator, and his results are more like Shoney's. He serves cake with too much icing, decorated with candies and candles. And then, after dessert, he gets out his camera, insisting on photographing his male guests, once the plates—and the rest of his family—have been cleared away.

It's almost always premed students he invites over—handsome, clean-cut, ambitious. In addition to being chairman of the biology department, Dad is the premed academic advisor. When he's out of the room, I've heard them say that they endure sitting for the photos because they get preferential class selection.

When I was small, these dinners were different, and I was proud of them, and so was Mom. It was the late 1960s, and the Ole Miss football team was nationally ranked, yet college football hadn't yet become big business. The players still had free time, gladly accepting TLC and a home-cooked meal from the community. Dad looked out for the pre-med football boys, like Bruce Newell, the quarterback who led Ole Miss to the Sun Bowl and headed off to medical school with a recommendation from Dad or Wyck Neely, the defensive back with the chiseled jaw and determined-to-win work ethic.

Wyck tosses a ball to me in the yard, and his girlfriend, Lila, is my first and best babysitter, telling Dad that I run fast, that I'm "a natural with a ball." Wyck wants to become a dentist, and Dad helps him get to LSU for dental school. We have framed Ole Miss game jerseys from Wyck and Bruce and pictures of Archie Manning bouncing me on his knee during a dinner. Archie is a Heisman Trophy finalist who puts Ole Miss on national TV in prime time. Most Americans only have a few TV channels in 1969, so if you get on ABC for a rare night game, it seems like half the country is watching. After we almost beat vaunted Alabama, coached by legend Bear Bryant, losing only by 33–32, Archie and Ole Miss win America's hearts, and by the time he leaves in 1971 for the NFL, the football boys are officially big deals and don't have as much free time.

The dinner guests keep coming, however, though with each passing year, their qualities change. Most remain premed students, but they morph from chiseled football players to girl-chasing fraternity boys with boyish faces to a mix of girl-chasing fraternity boys with boyish faces and fraternity boys with boyish faces rarely seen with girls.

Tonight, Barry and Robert are coming over. Both are premed and outgoing, of course, one talking openly about his girlfriend, which interests me. Girls are mysterious because I see cute ones I want to talk to, but then there's Eunice, who doesn't much like me and isn't so sure about our family. Eunice is three years older and rarely, if ever, sits with us for dinner or has friends over. I'm not even sure she *has* friends except for mine, as she self-invites herself into our neighborhood base-ball games played on the few open lots sprinkled around town.

Occasionally she'll take a plate into the living room and eat with her nose an inch from the TV while I sit with Mom and Dad in our kitchen at the yellow formica bar shaped like the letter *J*. Most nights, after dinner, she's in one kind of rage or another in her bedroom, screaming "fuck" and "goddamn it," lashing out at our mom (who stays with her for hours) about Dad.

These are not words I've heard anyone else in our house say. Mom and Dad don't cuss, and they don't drink alcohol. Our family goes to the Southern Baptist church up the street, where Dad's a deacon and plays the organ on Sunday.

"Why the fuck did you name me Eunice?" she screams.

From what I've learned at church, I've identified Eunice, possibly, as the devil. I don't hate her for it because I know she's trying to make sense of everything too. I was adopted from the same place she was, a Southern Baptist home for unwed mothers in New Orleans, but three years later.

Eunice wears denim overalls and a striped railroad engineer's hat pulled down low over her forehead on most days, so low we can't see her eyes. Dad urges Mom to put her into dresses, and Mom says she tries, but Eunice is beyond cajoling or bribing. She wakes up with her temper at a simmer, and the day stokes her anger. By nightfall, it spews out like a raging volcano of devil fury. I wonder if anyone still performs exorcisms. That movie scared all my friends and me, but it scared me for a different reason: I lived that story too many nights

When visitors come into the home, I wonder if they sense the danger and how lonely I am. Wyck, Lila, and the others who pass through, mussing my hair, giving me a friendly punch in the shoulder, I wonder if they sense that I want to leave this house, leave with them to never return. I wonder if they sense that I feel like somebody dropped me off at a strange babysitter's house years ago and never came to get me.

"Do you like science?" Robert asks, suddenly turning to me after a brief silence hits the table.

"No," I say, hoping he sees that I'm different from my father, the scientist. "I like basketball. And the weather. I want to be a basketball player or a weatherman."

Mom focuses on spooning gravy onto my plate.

"Robert is applying to Notre Dame for medical school," Dad announces, moving the conversation away from me.

I'm sure after dinner, Dad will insist on taking pictures. Dad acts like he's a professional photographer, combing Robert's hair aside with his fingers. It makes me squirm, and I can tell from Robert's tense shoulders that he doesn't like it either. "As long as you keep letting me enroll for the best classes before the football players," Robert says, turning his face toward me as if to explain.

There's a thump upstairs and a high-pitched, half-stifled scream.

"Excuse me," Mom says quietly, as she shoves back her chair. "I'll be back in a minute."

She won't be. She never returns once Eunice unleashes. She'll be in there for hours while Dad loads the dishwasher and puts away the leftovers and I get to talk to the college boys.

"We live down the street," Barry says, angling his thumb over his shoulder. "Come by anytime if you just want to hang out."

After our guests are gone, I clear my dishes and head straight for the stairs, even though I'll have to listen to Eunice's pillow-muffled agony and Mom's weary replies. I have homework, but I know already I won't be able to focus. Instead, I'll lie down across the covers of my twin bed, straight as a pencil, tuning my clock/radio onto Nashville's 15 WLAC. The AM radio station plays album rock, and the signal barely reaches our house, several hundred miles away, but the sound will be loud and clear enough to drown out Linda Blair next door.

I'm almost at the top of the stairs, wondering if I can dial into Gary Wright's *The Dream Weaver* to get me through the night when I hear Dad's loafers clomping up the stairs after me. This never used to happen when I was younger. I used to spend entire evenings without him speaking a word after our quick dinner. I slightly pick up my step, hoping to get to my room and close the door before he speaks to me.

"I hope you're applying my acne solution as directed," he calls from behind. "Let me watch you apply it. The experiment can't work without consistent application."

I want to take the pink sticky goo and throw it down the stairs. And I'd like to throw Dad down the stairs too. If he accidentally tripped, would I run after him?

But it's easier to give in, and besides, he's my father—even biologically, according to my legal birth certificate. The state of Louisiana decrees that I was born in New Orleans on November 27, 1965, to Betty Magee and Lyman Magee. Never mind that Betty and Lyman Magee were not in New Orleans on November 27, 1965, and she never gave birth to a baby. A fake birth certificate: the ultimate cover-up.

Mom and Dad met in Baton Rouge, Louisiana, in the 1950s at the First Baptist Church. He'd gone to a small Baptist college in Louisiana and now was a PhD student at LSU, with a part-time job as the church organist. She was the church secretary, a recent graduate of a small Baptist college in Mississippi. Since they were both single, church members encouraged them to date. Mom says she'd had a boyfriend in high school, but Dad had never had a date in high school or college, and she was his first kiss, a clumsy delivery she overcame to reach the second date.

In the early 1960s, they moved to Oxford, where Dad took a job as a biology professor at Ole Miss. They wanted a child, but Mom had a couple of early miscarriages and was diagnosed with endometriosis. The doctor said they weren't likely to have children, so they approached their church pastor, who recommended Sellers Baptist Home for Unwed Mothers in New Orleans.

Sellers was the regional adoption center managed by the Southern Baptist Convention. Families sent girls there in secret, telling friends and family they were sick or away at school, with plans for the girls to resume life post-delivery.

In a two-story dormitory on New Orleans' Peniston Street, Sellers housed thirty-six girls and staff. Opened in 1933 and modernized in 1960 with a red brick rebuild, Sellers was conveniently just around the corner from Baptist Hospital, one of the few excursions girls made during their stay. They had little to do but play card games, take short walks, and watch out the windows for cars coming and going, getting glimpses of the couples coming to pick up babies for adoption. They daydreamed about where they would go next and what tightly crafted script they would use to explain their prolonged absence.

"Everybody needs a story," director Allegra LaPrairie reminded the girls. "And Sellers isn't a part of your story. This is just a pit stop, and you will forget like it never happened."

At Sellers, girls were encouraged to stay on a first-name basis. While completing their dormitory chores and kitchen duty, they dreamed of baby names like Kimberly, Lisa, James, and Michael but left their babies for good after several days, leaving their baby behind to be claimed by someone else who would immediately give it a new name.

Mom and Dad let me know I was adopted early on. Same with Eunice. But even if they hadn't told us, we might have guessed. We don't look alike, and we don't act alike, and we mix like antagonistic species trying to survive in the same cage. But legally, we were born to the same mom and dad, according to the state of Louisiana.

Dad's family lives in Louisiana, so we don't see them much. My dad's father died about the time I was born, and his mother, Ma Maw, is aged and sick, meekly fighting off the cockroaches and mice thriving on the scraps she leaves for stray neighborhood cats. They had four children, and money was scarce.

Mom's mother, Mom-Mom, is different. She and Granddaddy live in East Mississippi at a crossroads called Prairie Point, with cotton fields in every direction and one general store with a post office. Money is scarce enough that Mom-Mom is the only woman school bus driver in the county, but not so scarce that she can't buy Eunice a

Honda minibike before she's big enough for it, and not so scarce that she can't buy herself a flaming red Buick with whitewall tires. Mom-Mom dyes her hair a flaming red to match every two weeks. Mom is their only child, and Mom-Mom dotes on her and Eunice, but she doesn't seem to like me.

Eunice calls me a crybaby, as does Mom-Mom. When together, Mom-Mom talks about me like she talks about the "nigroes," her term for the black folks who live in the frame houses with dirt floors and wallpaper consisting of yellowing newspapers on Granddaddy's 250-acre farm. The civil rights movement taught her the N-word wasn't OK, but she prefers the passive-aggressive "nigroes" to the more accepted "negroes."

When Eunice calls me a crybaby, Mom-Mom agrees loud enough that I can hear her, and I cry louder.

"She doesn't mean it," Mom says, attempting to calm.

But she does.

"I warned them about adopting someone else's child," Mom-Mom once told me during a Eunice tirade, as if forgetting that equation involved me too.

I have adopted friends who bond with their families, and I do, too, or I try, because I crave connection and because I don't have anywhere else to turn. But I know I didn't come from them, and I don't look or act like them. I can't help but wonder if somewhere out there are the people who made me, the people who would understand me. People who wouldn't shame me for being a crybaby but praise me for being sensitive. People who would want to discuss *Stuart Little* and football's greatest quarterbacks and the difference between hurricanes and tornadoes, people who love the Steve Miller Band and people who would laugh at my jokes. People who look like me, with my dimples and cowlick and my deep "Ha!" laugh that startles my parents every time.

In Cub Scouts, we make a communication device from tin cans and string, and I imagine it's powerful enough to connect to faraway places.

I take one can in my hand and place the other on my closet door. Sometimes, at night, I put the can to my mouth and whisper, "Hello, Dad? Are you there? It's me, David." No reply but my heartbeat.

Now, my adopted father has almost caught up with me on the stairs. This sure would be a good time for my birth father to make his appearance.

"David," Dad calls, only three steps behind me.

I don't answer but walk straight to the bathroom and pull a cotton ball out of the bag in the cupboard. I pour the gooey red syrup onto the cotton ball and begin to wipe it on my zits, which seem noticeably worse. No girl will ever be interested in this face. I'm a zit-covered loser.

Dread seeps through me as Dad leaves the doorway to stand close to me, watching my face in the mirror.

"I don't see how this goo can work without it sinking in. I think it's making it worse," I say, the words rushing out. My face turns red from anger and embarrassment and panic, not to mention the goo. Now I don't even look human.

"That's simply not true," Dad says. His confidence about being right is the thing I despise the most. If one of us knows something he doesn't, he's puzzled, questioning how we learned this fact that escaped him. Now, he's watching me with what might even be pride—in his concoction, not me. He's sure it's the cure the world has been waiting for, even though I can feel my zits growing more massive as I shellac my face with his Frankenstein lab goo.

I need a plan, which means I need Mom. She always finds the way to tiptoe around conflict. She's skilled at it due to long practice; she'll do anything to avoid confrontation or hurting another's feelings.

A couple of days later, as she's driving me to school, I burst out with my problem. "Dad comes into the bathroom every night and watches me put his stuff on my face. It's making it worse." As soon as I say it, I feel relief that somehow I communicated that it was both him and the medicine that was intolerable.

"We'll take care of that today," Mom says, "after school. We'll go to the drugstore and get the stuff that works."

Mom comes home from work, and instead of checking in with Eunice, who is already upstairs, she waves me into the front seat of her car, and we head a few blocks beyond campus to the town square pharmacy. Down the shiny linoleum aisle, I watch her sensible one-inch heels hit the mosaic floor with purpose. When she finds the right section, she stops.

"We can try a few to see what works best," she says, giving me half a smile, her full one pretty much cramped by all the guilt she can't shake.

I reach for Clearasil. "This one, for sure," I say, already picturing a clear face and soaring popularity.

Back home, I conceal my package. Mom has already told me where to hide it in the bathroom.

"Be sure to still pour a little of Dad's stuff on a cotton ball morning and evening," she says. "I'll take care of him coming in there."

Mom isn't at the dinner table again, though she sets places every night for herself and Eunice. It's like she wants anyone who might be looking through the window to know the family Christmas card isn't a total lie. "See, here's the table all set for everybody to sit down together."

I eat everything on my plate and pray Mom doesn't forget to tell him. I can't stand another night of him looking at me with that stuff on my face, which now looks like a pepperoni pizza made by a hungry drunk.

I stop on the stairs to eavesdrop. "Lyman," she begins, "you can't go up there and watch him every night. He's a teenager now. Show you trust him, and he'll be trustworthy. It's making him uncomfortable."

Yes, I'm uncomfortable. I want to scream like Eunice, "Stay the fuck away from me, don't touch my face, don't touch my hair, and don't touch me!"

Instead, I listen, then tiptoe up the squeaky steps to my room. I like what Mom says about being trustworthy. It sounds right to me, except that we are all lying, every single one of us, one way or another.

My acne improves with the Clearasil, but the evenings in our house do not. While Eunice goes quietly to school in the day, at night, she convulses behind a closed door. I know I should crack my books, but homework never works as an escape, never transports me from the house's turmoil.

I have a phone in my room with a long cord that reaches the bed, and after dinner, I dial up one girl after another, sweet-talking them in an attempt to cultivate a girlfriend and crumbs of affirmation. About the time they have to stop talking to finish homework, my adopted sister's attitude has really lathered up.

"He's gay, goddammit!" Eunice screams at my mother, the words piercing through her closed door and mine. "Don't you know that? What are you going to do about it? Fuck it. He makes me so fucking mad."

My stomach starts hurting. I can hear my mother's conciliatory tone but not her words. He's gay; my dad is gay. I'm not actually certain what gay is, aside from something no boy wants to be called. I know it's about boys liking boys or girls liking girls.

I know Dad wants to impress his male students the way most professors want to impress their wives. I've never seen him talk to girls, only boys. And then there are the photo albums on his hidden office shelf full of Dad's photos of Robert and Barry and Mark, a student who's sculpted like a bodybuilder and calls himself a model.

Mark came from a household of nine children and little money, and my father buys him clothes and food in return for taking his picture. Once, while visiting our house, Mark pointed at me. "You've got this handsome son," he said. "You should take his picture." Dad looked the other way as if he didn't hear.

At about the same time my face improves, Eunice's life does too. For her sixteenth birthday, Mom and Dad buy her a car, a silver Honda Accord, the first new car in our family in five years. He'd initially thought Eunice would get a used car, but she badgered him with pamphlets from a Honda dealership in Memphis until he shelled out the cash.

A couple of nights a week, she's now working at a horse stable owned by a couple named Paul and Cathy, who take Eunice in like one of their own. I'm jealous because she gets to start over with a new family. While I'm waiting for my birth family to appear on our doorstep, Eunice puts an escape plan into action.

She has new confidence, and she surprisingly offers to drive my friends and me to the movies on Friday nights. She has a few friends of her own, either because of the car or because the car makes her feel better about herself. Either way, she's starting to look and act a bit mainstream.

The house is quiet now in the evenings, and Mom and Dad don't seem to question how much time Eunice spends away. She's sometimes gone for days, eating dinner at Paul and Cathy's, then staying overnight. It's a relief for me, for all of us, but I sense the storm hasn't gone away.

But I'm thirteen with new hair growing under my arms producing a smell that Right Guard isn't rightly guarding. I'm exploring the neighborhood, too, on my own. Early one evening I knock on Barry and Robert's door nervously and find they're both at home. Robert grins and opens the door wide. "C'mon in, David! How'd you sneak away from Lyman?" I love it that they call Dad by his first name, like I'm one of the guys.

I find a space on the sofa and sit, looking around at the scattered books and papers stacked everywhere, the half-filled bottles of booze and wine as if they're waiting to be finished off. They each take a seat where they can find one, and sure enough, Robert finishes the shiny brown swig that's left in a whiskey bottle, then gives me an amused look. "We were just sitting here reminiscing about going streaking."

Barry finds his own half-empty bottle and nods. "Shit, that was fun," he says before tipping the bottle up.

I remember that streaking had been a fad. There had even been a hit song: "He's just as proud as he can be / of his anatomy . . ." Ray Stevens's ode to running naked with others went to number one.

"Cops ruined it," Barry says.

"Only because you got caught," Robert says, laughing.

"You streaked?" I asked, my cheeks warming.

"It's a great way to get close to naked girls," Barry says. "It was worth it."
Sweat breaks out on my palms.

"Worth breaking his leg!" Robert barks.

"What?" I ask.

"Yeah, I'm running naked down the street, following this girl who's got a great ass," Barry says. "I mean, amazing."

Robert fills in. "Yeah, running because the cops were chasing us. I got out of there like an intelligent human being, but Barry kept staring at this girl's ass jiggling in front of him, so he didn't see the curb. Down he goes, boom, and his leg bone snaps in half!"

I look at Barry for confirmation, and he nods.

"Yep, the police grab me, put me in handcuffs, and I can barely get to the cop car. I'm screaming in pain. So they take me to the hospital, and I get a cast from here to here." Barry indicates his entire leg. "So then I'm back in class the next day with the girl who has the great ass, and I ask her to sign my cast. She bends over me, her big boobs all in my face, and writes, 'Catch me if you can!'"

"Wow," I say, rubbing my sweaty palms together, sitting forward on the sofa, and dreamily repeating the line. "Catch me if you can." It's the most romantic thing I've ever heard. "Did you catch her?" I ask.

"Never did," Robert says, shaking his head in fake disappointment.

"Nope, never did," Barry says, smiling like maybe he did.

"Hey," Robert says, switching the subject. "Do you know what wine tastes like?"

"No," I say, frowning. Just when I felt like one of the guys, now I feel like a kid.

"Here," Robert says, uncorking a bottle and swishing it in front of my face. "Take a drink."

I involuntarily wrinkle my nose and shake my head.

"It won't hurt you. Come on, take a drink."

I turn the bottle up just enough for some of the wine to slosh against my lips. It tastes bitter and smells like vinegar, so I get up from the sofa and spit it into the kitchen sink.

"I don't like it," I say, sitting back down. My eyes are watering because of the taste and also because they're pressuring me.

"Fine," Robert says. "But next time, David, don't be such a pussy about it."

My face turns red, and I find an excuse to leave, a bit scared and a lot embarrassed. Also, determined. Next time, I won't be a pussy.

When Dad gets a sabbatical at the Dana-Farber Cancer Institute, I can't believe how happy I am. He's going to be in Boston for nine months! That's the best thing that could happen. If he cures cancer, that will be a close second.

Immediately I start imagining how normal my house will be, how great I'll feel without him hounding me. But that night at dinner, Dad announces, "We'll make it a father-son drive up to Boston." His plan is that we'll take in the sights during the three-day road trip, then I can fly home while he remains. Three days in a car with Dad? Before I can react, he adds the can't-miss incentive. "We'll even take in a Celtics game."

I've never been to a professional sports event, and though the Celtics are having a terrible season, I would have walked to Boston to see them play.

"That's great," I say, divided as always, even when good things happen.

On the day we head north, it's perfect fall weather, and when we reach Blue Mountain Parkway, leaves are glittering gold and yellow as I look out the window of Dad's Dodge Dart. The AM radio is trying to stay connected to Dad's classical music station, and I almost feel inspired by the air rushing through the vents near the floorboard. Maybe this trip won't be so bad after all.

"I found those girlie magazines you have hidden," Dad says. Talk about a natural buzzkill. Besides, those weren't girlie magazines. They were hard-core porn, and I'd given two-weeks' allowance to my friend Biff for them.

My face is red, and I feel sweat dripping from my armpits to my waistband, but I don't say a word.

"It's completely normal," Dad says, as if he's done the research. "But how often do you look at them?"

I'm silent, looking out at the leaves and the sun shining on them.

"Do you look at them every day?" he asks.

I grunt something that he correctly interprets as yes.

I'd look at them all day if I could.

"That's probably too much," he said. "I've been worried, with all these girls you phone and fuss over, and now these magazines. I believe that you are oversexed."

I could open the door and throw myself out, that's how embarrassed I am and how amazed by his always-confident, always-wrong interpretation. I've never done anything with a girl. I missed my chance to kiss Dawn, who had moved to town last summer. Because her father was a graduate student, we'd hung out at the university pool, her short blonde hair tucked behind her ears, her lips glistening with the gloss she nervously rolled on every few minutes.

Finally I'd been invited to her house to listen to her favorite LP by Kiss. When we were walking to her room and the lyrics from "Calling Dr. Love" roared from the turntable—"I've got the cure you're thinking of"—I'd tripped; that's how scared I was that an actual kiss might happen.

"I'm just saying," he repeats, "you may be oversexed."

I think I hate this man because he's making me hate myself. I feel clumsy as it is. My face has bruised, painful knots, my wet armpits are starting to stink, and now I'm sexually twisted.

I won't look at him. Nothing he ever does or says is comfortable to me. Biff's dad made me laugh uncontrollably when he told Biff and me to tape a "Pussy for Sale" sign on their family cat to make extra money. I keep thinking about it, not because I like the crude joke, but because I've never seen a father and son laugh together over something, ever.

Biff's father said "pussy." Barry and Robert said it too.

Pussy, pussy, pussy.

Are they oversexed too?

Dad doesn't try to talk again until it is dark and we're deep in Virginia, approaching the Days Inn we've booked. "You sure have grown tall in a hurry. I bet you grew five inches in five months. That's helping you in basketball," he says, stating the obvious.

He does come to watch all my basketball games, and I have to admit I look for his face in the crowd. But I don't know if he's there to cheer me on or ogle the other players. And I don't know why I even want him there, given his postgame commentary. Once, he urged me to pass more because he couldn't stand watching me shoot and miss.

"I read a story in a science journal recently that said when your pubic hair grows above your penis, you will grow five or six more inches. I wonder how much taller you will grow?"

Just when I'd managed to forget "oversexed."

"Has your pubic hair grown all the way across?" he asks.

"Yes," I say, still not looking at him. Not even the Boston Celtics are worth this humiliation.

"Are you sure?"

I clench my jaw. "Positive."

Fifteen minutes later, we check in at the Days Inn. We never eat out, not even on the road. Dad has brought bologna, a loaf of bread, and mustard that's beyond its expiration date for dinner. He squirts so much yellow mustard on his bread that it oozes between his fingers, and I can't watch. Instead, I decide to get ready for bed and watch TV. I stand at the end of my queen bed and strip down to my T-shirt and white Fruit-of-the-Loom briefs. Dad is standing over his bed, going through his suitcase, looking for something.

"I need you to show me," he says, turning to me.

"Show you what?" I can't help sounding perturbed. I just want to watch TV. Some *Charlie's Angels*, so I can think about that Cheryl Tiegs poster in my room where she's got her nipple pitching a tent in her red swimsuit.

"I need you to show me your pubic hair so I can see if you will grow five or six more inches," he says, "for basketball."

He's trying to make his voice light. I am bolted to the floor, standing beside the bed. "I can't know for sure unless I see it," he continues. "It depends on if it is fully grown all the way across, according to the journal."

"What does it matter?" I say. "It's not a scientific fact that I'll grow that much just because of hair."

"That's what the science says, David. This way, we'll be able to do our experiment."

I'm tired and I want to get in bed and I want him to stop—stop talking, stop pressuring me. To get it over with, I push down the top of my underwear just far enough for him to see pubic hair running fully across my pelvis.

He takes a step closer and bends over, pushing up his glasses, which have fallen on his nose. That's when he starts to extend his hand.

I release the elastic of my briefs and leap back, yelling, "Get away from me!"

"David." He steps back and raises his hands in the air, as if the police have told him to.

"Get away from me!" I yell. "I am not gay. Don't you touch me! Do you understand? Don't touch me ever!"

There's a second in which he gazes at me, his eyes stricken behind his glasses, his hands still in the air. Then he drops his hands to cover his face and groans into them. Suddenly, he is sobbing as I've never seen a man sob before. His shoulders are heaving. Strings of tears are sliding from the heels of his hands. "I'm sorry," Dad sobs. He chokes out a few more words. "I was just . . . I'm just trying to see if you are going to grow more . . . for-for basketball . . . Just . . . for basketball."

I envision how good it would feel to hold a basketball and smash it into his face.

Dad backs away onto his bed, sits down next to his suitcase, takes his glasses off, and keeps sobbing. I climb into the other and take my evening position—body straight, like a pencil, not moving—and I don't say another word. I don't realize I'm crying until I feel tears dripping into my ears.

That night, I learn how wanting to die feels. And if I cannot die, at the very least, I want out. Out of my body, out of my terrible knowledge. I want something to take me away, magical pills to transport me to another place, to the person I was born to be, David Whomever, until I was put up for adoption and this strange family came to claim me, changing my name and coercing me to pull down my pants.

Mom—*I could tell Mom what he did*, I start to think, but then remember how she reminded me to keep swiping cotton balls with Dad's pink acne goo, keep up the pretense every day and every night, avoid conflict, pretend nothing's wrong, fill the wastebasket with cotton balls and smile for the Christmas card photo. No, Mom can't help me either.

My dad is shaking the bed with his sobs. My anger burns clean, righteous, white-hot. I fight to hold on to it. But his sobs ratchet higher. I've never felt so conflicted in my life. I want to comfort my sobbing father. I remember how I felt in the ambulance speeding away from the golf course when I thought he was dying. I understood then that I loved him, that I didn't want him to die. That he'd tried his best. Even now, I can't help but pity him. He had grown up in a small Louisiana town attending a rural Baptist church, which his mother led as if perched upon a throne. Their rules were black and white: no dancing, no cursing, no drinking, no mixed marriage, no babies out of wedlock, and no homosexuals.

If you were gay, you'd go to hell.

But first, you'd get beat up and disowned.

Instead of being the person he was born to be, he became the most Baptist of all the Baptists, as a church organist and deacon. He married and adopted children. And filled photo albums with pictures of male students.

I pity him, and I love him, but I'm not sure I like him or like him being my father. It's a problem I can't solve, that night or ever. So I do what I do most every night, closing my eyes to end the nightmare so I can wake up for a new day, hoping for improvement.

The sun peeks through the motel room curtain the next morning, and I crack my eyes, seeing a box of doughnuts on the table.

"Eat some while they are hot," Dad says.

We spend the day walking the streets of Boston while I count down the hours until game time. Dad and I sit high in the Boston Garden rafters, a cloud of cigarette smoke gathering around us, which is perfect because I am floating in a dream.

The guy sitting next to us tells me that Aerosmith played here a few nights before, and I can't believe that I am not only looking at the real Boston Celtics, but that the real Steven Tyler was in this very building only days before. I scan the banners hanging from the rafters for my favorite players, watching these men who are literal and figurative giants pass and dribble, turn and sprint.

Dad orders us popcorn, hot dogs, and Cokes that fizz in their paper cups. He doesn't pay close attention to the game, but he has given me this moment, and we are both, in our way, delighted. As I watch the game, I can't help but wonder if my birth father might have been a pro basketball player. What if, in addition to the whiff of Steven Tyler, my real father is here, too, playing for the Celtics? In this moment, it feels entirely possible, and I imagine he's on the court, scoring, and he'll meet me after the game, taking me away from the nightmare.

I fly back home, and Dad stays in Boston. Immediately our house feels different, and I realize what I'm feeling is relaxed. I'm not braced for his footsteps on the stairs, his flashing camera zooming in on the male students, his sad eyes sizing me up.

So it makes no sense that on my next seventh-grade report card, I make four Fs and one A, in physical education. I had been so proud of my Stanford Achievement Test scores that year; I was in the highest percentile. How was I flunking every class with nobody noticing, not even me?

A few days later, my middle school football coach pulls me aside in the hall. "David," he says quietly so no one else can hear. "You made all Fs! Nobody else in the grade did that." My grade has more than two hundred students, so I get the scale of what he is saying. I have high achievement scores, and my father is a microbiologist with a PhD, and I am flunking intermediate school. "What happened?" he asks.

I have no idea. I was so out of it, I didn't realize I made all Fs. Instead, I drop my head and look at the ground.

"Is something wrong?" Coach presses. "Is something wrong at home?"

"I don't know," I tell him, tears welling in my eyes.

"Do you need any help? I can help you," Coach says.

I gather myself, wiping tears away. There is nowhere to begin to say what is wrong or how Coach might help.

"No," I said, trying to look him in the eye. "I'm fine. Everything's fine at home."

Chapter Two

Inevitable Outcomes

I'm walking home from a friend's house the summer before ninth grade, the sun scorching through my T-shirt. A car horn pierces my daydream of a cold drink and lunch, and a tiny Datsun pulls alongside.

The window rolls down, and my friend Donna yells from the back, "Get in!"

Donna is one year older, going into the tenth grade, and I don't know her well, but I know she's cute.

"Come on!" says an older girl in the passenger seat who looks like she's in college.

In summer, Mom and Dad let me go and come as I please, and they're both still at work on campus anyway. "OK," I say, then wedge myself into the back seat of the two-door Datsun. It doesn't quite make sense that Donna wants to bring me along on this joyride, and there's barely enough room for my legs, but I don't care. I'm between two older girls who are wearing tiny shorts in the back seat of a small car, and when Donna's older sister pulls out into traffic, their bare legs shift to rub against my own.

An AC/DC eight-track is sticking out of the stereo, and Donna's sister pops it in, cranking the volume. The Datsun vibrates like my heart. The song lyrics foretell our immediate future: "Don't need reason, don't need rhyme . . . going down, party time."

As we turn onto the highway, I learn this isn't just a joyride. It's my first beer run. Since Oxford doesn't sell cold beer and the county is dry, we are on our way to the Marshall County line, to Ben and Todd's, which sells beer to anybody, no questions asked. Donna breaks into song: "Hiiiighway to Hell!"

Growing up in the Southern Baptist church, where Dad is the organist, I'm warned each week about how the devil wrangles for my soul. He seems to be winning the tug-of-war with every clickety-clack of the tires along the highway, and I'm nervous. I've never tried alcohol or other drugs, and I'm afraid that if I do, I might get crazy and jump out of the window like that fellow on the after-school TV special.

"Ben's got tattoos," says the girl in the passenger seat, a freshman at Ole Miss. "I've heard he went to prison for murder."

The tattoo talk interests me. Few people in my small town have ink, and those who do look like they have gripping stories to match—Vietnam, a motorcycle gang, a murder charge. But this rumor about Ben might not even be real.

"Could just be a story," I say.

"True," says Donna's sister, backing me up. "It's like the Ohio Players and that song 'Roller Coaster.' They say that scream is from a girl murdered when they were recording. But I never believed it."

"That sounds true," says her friend. "Who could make that up?"

Donna's sister laughs, the smoke from a menthol cigarette stuttering out of her mouth. The windows are closed, and the smoke stings my eyes and clouds the car. I cough, swearing to myself I'll never smoke. Beer and AC/DC, perhaps. Cigarettes with all that nasty tar and nicotine, never.

Inside the store, Ben is behind the counter, packing a pistol in a holster that's buckled over his ragged T-shirt. Next to a barrel of pickled eggs and jars of beef jerky stands the triple refrigerator chock-full of beers so cold they look frozen.

I linger near the door with Donna and her friend. The college girls each buy an eight-pack of pony Miller Lites, then saunter back to the Datsun. Donna's sister hasn't even put the car in drive before the party starts. The girl up front gives us an eight-pack for the back seat and places the other between her feet. She looks back at me, spreads her legs apart, grabs a pony beer from the floorboard, and slides it between her legs with the bottle head sticking out. She clamps her thighs around the beer bottle. "This is how you screw," she says in a sultry voice, slowly twisting off the cap.

Blood squirts through my body. I want to kiss her, and I'm visualizing doing that as our smoke-filled menthol machine rolls its way along the Highway to Hell, fueled by the searing vocal gospel of Bon Scott.

"Damn right," I say, grabbing a bottle from our ponies, twisting off the cap, and turning it back for a swig.

Without making a decision, I'm a drinker, just like that; not because I want alcohol, but because I want girls.

Except the beer comes up as fast as it went down, choking my throat with the retch of a cat spitting out a hairball. The regurgitated beer tastes like how cold urine smells. I hold it in the back of my throat. This time, there's no sink to spit it into, and I can't throw up or I will forever be the pussy I was warned not to be.

I've got just one option. I close my eyes and force a big swallow that sends the Miller Lite back south. I try not to cough but can't help it.

"Ewww. You don't like beer?" says Julie, giggling.

"I love beer," I say, wiping my lips and hoping they don't see my eyes watering.

I manage to drink two on the way back to Oxford. Before we hit the city limits, I'm telling stories, singing along with the radio, and laughing so hard more tears, this time elicited by a different source, gather in my eyes.

"Hey," I say, tapping Donna's sister on the shoulder. "What does a cigarette taste like?"

She laughs and turns down the stereo volume. "Save something for later," she says.

When they drop me off, I say, "Hey, uh, that was fun," which is all it takes to get me invited for a repeat.

I go the next night. I go every time I can. I've finally discovered the way to stop worrying about Eunice's rages, Dad's oddities, stresses from school, chores, the strikeout in baseball. A few drinks and these problems become hazy as if viewed from a Datsun filled with smoke.

I've never seen my parents drink. They serve Cokes or punch when hosting church parties or students, though Dad once tried to make homemade wine in the basement from honey he'd collected from his hives. The experiment didn't go well.

Dad threw the honey wine out all without a sip, afraid its wayward fermentation might kill someone with a single swallow. I'd gone looking on a particularly bad day to see if any bottles had remaining drops but found only honey. Beekeeping was his most successful hobby amid a litany of flops. He tried to make deer hide rugs from hides discarded by poachers that Dad found near my grandmother's house, but because all the fur fell off, he was stuck with several barrels of bare deerskin in the basement.

But the honey tasted delicious, thanks to the clover that covered our lawn in spring. Dad hated that he couldn't get the grass to grow like a golf course fairway, but the lush clover helped sweeten our biscuits. I even thought Dad was brave, donning his white beekeeper suit with the smoker in hand and reaching into the hives amid thousands of bees, and he didn't cry when stung.

I watched from the back porch, and he'd pull out a chunk of dripping honeycomb and walk it over to me for a bite. I'd sink my teeth in, honey sliding off my chin, flowing through my system, pollinating me with happiness.

He wanted us, and his students, to be able to watch their magic, so he purchased an antique glass display case and placed it in our garage. In the case, he put the hive racks used in beekeeping and connected the case to the outside sunshine and clover through long, clear tubes extending through holes drilled into the garage. The concept worked for a while, and one spring, I sat in the garage for hours watching bees miraculously build racks of honeycomb. But somehow the tubes came loose. Bees escaped into the garage, stinging Dad dozens of times as he attempted repair, ending the experiment.

I've seen plenty of alcohol, even though Mom and Dad don't keep it in the house. I'll walk the stands at the Ole Miss football stadium with friends after home games, picking up plastic souvenir cups and discarded flags, the stench of bourbon permeating the air. And I've been to my best friend Jon's house.

Jon's mother, Dean, is the closest to a hippie I know. She is William Faulkner's niece. Since three years before I was born, he's been dead, but we play in his yard, and I know he was a famous writer, and she is a writer and an English teacher at a local community college. Divorced from Jon's father and remarried to another writer, Dean mesmerizes me during frequent spend-the-nights at Jon's house, smoking long cigarettes, drinking red wine from jugs, and listening to Chicago's latest album. Jon and I peek around the corner in T-shirts and briefs when we are supposed to be in bed, absorbed into the laughter and swaying.

One night the music gets so loud, the clouds of cigarette smoke so thick, that my stomach hurts. Jon has to ask Dean to call Mom to come and get me. She picks me up at ten in her pajamas and asks what is wrong.

"They do funny things," I said. Mom didn't ask for details, tucking me in with a "Night, night, sweet dreams."

Soon, I'm back, rapt, as if seeing my future.

Jon has more rules than I do. He has to say "Yes, ma'am" to his mother, and he can't make noise in the morning until at least noon because she's sleeping to ease her "migraines." Even I see the relation to the empty jugs in the trash.

Willie Morris moves to town as a writer-in-residence at Ole Miss after *Harper's Magazine* booted him as editor-in-chief, and Willie becomes Dean's best friend. He's at Jon's house most weekend nights. The game Trivial Pursuit is released about this time, and Willie and Dean and friends gather around the living room. Willie, the Rhodes Scholar, nails every answer, a master class in slurred trivia. Willie brings entertaining friends to Dean's house, including William Styron, the writer, and Jimmy Buffett, the musician. I've never heard of Styron, but I know every word to "Cheeseburger in Paradise" down to Heinz 57 and French-fried potato, and I'm impressed.

I wonder if Dean is hooked on alcohol since I rarely see her without either a drink or cigarette, usually both. I also wonder if she's some kind of saint because she has more social awareness and compassion than the other grown-ups I know. For instance, during our bicentennial summer of 1976, we're about to enter fifth grade. By day, we ride bikes to the square and buy gum at Blaylock's drugstore with bicentennial quarters, chewing on huge mouthfuls while peering into the Western Auto Store and dreaming about faster bikes. At night, we become stars under the lights in the local Civic League youth baseball games with our parents and friends watching. After the game, snow cones of red, blue, and orange color our mouths.

The Civic League's teams are named after the local civic clubs— Civitan, Rotary, Jaycees, and Kiwanis. These clubs are all white, and the teams are all white as well. Jon, however, plays in the City League, with its subpar facilities, the only white boy to do so. Even though the public school we attend is integrated, mixed nearly half white and half black, with some international students mixed in, we segregate by neighborhoods, church, and baseball on summer nights. It isn't because we want it that way. Instead, it's what we inherit from our parents.

When I start first grade, integrated just two years prior, a boy named Weasle becomes my friend. He's smart and funny and black. We save seats for one another in the lunchroom, we sit by one another in class, and we call one another on the phone after school. Weasle hears some boys talking about spend-the-nights, suggesting we give it a try. He'll come to my house on Friday night?

Sure, I say. I'll ask my mom, and he'll ask his, and we'll compare notes the next day on the playground. We're excited, but when I ask Mom, her brow crimps.

"Mom?" I prod.

"Well," she says, "no, not this Friday. We've got plans."

We don't have plans. We never have plans. "Not this Friday" meant "never." It makes my stomach hurt thinking about telling Weasle. But before I can deliver the punch, Weasle delivers his.

"Hey, David," he said, breaking into a smile. "I asked Mom if I could spend the night, and she said, 'Hell, no, you can't sleep at that boy house.'"

We never mention spending the night again, though our friendship endures.

Dean alone seems to be trying to improve social segregation in our town. She invites enough black boys to Jon's birthday party to create a near racial balance. She signs up Jon to play baseball those summers in the City League; he's the small white second baseman for the otherwise all-black Cardinals.

"Why do you play in that crappy league?" we ask Jon, reminding him that the girls come to watch Civic League games.

"Why wouldn't I want to play there?" he says. "All the best players are in the City League." Besides, he explains, his mom gave him just one option: play in the City League, where everyone is welcome, or don't play at all.

Dean called Jon "J-Bird," and Willie picks up on that, adopting J-Bird as his godson. He even writes an essay about Jon titled "Always Stand in Against the Curve." Willie asks Jon for details on all his games— he doesn't go since they are in the evening, which conflicts with his drinking. Willie doesn't much leave his house unless he goes to Dean's.

And when Willie is writing, he sometimes gets stuck in long binges of drunkenness, drawing the shades and closing the doors to visitors. Jon gets paid fifty cents a day to take out Willie's trash on these days, and often takes me along. We bang on the door of Willie's house, a small white clapboard cottage he rents on campus, but Willie doesn't answer.

"He sleeps past noon," Jon says.

Another victim of migraines, I'm thinking.

After five or six hard knocks, we enter. Inside, ashes and empty liquor bottles cover the kitchen, and we scoop the debris into bags while holding our noses from the putrid odor. Sometimes Willie peeks around a corner, his hair in every direction, face swollen, smelling like the kitchen. Jon explains that Willie is stressed because he's late on a book's deadline.

"Will he finish?" I ask.

"He's fourteen months late," Jon says.

✳ ✳ ✳

Eunice is staying at the horse ranch for most of the week, easing the tension around the house. I've shot up to six-foot-one, which helps out with football and basketball, and I've become more confident, which helps out with girls. I'm talking on the phone to several each night, ignoring homework to focus on finding the right girlfriend. When Eunice breezes through to get more clothes or her weekly allowance, she talks nonstop about Paul and Cathy.

"Paul made lasagna last night. It was *sooo* good," Eunice says. "I'll ask Paul if you can get his recipe."

"Mm, that sounds good," Mom says, joyful that she can sleep quietly another night.

When I see Eunice in these encounters, it's like seeing somebody else's sister. She's thriving in the attention of this couple, spared the pressure of our home. She's even got a bit of a glow. She's not so much a tomboy anymore. She's started wearing eyeliner and, every so often, smiling. Next year, she'll go to college, likely Ole Miss.

"I heard you won best all-around boy in the junior high," she says, as she's leaving again, with an overnight bag over her shoulder. "Huh."

"Yes," I say, barely able to believe she knows or remembers.

"It doesn't mean anything," she says, walking away.

Bitch, I think to myself. It means everything.

She's changed, but not that much.

Eunice wins academic awards, while I win popularity awards, which she disdains. Eunice never had a boyfriend in junior high or high school that I knew about, while I have started dating Ashley, the blonde bombshell with big dimples, the catch of junior high.

I've known Ashley since kindergarten, been obsessed with her since sixth grade, and the ninth grade is our time, Ashley and me—my life fulfilling its destiny, zits, stinky armpits, and all. We launch our relationship in the movie theater. Her best friend, Debra, is seated beside her, and Debra tells me when Ashley goes to the bathroom that Ashley wants me to kiss her, but she's nervous since she's never kissed before.

"Go slow," Debra advises.

With my arm laying along Ashley's shoulders, I slowly spin my head around. Ashley's brown eyes connect with mine, and I smell her watermelon lip gloss. As our lips touch, my toes tingle, and she pushes her tongue into my mouth. Not knowing what to do, I swish my tongue with hers, and our slobbery, watermelon-flavored kiss lasts for the longest time.

From that moment, I know she's mine.

More freedom comes when Dad teaches me to drive his red Dodge Dart, and I pass my driver's test. No, I didn't get a new car like Eunice. But when I ask about mine, Dad says we need to save more money.

I'm in bed that night, muffling my tears, when Mom visits my room. It's so unfair, I tell her—Eunice not only got a new car, she got to pick out the brand, color, and style. Mom rubs my back and explains that Dad is stressed at work, but she expects me to get a new car soon.

It's a lie—another lie from my mother to ease the pain of the moment, her specialty.

I refuse to drive Dad's embarrassing red Dodge Dart, which has no air-conditioning, so Mom lets me drive her Buick LeSabre over to Ashley's. Ashley's parents are getting divorced and are fighting all the time. She wants out of her house just as much as I do mine.

Ashley watches for me, so I barely have to put the car in park before she's skipping out her door, half-jogging toward the Buick. Knowing she's soon going to be next to me, smelling like watermelon, her skin so soft, is better than beer runs to Ben and Todd's. We never think about beer; instead, we make small talk, both thinking about the stretch of gravel road outside town where nobody drives. It's getting dark, and soon, the night will nicely cover us up.

I pull over in the dusk, the jagged outline of pine trees looking tall and protective against the purpling sky. Ashley undoes her ponytail as she climbs into the back seat so there won't be a lump under her head. I scramble back, smiling. She's looking at me with a smirk like she might just skedaddle if I don't get down to business.

Ashley has the biggest breasts in our grade, and she likes positioning them in front of my face for a reaction. We kiss and talk about things like the jet stream and football, and I get so lost in the conversation; sometimes she muzzles my talk with her chest. We start grinding our blue-jean-covered hips into one another, and all I know is I don't want to move from this spot, ever. When the lights of a passing car fill the windows with a wobbly yellow light, we don't even stop. Our car looks empty, like somebody just ran out of gas, and we'd hear the tires on the gravel if it stopped.

After we make out, we talk more.

"I want to live with Mom," Ashley says. She rarely talks about her parents' divorce.

"Is that what's going to happen?" I ask.

"Nobody tells me anything," she says. "And it's not like I can say I like it better when my Dad is gone. But I do. It's so much easier because sometimes I think I hate him."

Even though this is how I feel about my father, I can't find the words to admit it. She might ask why. I could never tell Ashley about that night at the Days Inn or that I suspect that, outside of work, the only times my dad is not at home is when he's visiting male students, taking their pictures and stroking back their hair.

But I ask questions about her parents because divorce seems like a beneficial arrangement. Her father has a new yellow Corvette, and rumor has it, a new girlfriend too.

"When do you think it'll be over? I mean, the divorce. Is it gonna happen soon?"

"Not soon enough," Ashley says, rolling over to stop our talk by giving me a deep kiss. She starts buttoning up her blouse, and I say a silent goodbye until next time.

As the most serious couple in the oldest grade at the junior high school, Ashley and I swagger down the halls, and I get the strangest feeling of liking myself. We're a couple, which feels like a new family.

In the spring, the Commodores come to town for a concert on campus at the coliseum. I'd only been to one show there, and that didn't go well. When I was ten, Mom heard a radio ad for "America" in concert. She assumed it was some type of bicentennial program and bought three tickets, taking Eunice and myself.

But this wasn't some "she's a grand old flag" program. We sat in the top rafters, dressed in our red, white, and blue Sunday best, surrounded by long-haired fans smoking marijuana. America took the stage, and lyrics like "You can do magic" and "A horse with no name" rang out of giant speakers stacked thirty feet high on either side of the stage. I was mesmerized, knowing the songs by heart from the radio, but Eunice was embarrassed by how badly we stuck out. When Mom hauled us out long before the encore, the crowd around us snickered and applauded.

As for the Commodores concert, I'm going to make sure the night is perfect. I don't plan on missing a note. Lionel Richie's soulful crooning is the soundtrack to our make-out sessions in the back seat of Mom's Buick. I tell Ashley she's my "Brick House," and she makes me feel sanctified in return.

"We're going to the Commodores next month at the coliseum," I can finally tell Ashley once I've saved up enough allowance and bought our tickets.

"Oh my god, David," Ashley says. We're in the back seat, and my face is getting smothered by her kisses. "Is that a good thank-you?" she asks.

Indeed. My life is good, I feel joy without worry, and we count down the days to the concert. When it finally arrives, we sit on the top row. The coliseum is small enough that we can see Lionel strutting around, dipping back his head, pouring his voice into the microphone while the band keeps the groove. The only problem is Ashley doesn't seem to want to be touched or stand close. We're both swaying with the crowd, and every time the first notes of a song play, she yells out the title and gives a little squeal, but when I go to squeeze her hand or kiss her, she moves out of my reach.

The music is everything I imagined it would be, so I try not to worry. But on the way home, Ashley's mood drops like a thermometer. "Let's stop at our place," I say, code for making out.

"No," she says. "I gotta get home."

It sounds like a lie, but I don't say anything.

As I turn onto her street, she says, "I just don't know, David."

"Don't know what?" I ask. But I do know. She means she doesn't know about us, our future. When I stop in her driveway, she reaches for the car door instead of my face.

The next day, I answer her phone call, trailing the long cord behind me as I plop on my bed, but she's talking before I even hit the mattress.

"I am breaking up," she says nervously, not even adding *with you.*

"What?" I ask, hoping she'll take it back.

I hear a male voice in the background. "Hang up," he says. It's a deep voice. An older voice. And not her Dad's, that's for sure.

Ashley pauses. I hear a quick intake of her breath, as if she might speak, then the blank dial tone. Ninth grade is over, and so are Ashley and me, my new family, my hope.

Mom tries to talk to me about it, but I shut the door, telling her to go away. Eunice seems happy about it—my turn to get burned. I lay in the dark for hours, days, weeks, listening to sad music. I pray Ashley might reconsider—maybe she's my "Goodbye Girl," "'cause, baby, goodbye doesn't mean forever." But I can't maintain my faith, connecting with the slower rock songs that I didn't connect with before: "heard it from a friend, who heard from a friend, who heard it from another you been messin' around."

I can't stand being alone with my feelings, how my father makes me feel, how Ashley makes me feel. I'm desperate to stop these feelings, even if it means feeling horrible the next morning. If I half-ass football practice, will it even matter?

So the summer before tenth grade plays out a lot like the summer before ninth. I go to Ben and Todd's with older girls. There isn't enough beer to drink, ever, but I'll drink all that's available, throwing up every so often. I spend as much time with my friends as possible, dodging my parents at home, and finding my way into parties where I'm usually the youngest kid.

There's a beer bong. Fun. There's vodka in the beer bong. Fun.

Barf.

"David," my mother says one morning, "you parked crooked in the driveway."

"I don't think so," I say.

And then I remember the night before and hurry out to find the empty whiskey bottle under the driver's seat and throw it away before getting grounded again.

Classmates vote me the friendliest guy in the entire high school. It should be an honor, but a fellow student has written on a ballot left on a voting table, "only when he's drunk!" which makes everyone laugh.

Winner! Yet, it's the first time I wonder how alcohol alters my life.

That afternoon I tell my mom about the school-wide ceremony where I'll be awarded the friendliest ribbon. I'm palming a sleeve of Saltines, thrusting every other one into peanut butter and pouring a glass of milk while suggesting where she and Dad can sit in the auditorium.

She says, softly, "We can't come this time." Mom stands five-foot-four, and I look down upon her furrowed brow, her eyes looking away.

I set my glass down without drinking. "You're not coming?"

"No." She shakes her head. "It's too much for Eunice." She sweeps some pretend crumbs from the counter into her palm.

"But, Mom, what about me—"

"She's still struggling," Mom says, straightening the elastic waist of her red stretch pants that match her top. Eunice is in her freshman year of college at Ole Miss, and she's joined a sorority with a few members, and she's drinking, trying to fit in. "But it's getting better. She's still going out to Paul and Cathy's during the week, and she says it calms her down."

She gives me a brisk smile that doesn't reach her green eyes. "We'll come to your next thing."

Onstage, when I'm presented with the friendliest ribbon, I look across the auditorium, seeing friends sitting with their families, and I don't see anyone there for me, and I have never felt so lonely.

* * *

I'm alone on a Friday night, strolling to Fraternity Row on the Ole Miss campus. It's a home football game weekend, and I'm wearing red Converse Chuck Taylors, blue jeans, and a white T-shirt with *Ole Miss Baseball Camp* stamped on the front, oblivious to the preppy dress code among the college students.

The fraternities have bands playing the night before home games, and the streets are closed for the crowds to mingle and wander from house to house with drinks in hand. I stop into the Teke house, where a party band is on break, and a guy offers me a drink.

"Sure," I say.

He walks over to a tall, dark green trash can and takes a cup from a stack on the floor, dips it in, handing me a drink of red liquid with a few chunks of fruit floating at the top.

I give it a look.

"Hey, dude," he says, "you're gonna like it. That's the best trash can punch on Frat Row, made with Everclear 95. When you finish that, just help yourself to more. It's here till the can runs dry."

Standing in a corner, I start sipping. Before the cup is dry, I have moved to the center of the room, approaching some girls. I introduce myself, telling them I am a high school senior. One, wearing a knee-length skirt and shoulder-length blonde hair that curls up in a flip, steps close. She touches my arm and says she's a sophomore. I blush.

Everything gets blurry.

I blink.

She's touching my face, running her soft fingers across my cheek. I open my eyes. *What happened?* I'm looking at the street, and all I can see are feet walking by. I'm lying on my side, my head rested in her lap, her feet resting against the curb.

"You're not really a senior in high school, are you?" she says.

"What?"

"You're not a senior." She's gently stroking my cheek.

I sit up, and my head sloshes, my vision smearing.

"No," I say.

"Can I call your mother?"

I look down at my shirt, covered in red vomit, and I look down at the street, covered in red vomit, and I looked at her skirt, covered in red speckles, as if spray-painted.

"What time is it?" I ask.

She looks at her watch. "Ten minutes after midnight."

"Midnight! What? I was supposed to be home by ten thirty."

"Well," she says, "you've had too much to drink, dear. You're late." She kisses the top of my head, helps me up, and gently wishes me good luck.

I walk home, throwing my T-shirt into a trash can along the way, and arrive by twelve thirty, shirtless. I unlock the door, creak up the stairs, and fall into the bed—my mischief undetected.

Weeks later, Mary, one year older in high school, has told her friend to tell my friend that she likes me. Mary has thick auburn hair and beautiful eyes, and when she invites me to a Sadie Hawkins Day dance, I count down the days.

I eat dinner at home before the dance. Mom doesn't enjoy cooking and doesn't venture beyond the casseroles in her church cookbook, figuring on saving time with dishes that squeeze meat and vegetables into one scoop, get seasoned with Campbell's condensed soup, and are topped with potato chips. On this night, she's made tuna casserole. I eat two-and-a-half servings. I always eat two-and-a-half servings, even of Mom's tuna casserole. I'm six-foot-one and lanky, and with the sports, I'm always hungry, drinking two Cokes at a time, eating an entire sleeve of Oreos or a box of vanilla wafers for dessert.

Mary knocks on the door wearing a knee-length skirt. Her hair is pulled back and tied with a bow, and I've never seen her so beautiful.

Before the date, Mary had asked me what I liked to drink, and I said vodka to sound experienced, and she nodded in agreement to look experienced. When we arrive at the party, she opens the Chevrolet's back door and starts mixing us drinks. She explains she'd never made a drink before as she fills my cup up half full of vodka before tossing in a few cubes of ice and filling the rest with orange juice until it brims over the top.

"Oh no!" she says, wiping the spilled drink off the back seat with her hand. "This is my mother's car. We can't get anything on it."

She hands me the drink, and I take a gulp.

"How's that?" she asks.

"Perfect," I say.

We walk into the party, sipping our drinks, and I look across the dance floor, seeing Ashley dancing close to James, her new boyfriend. I've heard they've gone all the way already, and from the way she's pressing her big breasts into his chest, I don't doubt it. I'd like to rush over and yank him off of her, but he's a senior and would crush me. Instead, I chug my vodka and orange juice.

Mary asks if I want to dance.

"Sure," I say. "But let's get another drink first."

We're back at the car, and Mary carefully refills my drink. Perhaps I fill again or maybe I don't; I don't recall. In fact, I don't recall the rest of the evening. Even when Mary tersely explains, days later, I don't remember that I fell, and she and her friends dragged me to her car, and I began to vomit in the back seat, spewing orange juice, vodka, and chunks of Mom's tuna casserole across the floorboard of her mother's sedan. She drove me to the back door of my parent's house, left me on the back steps, and rang the doorbell before going to scrub the car.

"I'm so sorry," I explain, but Mary walks away.

It doesn't go much better at home. Mom answered the door to find me puddled on the steps. It took all her strength to get me up the stairs and into bed, where she rubbed my back until I fell asleep. I remember cracking open my eyes the next morning, running to the bathroom, and vomiting again and again, before Dad called me down for a talk.

I tell him it was my first time drinking and that I was just experimenting. He seems to believe me but can't resist the teachable moment.

"David, when you swallow a drink, it enters your bloodstream through the stomach and small intestine," he says. "In your bloodstream, it flows throughout your body and reaches your brain where it reduces and blocks your neurons, or brain cells, from transmitting their electrical impulses. That's why you stumbled." He pushes his glasses up his nose. "You were poisoned."

It did feel like poison, yes. Dad is onto something.

"If it's poison," I ask, "why do so many people drink?"

He doesn't answer. He can lecture about the science of drinking all day but can't have the kind of father-and-son talk that might have helped, can't suggest that perhaps my birth father or birth mother, their identities unknown, might also struggle with alcohol, wherever they are. Instead of addressing my transgression as a warning sign or trying to get to the root of why I felt I needed to drink in the first place, he grounds me for two weeks with no driving or activities with friends.

"I hope you have learned your lesson," he says.

I learned my lesson. I never wanted to drink again. I felt awful about Mary, ashamed that Ashley probably saw me vomiting, and stupid for missing the year's best party.

And now I'm trapped alone with my feelings. I need to escape. So I call a friend to plan the upcoming weekend's drinking escapades.

✻ ✻ ✻

Late in the fall, Mom's eyebrows seem permanently drawn together. Eunice isn't living at home, so it's been quieter, but I have that feeling like I'm in grade school all over again, like the dark clouds are gathering. Early one morning, right before Thanksgiving, I feel Mom's hand on my shoulder, gently rocking me back and forth.

"Da-vid," she whispers, her voice breaking my name in half.

I open my eyes and roll over. Mom's face is puffy, her eyes redrimmed, her hair lopsided. "It's Eunice. Dad and I have to go to the hospital . . ."

Mom's voice trails off. I wait, watching Mom's face ball up in pain. She takes a deep breath to calm herself and begins again. "Her sorority sister found her lying incoherent. They pumped her stomach out. She's going to live."

"I'm sorry, Mom," I say, sitting up as Mom starts crying harder. It occurs to me that what I'm feeling includes a little bit of wonder and a little bit of jealousy. Could I do what Eunice did? Would I have the courage to finish it off?

"This is the worst day of my life," Mom says.

This, coming from a woman who's always avoided confrontation and relentlessly ignored negative feelings, is the most real thing Mom has ever said to me.

"It's awful how she feels," Mom broke off and swallowed. "And it's awful that I wonder if she'd be better off . . ."

Now I know Mom has the same thoughts that Eunice and I have. Maybe we'd all be better off if she died or if I died. Let's just undo this mess, reverse the altered birth certificates, nullify the false marriage, and cancel this family.

I remember a few years back, when Dad was flying to Texas on a work trip, he cried the day before leaving, telling me he hoped his plane would crash, then he'd be free from the madness at last. Confessing this seemed to make him feel better. Soon he wiped his tears and began stuffing balled socks into his suitcase. So then it was my turn to cry. I walked away and hid in my room, wanting to jump out of the window.

"Can you imagine," she says, "living in such pain that you'd rather be dead?" I want to tell her that, yes, I can imagine living in that kind of pain. I want to confess that it wasn't an accident in the fourth grade when pencil lead got jammed into an artery on the backside of my wrist. The truth is I'd heard that lead is poison and gave it a shove.

I want to tell her that I'm scared and alone. And I want to give her a big hug, but my arms stay immobile by my side. Still crying, my mom leaves for the hospital.

The next day is Thanksgiving, and since Mom and Dad are still with Eunice, my friend Chris's mom invites me over. Chris is a senior in high school, and his brother Charlie is in my grade, but I'm closer to Chris, who I know from parties and sports. I get dressed and drive over, numb but glad I'm away from my family.

His mother opens the door with empathetic eyes. "So sorry to hear about Eunice."

"Yeah. Thanks," I say, stepping around and through the door.

Thanksgiving lunch is turkey, dressing, green beans, and cranberry sauce, pretty much precisely the same food we'd be eating at home, and I notice something else similar. The rooms are dim, desperate for some light, and heaviness lingers.

When his parents clear the table, I'm alone with Charlie for a moment.

"I'm sorry about Eunice," he says, and I nod.

"How did it happen?" he asks, leaning in. "Pills?"

Later, Chris and I head to the local bar on the square downtown, leaving Charlie at home in front of the TV. The minute we walk in, I feel my shoulders untense from my earlobes. The bar is quiet because college kids have gone home for the holiday. There are two empty barstools. The perpetual Christmas lights behind the bar blink off and on against the liquor bottles. Chris is eighteen and can drink beer legally, and while I'm only sixteen, the bartender doesn't even look up from the glass he's polishing when we order a three-dollar pitcher of Stroh's Light.

Chris pours my mug first, making a nice head on it, especially for the cheap beer. As soon as the cold glass hits my lips, I chug half of it.

Ah, home.

"I'm applying to a couple of colleges up in Virginia," Chris says. "I'm ready to get out of this town."

I try to listen as Chris tells me about his preferences, but I can't concentrate. I just need to get through the holiday weekend. I can't even think about college yet. One day my time will come, and I will leave and not look back, escaping like the kid left for too long with the strange babysitter.

"Too bad Charlie didn't come with us," I say.

"He's a funny kid. Like, he makes me laugh all the time," Chris says. "But he's a homebody."

"Huh," I say, knowing home is the last place my body wants to be.

A few days later, it's finally Sunday, and I'll be back at school tomorrow. Mom comes into my room to talk, and I try to be patient. I know she's been through a lot, but I just don't want to know about Eunice.

"She's always been anxious," Mom says. "But I suspected there had to be something more, and now I know. Paul is inappropriate."

I can't help but shake my head. Somebody should go over there and whip Paul's butt.

Mom's face is tired, her neck folding in wrinkles I haven't seen before. Some part of her—the part that peeks over the blindfold she ties daily over her eyes—must have known you don't let an unstable teenage girl stay night after night in someone else's house. And here's the thing: she probably needed to believe that everything was OK over there because she so severely wanted respite from the hysteria and the vitriol, the girl screaming "Fuck" into her pillow like one possessed, the girl who kept asserting that Dad was gay.

I try to focus on Mom's face, her pug nose that looks like mine even though she's not my mother, and her curled brown hair she gets colored and permed at Polly's Cut and Curl. I know she's tried. Mom was my Cub Scout leader, good at planning the campouts and the service projects, the popcorn sales and the badge ceremonies. When I was a shy elementary school kid, Mom bribed me with a G.I. Joe helicopter to seduce me into playing sports. Mom took me to swimming lessons, even though she can't swim, and she clapped when I pedaled away on a bicycle for the first time, even though she can't ride a bike. Mom wrapped me in a blanket and put a cold towel on my head when I had a fever, and though she didn't succeed at gathering us at the table for family dinner, she set the table with four place settings every night in hope.

But Mom wore down over time. First, she married the wrong man. Then she got someone else's children, and they were wrong too. And so she made excuses and looked on the bright side and waited for things to improve. But they never improved, and after a while, the pretending and covering up became more real than the truth. She believed her own Christmas card.

Because my parents are tired, I figure they might be amenable to a plan to take their other problem off their hands: me. Surely they wanted to get rid of me, and I wanted to be gotten rid of. I pitch this idea: I'll leave the public school, where I've gone since first grade, and finish eleventh and twelfth grade in a nearby private school, thirty miles away. They agree.

I look upon this transfer as a fresh start, a way to outrun my superlative of Oxford High's friendliest drunk. And while some rumors beat me to my homeroom, I'm gradually able to convince the North Delta kids that they heard wrong. I meet a nice girl who doesn't drink, and we become steady. Mom and Dad let me go and come as I please. Instead of sneaking into college parties, I hang out with my girlfriend's younger brother, playing Atari. I get lots of playing time in sports. I make some tackles, score a few touchdowns, hit several home runs.

The school is planted between bean fields, just west from where rolling hills stop rolling. It has fewer than thirty students per grade, all white. It formed as one of many so-called white flight academies that sprouted in Mississippi when schools desegregated. There are no black students when I arrive in 1982. Until then, I'd been in a racially balanced public school, where race was a big part of daily interactions, with state mandates for balanced cheerleader tryouts and children who eat together at lunch but whose parents won't allow spend-the-nights.

Race doesn't come up at North Delta because we're all the same race. Instead, class is a more significant divider. Still, when I see Weasle back in Oxford, I know that just because race isn't discussed in North Delta doesn't mean it's not an issue.

"Congrats, man," Weasle says, referring to my touchdowns. At Oxford, he's still struggling to earn playing time as a running back. Weasle says he was proud of my accomplishments, then grins. "Wish I could play for a private school."

I wrap my arm around his neck. "You'd score all the touchdowns," I say.

This new David I try on at North Delta—sober, earnest, optimistic—begins to fit me better each day, like a worn-in letter jacket. But it doesn't last. During my senior year, something back in Oxford happens that I can't shake. I can't tell anyone at my new school, either. All they know is my home runs evaporate, and I fall into a horrid slump, swinging at wild pitches, striking out.

Chris has long gone off to college, but Charlie, his younger brother, is hanging out at the local bar more. And he's driving a familiar car: Dad has sold Charlie his Dodge Dart. I learn this not from Dad but from my old friends who laugh that Charlie's found his true love. He treats this old red car like a hot rod, except it's not souped-up. He's grown a scruffy beard, which fits like a Mississippi James Dean. He invites me out drinking, and when I walk to the driveway, he's revving the engine of Dad's old car. "How you like it?" he says, laughing.

"You wear it well," I say, smiling but wondering how this car sale came about.

Charlie and I take seats at a local basement bar, the only high school students here. There's an empty seat beside Charlie and an Ole Miss sophomore coed smiles as she lowers onto it. She orders a pitcher for herself, sipping and flirting for an hour. Charlie's laughing and talking, and I'm laughing and talking, and three is becoming a crowd.

When Charlie hits the bathroom, I follow. "OK," I say, "I can't tell. I think she likes both of us, so let's flip a coin on who gets to make a move."

"Nah," Charlie says, zipping up his fly and turning to the sink. "She's all yours."

"Really?"

He shrugs a shoulder, already walking back to the bar.

I follow and this time, I take Charlie's seat, next to her. But soon she's giving us each a sweet kiss on the cheek and saying her goodbyes. We're too young for her, turns out, or something.

"I'm going to find her next year," I tell Charlie dreamily, watching her walk out, "when I'm a freshman at Ole Miss. What was her name again?"

"Tedford," Charlie says, packing a dip of snuff in his lower lip. "Just think about Ted Bishop driving a Ford pickup truck," he says. "Ted-Ford," he says again, with grave authority to make the name stick, and slaps me on the back, making me laugh. Charlie is a character, the way he struts, the way he drives the heck out of the Dodge Dart, whipping it around in donuts, the way he tells his zany jokes.

Until, that is, he tells a joke that isn't funny. I'm not there, but I hear about it the next day. A bunch of guys went to a concert in Memphis. Afterward, everyone is drunk in the parking lot, especially Charlie, who falls into a friend and grabs his crotch.

"Get off me, man," the friend yelled, and Charlie teetered off.

And just like that, the rumor that Charlie was gay gained some legs.

That kind of rumor got you ostracized or worse. Sometimes I worried about my dad. It was a huge scandal when campus police busted a handful of professors meeting up in the men's bathroom in the library. I'd been relieved my father wasn't among the men arrested for indecent exposure. But he didn't escape the rumor mill. One Sunday morning, I was searching for a clean shirt to wear to church and found Mom in the kitchen. She wasn't wearing one of her ankle-length floral church dresses, wasn't wearing her pearls. In fact, she was putting on dish gloves, thrusting one hand then the other deep into the purple plastic with a thwack. When I asked what was going on, she concentrated on sprinkling Ajax in the sink and began scrubbing extra hard.

"Your father isn't playing the organ at First Baptist anymore. He needs a break—being a musician is really demanding, you know. All those choir singers with their song requests." She ground out several more manic circles, her jaw clenching though her voice breezy. "In fact, maybe we could all use a break. Sleep in on Sunday morning, you know?" This woman who'd never slept in a day in her life had nothing more to say about leaving the Baptist church she'd gone to her entire life. That night, her dry, choked sobs echoed through the closed doors of our house.

Charlie isn't the same after that night at the concert. He's drinking more and more, but instead of cracking jokes around the side of his wad of chew, the booze makes him dark and moody. One night at the bar on the town square, Charlie abruptly stands up and walks out. It's so strange that a few people go to the door to peer out at him. Heading toward the Dart in the parking lot, he turns around and yells to his friends, "I love you."

When Charlie gets home, he goes into his bedroom, closes the door, and loads a 12-gauge shotgun. He wraps a towel around his head and pulls the trigger.

It's late in our senior year, the moment when everyone is focusing on the future. But Charlie has no future now. I can't manage to squeeze that truth into my cranium. The red Dodge Dart that Charlie loved to corner too fast, would it never feel Charlie's fingers on the wheel again? All those road trips Charlie planned—would he never make a single one?

The next evening, I pass the Dart in Charlie's driveway as I walk to his front door. I stand beside the couch where his mom is slumped over a pillow and try to find words, but there aren't any. I look over her head down the hall, where the door to Charlie's room is closed. I wonder who cleaned the room. I think about that Thanksgiving dinner when he leaned forward, wanting details about Eunice's hospitalization.

Chris, home from college, motions me over with a jerk of his shoulder. "Want to meet up later when the crowd leaves?"

Yes, of course.

We take two open seats at the bar, order a first pitcher of beer. We drink deeply, that chill goldening our throats on its way down, and the more beer we drink, it is miraculous, a golden tourniquet cutting off that endless despair, bringing us to laughter even. Yes, we are laughing. We will never stop this drinking, drowning out death with each and every sip.

Chapter Three

Fraternity Row

I pledge the only fraternity in America with a swimming pool at an on-campus house. College, I can already tell, is going to be one long pool party.

And that's how it's starting out. It's the first day of classes at Ole Miss and, therefore, our first mixer, with the pledges of Kappa Kappa Gamma sorority coming over. The point of this beach luau is for my Sigma Nu pledge brothers and I to meet cute freshman girls in bikinis. The girls, clustered in small groups, have received two warnings from their trainer: One, don't drink the punch. Two, talk to the boys or the boys will throw you into the pool. We boys have received one warning from our trainer: "It's not a party until you've put a lampshade on your head."

Naturally, I'm happy to oblige. I'm warming up with a Bud Light in my hand. But instead of joining a group of pledge brothers distributing trash can punch in red plastic cups to our guests, I spot a Kappa with a dark complexion and dark hair standing beside the pool like a mirage. She's wearing a one-piece swimming suit with Bugs Bunny on the front, and she's fit but not flaunting it in a bikini. Her dark hair accents her big brown eyes. And I'm intrigued by her solitude, her sense of reserve, standing alone, no beer in hand.

Large black speakers surround the edge of the pool, vibrating the humid night air with Prince's "When Doves Cry." My pledge brothers move quickly among the scattered, jittery girls, handing out cups of red punch to those willing to accept them. I should join, but I can't rip my gaze from the brunette. Ah, what the hell. I take a swig and a deep breath and step to her.

"Hi," I try. "I'm David."

She looks at me with a broad smile but says nothing.

"Wanna drink?"

"I'm not sure," she says softly.

She extends her bottom lip, blowing air toward her forehead as sweat beads beneath her bangs.

"It's hot," she says.

"What?"

"It's hot," she says, leaning toward my ear so I can hear over the music.

It takes a little prodding, but eventually, I get her talking. She tells me she's from Arkansas, a two-and-a-half-hour drive away, where her father is a rice farmer.

I tell her how my home is mere blocks away, close enough to walk there and back before anyone misses me. But I explain that it's theoretically far away since I don't plan to set foot back in my parents' house for anything more than a quick errand. She gives me a puzzled look.

"I guess you're close to your family?" I ask.

"Yes," she says, "we're close. I have an older sister. She came to Ole Miss. So did my mother."

I smile, and she smiles back.

I tell her how my dad works on campus, promoted from professor and biology department chairman to associate dean of the school of liberal arts in recent years. "He's my academic advisor. It's odd but helpful.

I'm a liberal arts major, so he approves my schedule, and I can get all the good class times and teachers before they fill up."

She's impressed.

"It's not a big deal," I explain.

"Why don't you like to go home?"

"I've got a moody sister who's not technically my sister who has moved back home, living in her old room, and I think she hates me. Also, I don't have much in common with my parents." Beside us, one of my fellow pledges runs, whooping, to cannonball into the pool and we laugh, stepping back to avoid being soaked. "This is my home," I say, pointing to the fraternity house. "These are my brothers." I've been a pledge for all of four days.

Enrolling at Ole Miss wasn't an easy decision because it wasn't a decision. With a faculty and staff scholarship, tuition is free; Mom and Dad didn't offer other options. The fraternity bill is three hundred dollars a month, and it covers meals at the house and money to pay for the party bands we get for home football games and spring flings. Mom pays the bill without telling Dad how much it is. He gives me twenty-five dollars a week spending money, and I earn extra getting up at 6:00 a.m. on weekday mornings to DJ at the local pop radio station.

"Thanks for tuning in to WSUH," I proclaim on the air. "We've got all the hits, all the time. Here's a new one from John Waite—and listen, he ain't missing you at all." Getting up early for work when going to bed late, frequently after nights of drinking, isn't ideal, but the money helps me keep up socially, so I keep spinning the hits for extra cash.

The part-time job is doable since I don't require much acclimation to campus. I know the place intimately, having used it as a playground for as long as I can remember. I know which Coke machines you can fish your arm in to get free drinks. I know how to climb through the basketball arena's roof to play pickup games on the varsity court. And I know the dress code, jargon, and everything needed to fit in, thanks to an apprentice under the tutelage of the likes of Barry and Robert.

While my first official party on campus is familiar since I've been drinking here for years, it's all better now. I'm in college, not just a wannabe looking in, and I'm already talking to the prettiest freshman on campus. "I'm sorry, I forgot to ask. What's your name?"

"Kent," she says.

"Like the boy's name?"

"Yes," she says, rolling her big brown eyes. "Mother had a friend in college, a girl named Kent. She liked it and gave the name to me. Whenever I meet someone new, they get confused by my name. 'Kim? Is it Kim?' they ask. 'No, it's Kent,' I say again and again."

"Well, then," I say, "you deserve a drink, Kent."

"They told us not to drink the punch," she says.

"Good advice."

The pledge trainer sent me to the liquor store that afternoon with forty dollars to buy pure grain alcohol. I'm just eighteen, and the drinking age in Mississippi is eighteen for beer and twenty-one for liquor, but he assumed, correctly, that, as a local, I know which store will sell it to an underage freshman. He sent two other pledge brothers to the grocery store for jugs of Hawaiian Punch, fruit, and bags of ice, while assigning Skeeter, another pledge brother and a bit of a wild man, the chore of mixing it all.

"They say Skeeter peed in the punch," I tell Kent. "How about a Bud Light instead?"

We walk into the house to get longneck beers iced down in a bathtub.

"Cheers," I say, extending my bottle.

"Cheers," she says, rattling her bottle against mine.

We make small talk and smile, but way sooner than I like, she says she has to leave. "I've got class in the morning."

"I'd like to see you again," I say.

She gives a cute, shy smile. "OK," she says, then she's gone.

The music is still blaring; the night is young. Some are dancing, others are swimming, and I've got a substitute DJ at the station in the morning, and my first class isn't until 10:00 a.m. I see Skeeter standing by the trash can, holding a cigarette in one hand and a drink cup in the other, and walk over.

"Did you piss in the punch?" I ask, nodding to the trash can.

He laughs. "No." He tilts his cup, showing it's full of punch.

"Well, OK then," I say, taking a cup and filling it up.

Skeeter offers me a cigarette.

"I don't smoke," I say.

He smiles. Skeeter is a wise one.

The next day, I crack open my eyes and look at the clock radio beside my bed. It's almost noon. I've slept through class.

"Ugh," I say in a raspy voice, rubbing my hand across my forehead.

My mouth is so dry, my cheeks draw in tightly, clinging to my tongue, and my hair and clothes are reeking of smoke.

My roommate is studying at his desk. "Hey, pardner, how do you feel?" he asks.

"Fine," I say. "I'm fine."

I settle in at my new house, happy that Sigma Nu is a good fit. Before pledging, I'd gone on a drunken recruitment weekend to New Orleans with the Tekes, but they seemed more like good ole boys, called me "dude," and were into marijuana. I tried pot a few times in high school, but it made me hungry, sleepy, and paranoid.

Sigma Nu has a substantially higher chapter grade point average, and some members don't even drink. Nobody offers me marijuana in recruitment, even though I suspect some smoke. Members call me David, tell me about a weeknight chapter Bible study, brag about intramural sports success, and boast of notable alumni, including Archie Manning and Sen. Trent Lott. Archie is my hero, who once bounced me on his knee in our home, who became a Saint and got sacked time after time but got back up, determined on the next play. And my future plans include one day becoming a senator like Trent Lott.

I drink, but mostly on weekends. I attend the chapter Bible study and win a student body senate position. I make my grades, get initiated, elected to a fraternity office, and appointed to a student government cabinet position. I'm happy, energized, and focused on something besides patchwork family.

As a student government cabinet member, I'm the school spirit leader. The problem is the school has little spirit to lead. It's 1985, and the football team is losing. Even beyond that, morale is low because one of the students' favorite traditions has been canceled.

The tradition was that before kickoff, the cheerleaders threw bundles of small Confederate flags into the bleachers. The students caught the bundles, distributed the flags, and waved them in unison when the band played "Dixie" or the team scored a touchdown. Although the tradition was beloved by many, plenty of others, myself included, were ready to do away with the Confederate flag and its racist overtones. Ole Miss chancellor Gerald Turner received pressure from both sides and managed to cleverly score a tactical victory. He didn't outright forbid the Confederate flag, which would have outraged some alumni donors. Instead, he banned the wooden sticks that the flags had been stapled to. Suddenly the flags were cumbersome to wave and began disappearing.

But nothing has replaced them. Something needs to. And I've got just the thing.

I call the chancellor's office. "This is David Magee, and I'm a student and the director of school spirit," I explain. "I'd like to meet with the chancellor."

"What's this about, may I ask?"

"I'd like to talk about the flag," I say.

"Well, I believe that decision is made."

"No. I'm sorry. I should have explained. I agree with getting rid of the flag. But I have a solution to fill the gap, something that might improve school spirit."

The chancellor takes the meeting, in which I suggest the school purchase red and blue pompons for cheerleaders to hand out at games.

I sense he likes the idea, but he won't approve it, sending me to the athletics director for another meeting.

Warner Alford was an All-American lineman and co-captain of the team at Ole Miss in 1960, the year they won the national championship. As a player, Alford helped Ole Miss become a national power in an era of all-white teams. As an athletics director, he is working to help Ole Miss diversify. He wanted the Confederate battle flags gone, so perhaps he'll be open to my idea, but I'm nervous.

When I go to his office, Alford shakes my hand firmly, then points to a chair for me to sit. His desk is stacked with reports and paperwork, and he drums his fingers on the folder in front of him.

"Just tell me what it is, son; I've got a busy day." His voice is deep and loud.

I slide an open catalogue across to him, point with a finger that seems to be shaking to a photo I've circled showing red and blue pompons.

"I've already checked," I say. "If we order them soon, they can be here in time for the cheerleaders to hand out at the opener against Memphis State."

He pulls the catalogue close to study it with a frown. "Son," he says, "you are going to need almost $15,000 to buy that many pompons. Do you have that money?"

"No, sir, I was . . . I was hoping the university will pay for this."

He shakes his head. "I appreciate what you are trying to do, son, but there's something you've got to understand. And I need you to listen and listen well. You are going about this all wrong." He leans toward me, his voice growing even louder. "If you and I sit here and make this agreement and we hand out pompons, the cheerleaders might get booed off the field by folks who want that rebel flag back. If you're going to get this done, you've got to build in grassroots support. You need to get buy-in from the students. They've got to want this. So"—he leans back and his chair squeaks—"I tell you what. You get the students to raise money and bring me $7,500, I'll match the other half." He slaps his desk. "We'll buy these pompons, son. We'll get your tradition started."

We shake hands as we did when I entered, but this time his eyes are on me, not the folder on his desk. "I believe you can do this," he says.

I ask Sigma Nu to donate the first $1,000 needed, and they commit. Next, I write letters to other fraternities on campus. Checks roll in from all but two, which explain in their replies that the battle flag is preferred while the effort is appreciated. I count up what I've got: $6,000. I take the money to Alford with a few days left before the ordering deadline. "Sir, I've had a good response," I tell him, "but I'm still a little short."

"Well, son," Alford says, "let me tell you what. I'm going to match this money you have raised, making up the difference for that $15,000. We're going to start this new tradition and hand out red and blue pompons at football games this season."

He stands up and extends a hand, delivering a firm shake, followed by a pat on the back. "That's some good work, son. I like your leadership skills."

It's the highest compliment anyone of authority has given me. And I'm gratified to help the university take another step away from the battle flag. My Sigma Nu brothers are proud of me, and my fraternity advisor suggests I might have a future in politics.

"You can be governor one day," he says. "You can be whatever you want to be."

And I want to succeed to prove Dad wrong. He's never been convinced that I would amount to much. When I told him in high school that I wanted to write books after college, he said, "Oh, well." The next day he suggested a career in sales. "You're so handsome," he said.

As my academic advisor, he steers me away from challenging classes. He doesn't ask about my grades. When I meet with him, I'm back out in the hall within five minutes. I know he spends more time with his other advisees.

So I'll succeed in spite of him. Or I'll succeed to spite him.

It's my sophomore year, and I'm holding office as a recruitment chairman, imagining one day my name will be added to the fraternity's list of notable alumni. I've traded my DJ job for work on campus as a sorority houseboy, which means busing tables at lunch and dinner. My compensation is free meals and lots of smiles from the cute sorority girls. I'm loosely dating a freshman, but I'm unimpressed with how much she drinks, clumsily falling on me late in the night and mushily whispering close to my face with her beer breath. I don't want that, for her or for me.

My life is tracking toward everything I hope to achieve. But even here, my family drama intervenes.

Dad's now driving the family Buick LeSabre; he started sharing it with Mom when he sold Charlie the Dodge Dart. From the parking lot at the Sigma Nu house, I can see the lots for adjacent fraternities, and I've been spotting the LeSabre.

Dad never stops by to see me, which is good. But he's visiting the other houses. He's visiting more frequently after work and on weekends. Eunice is living at home again, and Mom tells me her fits are back. That's undoubtedly pushing Dad out, but now he's creeping in my space, the only place where I've felt free to become myself. I take to peeking out of the windows, scanning the lots for his car, feeling a little jab when I find it, the LeSabre living up to its name. If I have to pass it on the way to class, I feel the urge to sprint. I try to deduce what students he's visiting and avoid them.

One evening, I need to pick up some clothes, and Mom says she'll be out at a ladies club meeting, but I'm welcome to come anyway. She'll leave a clean shirt in the laundry room, pressed.

Walking through the back door and into the kitchen, I find the sink is full of pots and pans, the remnants of a multi-course extravagant dinner.

My heart beats faster, realizing I'm an uninvited guest.

I walk into the den, and sitting close to Dad on the couch is one of my classmates. He's a premed major, and he's got a boyish face that Dad so loves. They are bent over a photo album.

"Oh," Dad says, jumping off the couch. "I'm showing Chad some of the pictures I made."

Chad sits still, his cheeks and neck flaring red.

"OK, well, I'm just here to get a shirt," I say, scurrying away.

Another day, a beautiful Friday afternoon in October, I'm strolling down Fraternity Row, waving to some friends driving by, when I see Dad's car parked outside Chad's fraternity house. My stomach twists like I could throw up, but I keep walking. My dad's not breaking any rules. Visitors are allowed at fraternity houses, and Chad is nineteen, old enough to make decisions. It's also hard for me to imagine Dad doing something that Chad doesn't want done because Dad's always been timid. Mom likes to tell the story about Dad arriving at Ole Miss as a professor. He came from a small Baptist college where they didn't have fraternities, but when requested, he agreed to be the required chaperone for a fraternity that needed to host a party. Mom says that Dad asked for the rules and read them word for word. When he saw some students with alcohol, he made them pour it out and cited the bylaws. They didn't invite him to chaperone again.

I'd like to ask him to leave Fraternity Row now and never come back. Instead, I swallow down my queasiness and walk into dinner at the fraternity house with a smile, delivering high fives like everything's perfect. We're all excited because it's homecoming weekend, and the Sigma Nu party is my responsibility as the social chairman. I've booked The Malemen to play. The all-black show band has been around for years, playing cover songs from the Commodores, The Gap Band, and Prince, with a few originals: "The Malemen do deliver." They've got a lively stage show with costume changes and horns and backup singers.

I check on the band in their large bus parked out back, then get dressed in a white button-down shirt topped with a sleeveless argyle sweater and khaki pants. Then I help welcome the students who crowded into our courtyard to listen, dancing and drinking, loving the vibe. I'm slugging vodka and orange juice and scanning the crowd, accepting high fives from my brothers for the big win.

The crowd keeps growing until there are several thousand students. I've got sixteen $100 bills in my pocket to pay the band, and I'm feeling dangerous, like a gangster seeking trouble, the vodka misfiring more neurons with every passing minute. I'm mad at Dad. I'm mad at Mom. I'm mad at myself, and I'm eager to throw it all away, to become who I started as in the adoption home in New Orleans: nobody. The final set ends, and I half stagger, half swagger to the band bus.

An older member, dressed in his orange polyester show suit with ruffles and white shoes, opens the door when I knock.

"I've got your money," I say, handing over the bills.

"Thank you, sir," he says, without bothering to count them.

"Hey, uh, do y'all have any weed?"

He looks surprised and doesn't answer.

"C'mon," I say boldly into the bus. "I know you got some weed. I just need a joint. Just one."

The band member explains he'll be right back. Minutes later, he's back at the bus door with a smile.

"All right," he says, "where we gonna do it?"

"Well, hmm. Let's go to my room," I say.

The music has ended, but the party is still going strong, in rooms, in hallways, in the courtyard. Everyone is drinking, but marijuana is not allowed in the house, a rule rigidly enforced. I live on the second floor with a roommate, who's busy in the courtyard. The band member follows me to my room, the size of a small storage stall, and I shut the door behind us. The beds are elevated to fit our hand-me-down couches beneath, and we sit.

"This ain't much," the band member says, laughing, as he pulls a fat rolled joint from his pocket.

"Yeah," I say, "but it's home."

"We can do this in here?" he asks, gesturing at the room with his lighter.

"Sure," I say. "Why not?"

He lights the joint, takes a big puff, then hands it to me. I take two puffs, coughing on the second, and smoke fills the room, seeping beneath the doorjamb into the hallway. We keep smoking until we hear a yell. Someone is yelling, coming toward us down the hallway. The band member looks at me, mid-toke, with wide eyes.

"Alarm! Alarm!" calls the voice. Now I can hear who it is: David Scott, our chapter president, a non-drinker who leads our Bible study.

"Someone is smoking marijuana in the house!" David Scott yells. "It needs to stop now!"

The band member stubs the joint into our carpet, twisting his shoe into it before dashing toward one of the closets. He gets in, crouches beneath the hanging clothes, and pulls the door closed as David Scott's screaming continues.

I'm standing in the middle of the room, pleading to the closet. "It's OK," I whisper. "It's not a big deal."

"No," he says in a frightened voice, from behind the closed door. "I can't get in trouble with the law. No police. You gotta get me out of here. No police."

"Sir," I explain, "the police aren't going to get us. Nobody is calling the police. It's just David Scott. He's gonna be a doctor or a preacher, or maybe both. No police."

"No police," he says.

"Listen, I've got a plan. When David Scott gets to the other end of the hall, we'll run out of here. You get into the bus, and I'll take it from there."

David Scott, still looking for the culprit, still shouting "Alarm! Alarm!" turns the corner and we bust from the room, sprint down the hall and out the door.

At the bus, I slur an apology. "I didn't mean to get you into trouble."

"That's all right," he says, before shutting the bus door. "I shoulda known better than hitting a J with a white boy."

The next afternoon, I receive a summons to David Scott's room.

"Come in," he says, when I knock. "We've got something to talk about."

I stand in front of him and he glowers at me. "Someone was smoking pot in the house last night," he says. "The smoke came from the vicinity of your room. Do you know anything about it?"

"Um, no, I . . . I don't know anything about that," I stammer, "other than what I heard. Everybody was talking about it. Wonder who it was?"

I am a fraud, just like my father.

On Monday, I skip class and ask around the house for someone who wants to go drinking. One night turns into a week, and a week turns into a month. I skip my classes and squelch my despair with a party persona, all false laughter and zeal. I can't seem to destroy my prospects fast enough. By the end of the semester, I'm in full tailspin and failing my classes. I resign from my student government leadership post and my fraternity office and call my father for a meeting.

I'm in his office at the Lyceum, seated in a chair like the other students he advises. He's heard from the dean of students that I'm struggling, but he doesn't know how seriously. I explain that I haven't been to my classes for a month. He says he worried the fraternity environment would be more than I could handle.

"If anything," I explain, "the fraternity motivates me to succeed. It's more me letting the fraternity down."

"Well," he says, "there's just one option. I'll get you withdrawn from classes."

"Isn't it past the withdrawal deadline?"

"I'll get it done. I want you to take the time to think about what you are doing, who you are hurting. It's hard to see you like this."

I want to say something, but my eyes get teary, and words stall in my throat. I leave Dad's office determined to get away, for good. I need a new life, one where the pain isn't staring back at me across the fraternity parking lot.

I'll quit school and work full-time. That's my plan. Maybe I'll join the Air Force. They can send me far away, I'll earn my own money, and in a few years, perhaps I can start back in college somewhere else.

Meanwhile, I'm living back at home and so is Eunice, and the November days are gray and lonely. My twentieth birthday approaches. I don't like my birthday, which says abandonment at Sellers more than cake and ice cream. The best birthday I recall was my tenth, when I celebrated with my friends. Mom got a room at Pizza Hut and my friends gave me a bunch of cool gifts, including a new football and a Miami Dolphins replica jersey ordered from the Sears catalog, and we ate pepperoni slices until the back of our throats burned from the salt. Birthdays since have been mostly painful. Besides, Dad bakes the desserts in our house, making cheesecakes in an assortment of flavors with varying success, and I've seen him deliver those same cheesecakes to countless boys since I can remember. I don't want his cakes.

I'm waiting tables at a local restaurant and saving money, with plans of leaving in the spring to find work and solace. Eunice sleeps till almost noon every day, so I can get in the shower and out of our shared bathroom before I have to see her. She's up late at night while I'm asleep, so our paths barely cross. When I'm not working, I stop by the fraternity house and visit friends to avoid home. There's an end-of-semester party, and I don't go for very long because I don't want to drink, realizing that alcohol makes it all worse. I merely stop by to greet the arrivals for a hello.

I see Kent's friend, a Kappa, and give a wave. She walks over and asks how I've been. I explain that I'm working, living at home, that my party days are behind me. She nods while I'm talking.

"You should call Kent," she says.

I want to, but I'm not sure she'll talk to me. I've called her a few times to ask her out, and she agreed once. We went to a movie, but I was too nervous to talk and so was she, and it was clumsy.

"Kent's been waiting for you to settle down," the friend says.

"I have settled down."

"Exactly. You should call her."

Kent lives at the Kappa sorority house, where rooms don't have phones. To reach her, I call the main line in the foyer and hope someone answers, and I ask them nicely to walk up the stairs to the second floor and shout, "Kent, phone for you!"

On this day, I get lucky, as five minutes later, in a breathy voice, Kent picks up the phone.

We see a movie, and I'm still nervous but this time succeed in talking to her. And she is able to talk back. I like the way she doesn't try to build herself up and is interested in the little details, like the song playing on the radio and where we will eat. I like everything about her. We share lunches and dinners together, with hamburger steaks and hot sandwiches. When we take walks around town, I look at houses with "For Sale" signs, and I imagine living in one with her. I imagine that instead of my messed-up family, we'd have happy kids, harmonious dinners. I'm becoming convinced that this soft-voiced rice farmer's daughter is the key to my future happiness.

When Kent goes home for Christmas, we talk by phone, but it's not the same. She says I sound lonely.

"What will y'all do for Christmas?" she asks.

"Try not to jump out of the window," I say.

She calls back the next day. "Come to my house."

DeWitt, Arkansas, population 3,293, is a farming community that's known for mosquitoes so thick in the summer you can't walk outside, and migratory ducks so plentiful in the winter the head of Ducks Unlimited spends his hunting time nearby. Kent has told me there are two banks in town, a handful of churches, one public school system, and a small, mostly empty town square. We'll celebrate Christmas at her grandparents' house, along with her mother, father, sister, aunts and uncles, and first cousins—nearly twenty in all. I'm nervous driving through the flat Delta farmland, flooded fields in every direction, the sky dotted with flying geese like Morse code.

When I arrive, Kent is waiting for me outside. We hug, and I kiss her cheek. She points across the highway. "That's my house," she says. "We live across the street."

A tight-knit family, many of whom graduated from Ole Miss, so this should be friendly territory, but Kent can tell I'm nervous.

Leading me toward the door, she asks, "Are you ready?" The opening of the Ole Miss Hotty Toddy Cheer.

I smile. "Hell yes," I say, continuing the joke.

I'd learned the words to Hotty Toddy before I learned to read in school.

Are you ready?

Hell yeah! Damn right!

Hotty Toddy, Gosh almighty,

Who the hell are we? Hey!

Flim flam, Bim bam

Ole Miss, by damn!

In the living room, Kent's entire family is gathered around a roaring fire overheating the room. As one, they turn to appraise me, and I feel my face flush.

"Hotty toddy," says someone from the back of the room.

"Damn right," I say, and blessedly, everyone laughs.

Most in the room are drinking beer or wine, and lunch is still cooking. Someone offers me a beer, but I turn it down. Kent's mother shares a story from her Ole Miss days about driving to the Marshall County line with her friends for cold beer, and I smile.

Kent is a tenth-generation Arkansan, and she has her father Bill's dark complexion and quiet personality. Bill grew up in DeWitt, son of the local town doctor, graduating with a degree in agriculture from Texas A&M. He's farming rice on several thousand acres and likes to duck hunt, but his girls aren't interested; the shotguns are too loud.

He invites me to go in the morning—my first invitation for hunting. For years, I've watched my friends hunt with their fathers and I pretended I didn't want to go, but Dad was scared of guns and had never been himself, so I'd sleep late in deer and duck seasons and proclaim hunting held no interest.

"I don't have a gun," I explain.

He smiles. "I've got plenty of guns. Everything you'll need."

Later, when we're walking across the street to Kent's house, she slips her hand into my elbow. "Dad likes you. He's been waiting on you. Someone to hunt with," she says, and gives my arm a squeeze.

It seems like I've barely closed my eyes that night when I hear the bedroom door crack open.

"Time to get up," her father says. "Shooting time is in an hour."

He loans me a coat, hat, coveralls, and rubber waders with boots. We load guns in his truck and drive twenty minutes outside of town, turning off on a dirt road. Rabbits flee in the truck lights ahead before we come to a stop. We walk down a slippery levee, barely keeping balance in the dark, arriving at a hay-covered steel pit in the ground. Kent's father kicks back the lid.

"This is it," he says, nodding.

We climb down, lower the lid, and take a seat on the wooden bench inside.

"Are the fans mad Ole Miss isn't going to a bowl this year?" he asks.

"Absolutely," I say. "The defense is good. If they could just get the offense moving."

He glances at his watch, then pauses.

"Listen," he says.

Flapping wings whistle in the wind, and I hear ducks calling.

"Mallards," he says.

"How do you know without seeing them?"

"By the quack," he says, picking up a wooden call that's strapped around his neck. "Mallards have that deep quack, like this," and he imitates them perfectly.

He glances again at his watch. "Shooting time," he says, and cracks the pit lid to peer outside. It's thirty minutes before sunrise, and I'm basking in the thin light of dawn, seeing it all so clearly. "Here they come."

He lifts the call to his mouth and bellows across the Arkansas prairie.

"Get ready," he says.

My heart flaps alongside the whistling wings, and they are growing closer, closer. I click the shotgun's safety.

"Now!" he says, and flings open the lid. "Let's get them."

I aim and shoot twice in quick succession.

Two ducks with green heads fall to the water. Mallards.

"Good shot!" he says, smiling.

He may have hit them both, but he's giving me credit.

"Thanks," I say, pride surging through my chest behind my borrowed coat. I'm already reloading the gun.

The next semester, I'm back in school, drinking less and responsibly, serious about my new girlfriend, Kent, and my new major, journalism. I'm not living in Sigma Nu but alone, in an apartment. I pay my rent with a job at the small local newspaper writing sports stories. I have wanted to write since high school. Dad hands me clippings of my stories from the paper every few days, not because he's making a scrapbook but because he's circling my grammatical errors, correcting them with black marker. He's right, of course, and I do want to improve, but he manages to leach the joy out of publication.

I write a three-part series for the newspaper on drug use among college students, interviewing my peers. These are A students heading to graduate school, and we've been friends since my freshman year, yet I am surprised at their experiences with ecstasy, marijuana, and cocaine. Because I agree not to use their names, they share details and describe the guilt and anxiety the drugs cause them.

I win an Associated Press regional award for reporting. Still, the one professional source on campus who talks to me on the record, the director of a drug education program, gets chastised by the administration for speaking out. "Your stories were good," she tells me. "But I might lose my job for talking to you."

I don't want her to suffer repercussions, but I like the feeling of bringing to light the things we need to be thinking about, talking about. My life began with a lie. I begin to think journalism could be the antidote to that false birth certificate: paper that tells the truth instead of covering it up.

I pursue more stories, writing mostly sports, and receive fewer black-circled errors in clippings from my father. And I begin to think that I could build a life for Kent and me through this skill I'm honing, late nights at my desk I used to spend drinking pitchers of beer at a bar. Kent says I write well and offers tips on my stories without sounding critical. I'll show her a draft and she'll proofread one and point out a typo or read a sentence and say she doesn't understand.

Sometimes I fantasize about what our future will hold, me writing stories others want to read with her offering support and guidance.

"I'm gonna do something big," I tell Kent. "Wait and see. I'm gonna be the best husband, the husband you deserve. And we're gonna have an amazing family." I kiss her temple. "The best."

"I just want us to be happy," she says.

I'm hired full-time as a reporter at the small newspaper, earning $225 a week. I ask Kent to marry me, and we wed our senior year of college at First Baptist Church in DeWitt, where Kent attended growing up. The reception is held at the local country club, a small brick building overlooking a swimming pool and a weedy, nine-hole golf course. We dance to a four-piece band playing jazz music. The groom's cake is red and blue—Ole Miss colors—and there's a keg of Miller Lite beer in the corner, but I'm too excited to drink.

Dad has his camera, pretending he's a hired photographer. I wish he'd just stop and talk to guests, but he's hiding behind the lens. I cringe when Dad lines my groomsmen for individual photos in a back corner. I know my friends don't want to be photographed, but he's my father, so they don't say no. He snaps dozens of pictures, enough to fill another photo album. Kent notices he doesn't bother taking bridesmaids photos.

"That's Lyman," I say.

She must see sadness flicker across my face because she leads me to the dance floor and slips her arms around my neck. "We're married!" she says, grinning.

"Damn right," I say.

We make our getaway as the jazz band plays a few "Dixie" bars, and friends and family shower us with her father's homegrown rice.

Our son William is born at the Oxford hospital two years after Kent and I marry. With the first name after her father, William has my last name, my own family at last. The nurse who is checking our baby's vitals smiles at me. I have baby-smooth skin and a few last teenage pimples, and she tells me I'm too young for fatherhood. But I am ready, wanting it more than I've ever wanted anything.

The nurse puts William into my arms. He weighs more than eight pounds and is wrapped tightly in a blanket that frames his precious face. I peer down, seeing a tiny nose and a wide mouth, familiar-looking.

"He looks like you," the nurse says.

I tingle, and a tear drips down my cheek.

One tear turns to many; they are streaming down. William is the first person on earth I am related to that I've met.

January 16, my son's birthday, coincidentally Eunice's birthday. I fear it's a curse, but I talk myself out of that. Eunice doesn't visit the hospital. Mom makes up some story about Eunice thinking she has the flu. It's just as well, though, since this moment is ours.

I look at Kent, sitting upright in the hospital bed, backlit by the heat lamp. She's weeping, managing to look both angelic and exhausted. I clutch William tightly, whispering a promise. I tell my son I will be the best father ever. I will take care of him, his mother, and other siblings to come. I will give him everything. I will build him a childhood better than I had, without the secrets, without the darkness.

And staring down at my son's perfect face, I realize there's someone else who needs to meet him: my birth mother, his paternal grandmother. There's no way she doesn't want to meet him. And there's no way she doesn't want to meet me again, having last seen me when I was a few minutes old like William. If I want to create the perfect family, if I want to end the days of being stuck with the strange babysitter, I have to get rid of all the secrets. Right then and there, with the best eight pounds in the world in my arms, I vow to find her.

I announce my plans in a newspaper column. "I want to know where I got my eyes, my hands, my laugh, but the state of Louisiana has my information locked away." I'm hoping someone might pass a clipping along to another, leading her to me. The column helps me win a journalism award as one of the top three newspaper columnists in the state, but the telephone doesn't ring. I can't contact Sellers directly because it has long since closed. Instead, I contact the state agency in Louisiana that holds the sealed records. A social worker answers, saying the law won't allow the release of any identifying information. But there's one hope, she says. If either birth parent has contacted the agency looking for me, they can make a connection.

"Hold on," the social worker says, "and I'll check your file." I hold on and hold my breath. But when she picks up the phone again, she apologizes. "It doesn't appear anyone is looking for you."

Of course not. "Is there anything you can do?"

"We'll mail you non-identifying information that may be useful."

The next week, a letter arrives. "Your birth mother was a high school graduate. She had green eyes. Her father was in sales. She had two sisters. Your birth father was a junior in college. He had one sister. His father was an elected school superintendent. He played basketball."

It is nothing, really, information so vague and trivial that finding my birth mom is still a long shot. Yet it moves me profoundly. I am somebody because I came from somebody, and my family is out there, somewhere.

∗ *Chapter Four* ∗

Anxiety

That's me, in the front yard, surrounded by my three children, eighteen months apart from oldest to youngest, William, Hudson, and Mary Halley. I'm in my early thirties, and our 1928 house, recently remodeled, is mostly paid for. It's just a few streets off the town square on one side and touching the edge of Ole Miss on the other side. Kent is in the kitchen, and when I look up at the window, she waves with her spatula. Tonight she's making poppy seed chicken, one of the family favorites.

My children rarely, if ever, fight. We've taught them to say "yes, please" and "thank you." They sit snugly on the church pew with us on Sunday mornings, wearing the matching clothes that Kent smocks. They attend the same public schools I did, with many of the same teachers, who call William "David" by mistake—that's how much we look alike—though he's a much better student than I was.

Mom and Dad live in the same house several streets over. They babysit, and the children call them BeBe and Granddaddy. BeBe hosts them for Easter egg dyeing and playing board games with no rules, doting on them. At least, that is, until Eunice storms unexpectedly into the house. Then, Mom drops everything, focusing all attention on Eunice.

Eunice is living in a farmhouse five miles outside of town on some acreage that Mom and Dad purchased for her, driving a truck that Mom and Dad gave her. I try to remind myself that I don't want handouts, that I'm proud of my self-sufficiency, but it's funny how old family dynamics trigger us. A while back, Dad agreed to cosign the banknote for our house renovation. I suppose he agreed in order to create balance, or the illusion of balance, between his kids. I'm responsible for all payments, happily so. But every month, he stops by to find me alone, asking when I can take him off the house note. So I do. It rankles, but I say nothing, reminding myself that Kent and I and the children we've created don't need anybody else.

The promise I made newborn William is still before my eyes at all times: I will provide the happy home I never had. And it's no chore; our children seem glad and easy to be on the receiving end of my attention, and they look deeply into my eyes when I speak, giggling at my jokes. Kent is the quiet counterbalance to my louder impulsiveness. We're an affectionate family. In the yard or family room, I like to scoop them into my arms or clutch the back of their necks and tell them some of the ways they've made me proud.

* * *

Now it's 5:00 p.m. on a Friday, and I've got a beer in one hand and the football in another. I am teaching the boys how to cut and run and catch. Five-year-old Mary Halley yells that she wants to go put on her Ole Miss cheerleader uniform and she'll be back to root for us.

We're playing our favorite, "offense-defense," one-on-one football with William against Hudson with me as the all-time quarterback. Whoever is playing defense has to wait alone while I call the play with the offensive player. Crouched down, I'm almost kneeling as William pulls my face close to his ear so he can hear but Hudson can't. It's more of a snuggle than a huddle, more of a compliment session than play calling.

"OK," I tell him, "you had an amazing week of school, and I'm so proud of your high score in reading." I kiss him on his cheek, warm from sprinting. "Let's go on a three-count hut, then you run across on a drag pattern, OK?"

"Got it," William says, pushing his wire-frame glasses further up onto his nose. He's got astigmatism, which makes catching a ball hard, but if he catches it, neither Hudson nor most anybody else can outrun him.

I throw a soft pass across the middle, and William grabs it, turning on the speed to score.

Now Hudson joins me for his turn at offense. I pull my face close to his to deliver praise.

He giggles. "You smell like beer!"

"You smell like a sweaty boy!"

"Are you ready?" I say, and we break, heading to positions with great seriousness.

I underthrow a wobbly pass to Hudson, and he reaches over William for a dramatic catch and touchdown. Tie game.

Mary Halley is back, wearing her red and blue cheerleader outfit with white tights and tennis shoes. She hops down the front steps, her soft shoulder-length blonde curls bouncing.

"I've got news!" she announces.

"Come to the huddle," I say.

She joins William and me for the play call.

"OK, tell us the news," I say, putting my arms around my oldest and youngest.

She whispers, "Mom says dinner is ready."

I straighten, announcing to Hudson, "Last play before dinner. It's a tie game," then I return to the huddle.

"Dad," William says. "We need to run my play."

I know what he means, but I ask anyway.

"What play?"

"The cookie cutter."

I nod, and we break. Mary Halley runs back to the steps but can't keep the secret. "It's cookie cutter!" she exclaims to Hudson, erupting in giggles.

We'll run the play anyway. He zigzags down the lawn, crunching freshly fallen acorns, hoping to shake Hudson with his speedy pivots. I loft the ball soft and high toward the end zone so he can make the winning catch.

Bingo.

"Touchdown," he says proudly, after securing the ball under our goal-line oak tree.

Hudson delivers William a congratulatory high five as we head inside for dinner, all smiles. The kitchen smells wonderful, and Kent is bending over the table to light a candle, the flame's glow illuminating her beautiful face. I grab another beer and head upstairs to change my shirt and splash some water on my face. I place the beer on the vanity and look at myself in the mirror. *This beautiful life*, I think.

We're doing everything I hoped, giving the children the experiences I'd always yearned for. When I was a boy, I used to envy my friends who got to go to Alpine Camp for Boys on Lookout Mountain in the hills of North Alabama. This Christian camp was led for decades by Ole Miss alum Dick O'Ferrall, and I was jealous of my friends' stories of Mr. O, the kind of man who gets to know you, teaches you how to tie good knots, identify berries, and pull apart an owl pellet to identify the field vole it ate. The type of man who doesn't touch your hair or ask to take your picture.

Two summers ago, we packed William's clothes in a trunk and sent him away for a month to Alpine Camp. He's shy around strangers, nervous in new situations. I was worried that he'd be too anxious to enjoy himself, and I was worried that I couldn't stand having him away for thirty days. When we finally got to pick him up and were driving away, he broke down in tears when Kent asked about his clothing. He revealed that he wore his only pair of boxers every day for twenty-six days because none of the other boys in his cabin wore tighty-whities. Wearing dirty underwear for nearly a month at camp beat getting picked on by other boys.

Once tears subsided, he talked the rest of the drive home about his bunk mates and campfires and forest hikes.

"Can I go back next year?" he asks. We promise that he can and exchange a smile when he finally drops off to sleep.

Because I never want to be the type of person who avoids conflict at all costs, I'm drawn to conversations that bring light to moral dilemmas. Perhaps that's why the young adults seem to like the Sunday school class I lead for them at our church. I'm not good at following the prescribed lesson plans or regularly integrating scripture, but I prod them to debate the ideal work-life balance or consider what a Christian approach to racial injustice or economic inequality might look like. For Martin Luther King Jr. Day, I ask the class to consider if his reported marital infidelities dilute his society-changing work.

"King has been to the mountaintop, and he's lived in the gutter," I say. "One destination doesn't negate the other, and it's not our place to judge. But we can learn."

Unless I've stayed too late at a Saturday night function, teaching with red eyes and alcohol on my breath, we have robust conversations and lots to ponder for the next six days.

Weekdays, I'm working but home early enough to engage with each child, help with spelling words and baths, and tuck in. I'm also coaching my children's City League sports teams—now integrated, thank God. I coach all three of my children in basketball and soccer, and in addition, I coach flag football and baseball for the boys. It occurs to me that I've coached over twenty teams and have zero championship trophies. But the truth is I'm less concerned with winning than building self-confidence. The boys and girls give me heartfelt hugs after games. Those are my trophies.

Despite all of this affirmation, I feel restless. Impermanent.

I was named news editor at the paper, the youngest at a daily in the state, but I can't help wondering what else is out there. I notice a business opportunity in Oxford. While our town is too small for a Kinko's, we're big enough, with university work included, for a copying and printing center. I also know the small, family-owned newspaper has no more room for growth, so I leave the paper. I miss writing, but my business gamble was a good one. A line stretches out the copying center door. That's gratifying, sure, but I find I'm uninterested beyond that and wonder if I'm going to get stuck in job jail. Again, I'm looking around. Opening the copy center has taught me a valuable lesson, though. There are lots of good ideas, but only those checking almost every box are worth pursuing. So I just have to find out what boxes I'm missing.

I run for city council, winning a close election against someone older and more qualified. He put signs in all the yards, while I avoid signs, which leads Dad to predict my better-qualified opponent will win. Instead of spending money on yard signs, I spend time handwriting letters. I write to many of the 1,600 district voters, complimenting each about some unique achievement or characteristic I know about them. I eke out a victory by thirteen votes. On the council, as a swing vote, I'm making a difference in saving this town I love. I help establish a historic district and shut down corruption by turning away a bribe on a construction project. I enjoy this work more than the copy center, but it doesn't change the fact that I'm thirty-four and wanting more. I can't shake an anxiousness that others don't seem to feel. When something goes wrong, even something small, I feel like I don't have the resiliency to cope or put my disappointment in perspective. It's like my psyche got damaged so when the curveballs of life come along, I'm just striking out.

A particularly vicious curveball nearly flattens me when I learn Kent's father has colon cancer. This man, who taught me to love the predawn Arkansas sky shuddering with the wings of migrating mallards, has been a mentor to me. He not only introduced me to duck hunting, but he taught me to be a man of integrity, a man who follows the rules and is also willing to lead in setting the rules. Not being the type to complain or worry others, he ignored the signs of cancer until it was too late. His death, at fifty-four, is cruel and swift. Kent's mother is not the same; she can't recover, and Kent and her sister feel the strain. I feel it also. I try to go duck hunting without him, but I've lost interest, lost heart. I put away my hunting coat and hang up my rubber waders.

The death of this man contributes to my feeling of instability. But that's not entirely it, nor is it Kent's inaccessibility in her grief, nor is it my resentment in seeing Mom and Dad sacrifice for Eunice. Sure, these things matter, but there's something that makes me feel skittish and unsettled on the planet. It's that I don't know who I am.

Sure, these precious children are mine. They even look like me. William has my wide mouth, Hudson my lanky frame, and Mary Halley my pug nose. But who did I get these traits from? And who did they get them from? And it's about more than the shape of noses and mouths. Why do I drink when Mom and Dad don't? Why am I a storyteller when Mom and Dad aren't? Why am I an athlete when Dad can't walk nine holes without heat stroke? Why can't I stop asking why?

When I announced in a newspaper column eight years ago that I was seeking my birth mother, it was a Hail Mary. Now we've got this new thing, Google search. I enter into its bar of possibility: "private investigator in Louisiana." The first result, Sly Cat Investigations, leads me to Burt, the owner, and I mail him a thousand-dollar check to get started.

Burt has searched for a Sellers birth mother before. He says the agency took in girls mostly from Texas, Louisiana, Mississippi, Alabama, and Florida. He says the odds are high that my birth parents are from Louisiana because of the non-identifying information I received, which claimed that my birth grandfather was "an elected school superintendent." Counties in Louisiana elect their superintendents.

Three months later, Burt has used up one thousand dollars of time. He's shared a few possible candidates, including their photos, but none

create a spark. And with three children, a mortgage, and a small business, I don't have money to throw around unless I'm sure to get results.

"What's your best advice?" I ask.

"Well, perhaps instead of paying me," Burt says, "you should try
calling someone at the state with access to the records. Offer them the
one thousand dollars for information."

"That sounds like bribery," I say. "I've suffered enough from this
adoption thing. I don't want to end up in prison."

"Call it what you want, but this is Louisiana. It works."

Burt gives me the phone number for the state office that holds
the Sellers sealed records, received when the agency closed down in
the 1980s. When I phone, a bored bureaucrat answers. I explain how
I decided eight years ago to find my birth mother and how I hired a
private investigator who discovered only dead ends. He responds that a
volunteer registry can provide information when both the adoptee and
birth mother are actively searching.

"Tried that," I say. "Listen, about my birth mother, I don't want anything from her. I'm successful enough that I don't want anything but to
know her. And I've been searching for years."

He says, "Maybe it's meant to be this way."

"I—I just can't accept that somehow. I need to find her."

He sighs, but not unkindly. "I'm sorry," he says, "but I can't provide
information from sealed records. I could lose my job."

"Where are the records kept? Right there in your building?"

"Yeah," he says. "About one hundred feet below where I'm standing.
They're in the basement."

"So close. The answer I've been searching for, right below your feet."

He doesn't say anything.

I'm trying to get the courage to offer a bribe. Instead, I try a bluff.
"Sir, the private investigator did give me the potential name of my birth
mother. How about you go to the basement to get my records, and we
see if the name in the file matches the one he gave me?"

He pauses.

"Please," I say. "I need this."

"Can you hold on?" he says. "This may take fifteen minutes."

"I've been holding on for thirty-four years," I tell him. I hear his footsteps fading into a quiet, and my pulse pounds in the ear I press to the phone.

Fifteen minutes later, the footsteps return. "I'm back," he says, clearing his throat, "and I have your files."

This man I don't know holds my truth in his hands.

"Here's what I'm going to do," he says. "I'll read through and tell you some non-name and non-hometown information, and maybe that will get you started." I hear the sound of paper. "OK, so . . . It looks like your birth father was in college. He had blue eyes. He was twenty-one years old. He has one older sister. His father was a school superintendent, elected. His father was a good basketball player. It doesn't say where.

"Your birth mother was eighteen. Her name is Janie. She had green eyes. It looks like she had graduated from high school, had you, then planned to go to college. It doesn't say where. Her father was in sales. She has two younger sisters."

"Her name is Janie?" I ask.

"Yes."

I smile. He's given me a name. "Janie," I say. "Yes, that's the name my private investigator suggested."

"Hmm," he says, "this is interesting."

"What?"

"I'm reading notes here in the file. Your birth mother, Janie, named you. It says she visited you in the nursery and held you. She called you John David. Didn't you say your name is David?"

"Yes!"

"It says that she said she didn't want to give you up, but she didn't know what to do for you. She didn't have any way to support you."

Some strange sob is yanked from my throat, a sound I've never heard before.

"I'm sorry," he says awkwardly.

"It's fine, really," I say, trying to control my voice. "I'm just glad to get information."

"I know this is hard."

His voice is no longer bored. He's engaged in my story. I decided to press my advantage. "Sir," I say, "Janie gave me up more than thirty years ago. If she wanted to keep me as a young girl, I suspect she'd be fine hearing from me now. If I research every elected school superintendent from Louisiana, eventually, I'll find her without your help. But how many more years will pass while I search? Who knows if she'll even still be alive by then? This would be much easier if you just tell me her name. I promise I won't tell anyone who I got the information from."

He pauses, then sighs in a lengthy exhale.

"Her name is Janie Cooper, and she is from Monroe, Louisiana."

Click. He hangs up the phone.

Like most clichés, the saying "it's a small world" endures for good reason; even the long-lost mother who gave you away for adoption is more closely connected than you could have imagined.

My first move, once the news settles, is telling Mom and Dad. They are happy for me, confident that I'll meet Janie, certain I'll find peace at long last by meeting my blood family. Mom says it is strange thinking I may call another woman "Mother" but that she wants to meet Janie in the future.

"If I meet her, I have something to tell her."

"What's that, Mom?"

"I want to tell her thank you," she says, "thank you for sharing her wonderful son with me."

We cry, and she gives me a tight hug.

"You'll always be my son," she says.

My next move is to call my friend Mike from Monroe. Mike is a coach at Ole Miss, and we go to the same church. His wife, Allison, was my college classmate, but he's eighteen years older. Janie was eighteen when she had me, and Mike is a people person, making the odds high that one call does it all.

"Mike," I say, "did you happen to know a young woman from Monroe named Janie Cooper? I think she is two years older than you."

He pauses. "David," he says, his voice filling with wonder, "I sure do. You look just like her. She must be your mother. Praise the Lord. How about that." Mike starts citing what he knows. "Janie went to Neville High School. She was a cheerleader and a class beauty. Full of personality. But I sure did not know she had a baby. It was a different time. These things were secret. There may have been rumors, but I don't know."

"I wonder where she is now?" I ask. "If she's married, she may have a new last name."

"I remember Janie well, and I had a cousin who dated her some, but I haven't heard anything about her since high school. You know what, though? I bet I can get my hands on my yearbook pretty quick."

Mike brings it to our house within the hour. Kent and I lean over the photo he flips to, which shows a girl in a red and blue cheerleading uniform at the top of the cheer pyramid. She looks like she could fly, grinning, invincible. And her eyes, nose, and forehead look familiar. I look at Kent and I can tell she sees it too. This photo, from Janie's senior year, was six months before she got pregnant with me.

Mike also slides me a piece of paper. "My cousin knows where she lives," he says. "He said they didn't date after her junior year, but he knows her married name and where to find her."

"Janie Williams, Jonesboro, Arkansas," I read. I turn to Kent, whose sister lives in Jonesboro. "Williams," I say. "That name sounds familiar."

"That's because you've heard it before," Kent says. "My brother-in-law's practice. The other physician has that name."

She calls her sister, who confirms that her husband is a medical partner with Janie's brother-in-law. For all these years, I've wondered where my birth mother lives. It turns out she's only two degrees of separation away, with an in-law in medical practice with my wife's in-law while living only several streets away from my sister-in-law, not to mention having grown up with a friend.

Kent's sister tells us what she knows. Janie has three children—my half-brother and two half-sisters—and she's confident they don't know a thing about their mother putting a child up for adoption three-and-a-half decades ago. And there's this: Janie is involved in a long and messy divorce involving lots of money. Kent's sister isn't sure how Janie will greet my reemergence.

Soon, I will learn. Not well. Janie doesn't handle it well at all.

I find her number in the phone book, but it takes me several days to build my courage to dial it. When I do, Janie answers with a perky voice.

"Hello," I say, "this is David Magee." I've practiced this in my head. "I believe I am your adopted son."

Silence.

"I'm sorry to catch you off guard, but I don't know how else to do this . . ."

No response.

"If you put a child up for adoption at the age of eighteen, it's me, David."

She stammers, audibly shaken. "Well," she finally manages, "I guess that's right. But I'm sorry. I can't talk right now. My sister is here, and we're headed up to Oklahoma for the weekend."

"OK, can I call you after your return?"

"Well, that's not a good idea. The adoption isn't information anybody knows." Her tone changes just a bit, grows an edge. "How did you find me, anyway?"

"I got information from the state, which keeps the old Sellers records."

"Have you told anyone?"

"Just my sister-in-law."

"OK."

"But there's something you should know. Her husband is a medical partner with your brother-in-law. And my sister-in-law lives down the street from you."

She's silent again.

"I need to go," she says. "They're waiting on me."

"Can I call when you return?"

"No," she says. "That's not a good idea. Why don't you give me your number, and I'll call you when I get back to town?"

I count the hours and the days, but she doesn't call.

Kent asks if I'm OK.

"Sure," I say, "I'm fine."

After work, I stop by the convenience store, picking up a six-pack. I rarely consume beer on weekdays, preferring to focus on family and coaching youth sports. Initially, I drink two beers, maybe three. In time, I drink three, perhaps four. I figure that Kent's mother drinks two beers, maybe three, every day. If she drinks two or three and weighs seventy pounds less and nobody thinks it's a problem, then I can most certainly drink three or four, and it's not a problem. Some of my friends do worse. They drink whiskey, vodka, and gin during nightly cocktail hour, so my beer consumption can't possibly be troubling. Besides, I'm still tucking our children in at night, planting loving, beer-breath kisses on their foreheads.

I'm at home by myself early one evening, finishing a second beer, when I get a flush of courage, picking up the phone and dialing Janie. She answers and talks a little. I wonder if she, too, is drinking courage, but it doesn't matter. Whatever it takes.

"This is hard, David," Janie says. "Very hard. But I want you to know something. I love you. I've always loved you."

I try to respond, but my voice cracks.

"Can I ask you a few questions?" she says.

"Sure."

"Did a lawyer call you?"

"What?"

"Did a lawyer put you up to this?"

"No," I say. "I found you because I want to meet you. I want to know who I come from."

"I can't trust anyone," she says. "They are watching me. They'll do anything to make me look bad."

"I don't think this is bad," I say. "This is good. I think it is, anyway."

Silence.

"Ask me something else," I say.

"Isn't your birthday in November? Maybe November 23?"

"It's in November, but November 27."

"Gosh, they told us to forget everything. Funny. I've forgotten the date. I just knew it was around Thanksgiving."

"Yes, well, the date of Thanksgiving changes every year since it's the fourth Thursday of November."

"Well, sure, it does," she says, laughing. "That's right."

"And it wasn't Thanksgiving Day in 1965. I've looked at the calendar. I was born on a Saturday, two days after Thanksgiving."

"Well, I'm thankful for that," she says.

"What?"

"I'm thankful for you, that's what."

She says she's ready to meet within a few weeks, and I'm ecstatic. Finally, I'll meet my birth mother.

"I'll call back soon and set it up," she says. "But remember, we need to keep this quiet. Nobody can know. I've never told my children. I never told my ex-husband. Let's keep this a secret, OK?"

"Sure."

"If you tell," she says, "I won't be able to meet."

"I'll keep the secret."

Three weeks pass, but she doesn't call. Eight months pass, and she doesn't call.

I walk by the phone, and if nobody is watching, I'll pick it up, and scroll the caller ID log—no calls from Janie. Kent senses my increasing anxiety, my ridiculous shame at being unloved, unwanted.

"I know this is hard," she says.

"No, I'm fine."

She takes the children to visit her mother, who has moved to the lake in Hot Springs. Alone in the early evening, I'm hungry. I walk to the town square, taking a seat at the bar for a few beers and dinner. There's a university professor I know seated to the right. His wife is out of town. For three, maybe four beers, we talk.

I order a hamburger and fries, and the bartender brings my check.

The professor leaves.

A young woman in her mid-twenties takes a seat on my left around the bar bend. We begin to chat. She's a decade my junior and pretty, with shoulder-length blonde hair and green eyes. Her smooth legs extend from a miniskirt that I can easily see around the bend.

"Sir," I say to the bartender. "I'll have a glass of merlot."

I'm too full for another drink but unsure of how to navigate the moment without one. After that glass goes down, I'm less full, ordering another, then another. She's laughing at my jokes, flipping her hair, telling me I'm charming. Our barstools seem closer together somehow, or maybe I'm just tilting. My glazed eyes focus, embarrassingly, on her white halter top.

"I need to go," I say.

I look at my watch. It's a weeknight and getting late.

"Aww," she says. "Are you sure?"

I flash a smile of wine-stained teeth.

"One night never hurt anything," she says, leaning toward me.

The next morning, I open dry, bloodshot eyes, and she's gone. I don't remember her last name, and I barely remember the events after leaving the bar. My stomach hurts from the drink, from my guilt. I've just been awake for minutes, yet I already know she was wrong.

One night hurt everything.

Maybe every family is crazy, just crazy in a different way. Jon's mother drank too much and was a chain-smoker. Weasle lived with his mother, Bessie, who worked sixty hours a week, several half-siblings, and barely saw his father. Ashley's parents fought bitterly before her father peeled off in his new Corvette. My family's crazy too. So what? That doesn't make me rare and precious. But I can't seem to get past it. My response is what's not right. I'm allowing it to slowly poison everything I love.

I somehow feel that Janie is the key to finding peace with who I am, yet I'm uncertain if I should keep pursuing her when she's so clearly conflicted. I suspect walking away from her may be the best path, but once you've heard the mother you've never known say, "I love you; I've always loved you," turning back is nearly impossible.

Janie has moved to Plano, in the Dallas area. I find her number through information, surprised it's listed if she's trying to avoid me. I call; she doesn't answer. I call again; she doesn't answer. One day, nearly a year later, I call again.

"Hello," she says, in a different voice than what I've heard before.

"It's me, David."

She sucks in her breath. "I'm sorry," she says.

"No," I say. "Let's not go there. No apologies. This is a difficult situation."

"You've got that right," she says, with a deep chuckle.

"I don't want to push things, but I want to meet you. You're my mother, and too much time has passed. We should give it a try."

"Well, now," she says, "I'm not your mother. You have a mother."

"That's true, but my mother wants us to meet," I say. "Listen, I'll make it easy. I'll come to you."

"Well, I'm good for the next few days. Pick one and come then."

I want to leave now, this very minute, before she changes her mind, but the day after is the best I can do. "I've got a city council meeting tomorrow night; I'll hit that, then fly out of Memphis into DFW Wednesday morning if that works?"

"That works."

I land at the Dallas airport before lunch, picking up a beige Lincoln Town Car at the rental desk. I took two upgrades above my usual base rental because I need all the breathing space I can get. Here's the planned schedule: I'll drive to her house where we'll meet, then we'll find a restaurant for lunch, visit more, then I'll catch a flight out at 6:00 p.m.

Janie lives along a golf course of a posh club, and the number one fairway runs behind her house. I turn into her driveway, the Lincoln's wheel slipping through my sweat-slick palms. I'm wearing khaki pants, tennis shoes, and a striped golf polo. I'm afraid I'm too casual, but there's no turning back now; I'm reuniting with my birth mother thirty-five years after she left me at the adoption home.

I knock on the door, and Janie opens it with a sweeping, "Well, hellooo."

She takes a step back. "Let me get a good look at you." I'm aiming for a good look too. She's smiling, her hair short and blonde, and she's wearing a sleeveless denim jacket and jeans.

"Yep," she says, "there it is. You have our family look. I see that nose. My nose. And your eyes. Gosh, you look a lot like my father."

"You look a lot like my daughter, Mary Halley."

We smile at each other.

"DNA is powerful," I say. The moment seems to stretch forever.

"I remember holding you," she says, and thumbs away a tear. "I told them at the adoption home that I wanted to see you. They brought you from the nursery up to my room. I held you in my arms and told you I loved you. I told you I wanted to keep you, but I didn't know how; I had nothing." She shook her head. "I was just a scared girl."

It occurs to me that she needs to say that as much as I need to hear it. She almost looks relieved that I'm not angry at her. I'm not. I just want to be with her.

She leads me inside, where we sit on a couch. I look around. The furniture in the house is new with white upholstering. She seems to notice me noticing.

"When you go through what I've been through, you need a fresh start," she says, gesturing at the furniture.

"We could all use a fresh start," I say.

Our eyes meet, and it's almost like there's an invisible tether between us, the connection is so strong.

"I can't stop looking at you," she says. "You are a Cooper."

"I'm half Cooper," I respond with a smile.

"I'm not ready to go there," she says.

I nod. We move on to a few neutral topics before I ask, "Your other children. Do they know about me?"

"No, no," she says, "they don't know, and I'm not ready to tell them. I may never be ready. It's too complicated."

"Maybe not," I say.

"Yes, it is," she insists.

Between each conversation, Janie pauses and looks at me, voicing amazement at how much I look like her father and how much I look like the baby she signed away for adoption in 1965.

"I can't take my eyes off you," she says, again and again, as the time ticks by.

Janie says she left Sellers a week after giving birth, spending December at home in Monroe. In January, she enrolled at the University of Arkansas in Fayetteville. "Nobody in my family had been to college," she says. "I was determined. My grandparents paid for it and my father drove me up to Fayetteville in the snow and ice.

"He told me, 'Janie, you've got to pick yourself up and keep moving. You've got to move past this.' And, that's what I did."

Three years later, she had married Tom and was pregnant with my brother Jimmy, who's three years younger than me. Janie graduated from Arkansas with a degree in education, then had Susan, four-and-a-half years younger than me. They moved to Jonesboro, where Tom set up a law practice. Tonya, her youngest, was born ten years after Susan; she's nearly fifteen years younger than me.

"How did you end up at the University of Arkansas?" I ask.

"Because it wasn't LSU," she says.

I want an explanation but don't want to press my luck. At this point, we've been talking for hours. Without discussing it, we dropped the idea of going out to eat. I'm not sure I could have swallowed a bite anyway.

"Was it awkward, showing up on campus the second semester of your freshman year?"

"You bet it was," she says. "You didn't do that then. I missed rush at the sororities and had to answer why."

"And?"

"I said I was sick and in the hospital. That part was true. I was sick about it, and I was in the hospital."

"I'm sorry," I say. "I can only imagine how difficult."

"After the delivery, they put me in a room with three other new mothers," Janie says, looking toward a window, away from me. "Nurses were bringing those girls their babies every few hours. But the nurses knew I was from Sellers.

"One of the girls asked me, 'Why aren't you getting your baby? Is something wrong with your baby?' I just nodded yes, rolled over, and pulled the covers up over my head."

There are no lights on in the house, and the sun shining through the windows and doors to the patio is fading as the day turns into dusk.

"I'd like to meet my brothers and sisters," I say. "I've always wanted real siblings."

"No," she says, her demeanor changing, "absolutely not. You cannot meet them, or this relationship will end."

"I understand, but I don't agree," I say. "I mean, yes, I'll keep it a secret, but times have changed. They'll understand that you were just a girl, that you had no choice. That you were told to pretend it never happened."

"No," she says.

I look at my watch. We haven't moved from the couch for five hours, and my plane is leaving soon. "I have to go," I say.

"No, please. Stay here tonight. I've got a guest room. I don't think I can handle you leaving. I've said goodbye once before. I can't do it again."

We take the Lincoln Town Car to a nearby Ruth's Chris Steak House, ordering the same: filet, mashed potatoes, asparagus, and a glass of red wine. She stops after one, and I have two. Back on the couch, she tells me about her father, my grandfather.

"You need to meet him," she says. "Soon. He'll be tickled."

"My mother-in-law sees him," I say.

"What do you mean?"

"She lives in Hot Springs. I believe he does too."

"Yes."

"My mother-in-law plays golf. She sees him at the country club, sitting at the bar."

"Well, I'll be."

"She says he drinks Bud Heavys. Says he's been at the bar every time she's been to the club."

"Yep, that's my father."

I look at my watch. It's 1:00 a.m. "I need to turn in."

I get up at 7:30 a.m., and she's waiting for me in the kitchen with coffee. I've only got time for one cup since my flight leaves at nine thirty.

"I didn't sleep at all," she says. "I couldn't stop thinking about holding you at the adoption home. It was so hard saying goodbye. I don't know if I can do it again."

"Well," I say, "if you still want me to meet your father, just set that up for soon."

"I do. I'll call you in the next day or two with the plan. It will be so good; I can't wait. Yes, that will give me something to look forward to. I'll give you a day to get home, then I'll call to set up a day to meet in the next two weeks."

"I'll be looking for your call."

"I love you, David," she says. "I've always loved you."

Back home, I share the full story with Kent, how she showed me a picture of her father, my grandfather, and how he looks like me, how we both ordered our filet cooked medium-rare.

"She's calling the day after tomorrow," I say.

A little hyphen forms over the bridge of Kent's nose.

"She is," I say.

Kent lays her hand on mine and squeezes.

"She is."

But she isn't.

After a week, I call Janie. No answer.

After a month, I call Janie. No answer.

After that, I stop calling.

* *Chapter Five* *

Medication

I've developed a crush on red wine. Fermented grape is less filling than fermented hops, and its sugar hits my bloodstream like a Snickers. I stop by the liquor store daily after work for a bottle. Kent will drink one glass at dinner, and I'll drink the rest. If, on a rare occasion, she tops off her glass, I watch her pour, anxious that there won't be enough for my third glass.

Not that I'm addicted or anything. No way. I've seen the frail, toothless man begging for money outside the liquor store. I'm nothing like him. It's just that I have a stressful job, that's all, and when I come home, I take the edge off.

But I dread the moment when the last drop falls from the bottle like a tear. So I pregame with a beer, slugging that down as Kent preps dinner, and I talk to the children about their school day and homework and their sport-of-the-moment.

Eventually, the beer-then-bottle is not enough, so the solution is clear: buy bigger bottles. Now I tote home the 1.5-liter magnums that pour eight or nine glasses. We rarely polish off a magnum in one night unless friends have stopped by, but having the extra for one more splash in the evening eases the last teardrop jitters.

I'm still drinking just two or three glasses of wine a night, but I use those big glasses designed to let the cabernet breathe, and I pour them way past the halfway mark. Maybe the wine doesn't breathe as well, but I sure do.

And I've added in something else. At parties, when I see friends on the patio smoking, I'll join them. "Can you spare?" Soon, I'm embarrassed about mooching and buy packs. I don't smoke daily but in party moods. When counting pours isn't required, I'll smoke four or five, balancing nicotine, the stimulant, with alcohol, the depressant: the perfect double-edged sword. The more I drink, the more I smoke. The more I smoke, the drier my mouth, so the more I drink—a gnarly wet-dry saga leading to mornings of headaches, a hacking cough, and teeth that feel like they're wearing fuzzy little sweaters.

I think of Dad's admonition that alcohol is poison, recall the blackened slice of lung framed on his study wall. Yet, several times a month, I find excellent excuses to binge: a neighborhood Christmas party, a football tailgate, a golf tournament. Those are times of hilarity, storytelling, and bonding with friends, or so they seem at the time. Someone always gets feelings hurt before night's end.

"Can we please go to one party without you saying something that embarrasses me?" Kent pleads. "Please?"

But surely, she's exaggerating. And after all, everyone is doing it.

With each passing month, I lose a little bit more of my self, sucked away by a sort of vacuum cleaner that never turns off. I'm vaguely aware of the deterioration because I feel melancholy more often, irritable after drinking bouts, ready to get the day over with because I'll feel better when I have that evening's first drink. I still experience joy routinely, mostly with my family at a gathering, trip, or ball game, but I'm left alone with my isolating thoughts when those moments are over. Janie never calls and doesn't want to know me, which must be because I'm inferior, unlovable. Which must be why, when someone like that mini-skirted blonde at the bar lays a hand on mine and tells me she could listen to me talk forever, I'm so vulnerable. Lord, I am tired of the shame. I vow to change. Tomorrow, I'll get up early, exercise, get those natural endorphins buzzing around my body, maybe have a little check-in with God, read my Bible. Tomorrow, I'll choose a dinner restaurant that doesn't serve wine. Instead, tomorrow I'm even weaker. I medicate the stress of my misdeeds. I'm even medicating the stress of parenting.

I try to delay my drinking, pouring an extra tall glass, until after the kids are in bed, and I hide my smoking entirely. In the fifth grade, William is still my buddy. He goes to Nicaragua with me for two weeks on a church mission trip. The other forty missionaries are adults, yet William becomes the star of the group. He closes his eyes for nighttime prayer without prompt, and he says, "Yes, sir," to the other men. He works harder than anyone, handing out medical supplies like bandages. We take breaks together in the commissary, buying Cokes sweetened with cane sugar and splitting a candy bar. At night, we pull our sleeping bags close in the empty cinderblock room, hoping scorpions don't join us.

Yet he's at that age at which the innocence and sweetness of elementary school years are toggling more and more into the self-consciousness of puberty. He wants to quit the violin, abandoning several years of lessons. He's wearing contacts to school, brushing his teeth without prompt, and writing notes with one of the cutest girls, and they call themselves going out. We hope he's gaining confidence from that and from the football. Nobody can catch him in the city flag football league; he's scoring multiple touchdowns a game, racing past the college football coaches' sons, racing past everyone.

He should feel good about himself, but he seems to be unsure where he slots in socially. At Alpine Camp, he's one of the boys. He's the boy who wears glasses at school, reads too many books, and hangs out with the smart international boys, sons of university professors. That's OK by us until we get a call from the principal.

"You need to come in," she says, "so we can talk."

We're at her office within thirty minutes. She greets us and invites us to sit, using a calming voice that feels maybe a little patronizing.

"Just tell us what happened," I interrupt, which earns me a look from Kent. "Is William OK?"

"He's fine," she says. "But there was an incident." She tells us that some boys from his grade surrounded William during recess on the playground and dragged him down a hill, out of view of the teachers. They pushed him around, backed him against a tree, called him names. Somebody either kicked him or threw him to the ground. A teacher spotted the group and came over, found William crying, his face muddied, his jeans grass-stained, his T-shirt a bit torn. But, beyond skinned knees and hands, he was basically unhurt.

"Who were the boys?" I demand.

"William isn't saying." The principal folds her hands. "He's upset and shaken, but he doesn't want to tell on them. He wants this to go away."

"Who were the boys?" I demand again.

The principal pauses, then tells me their names. One is the son of an Ole Miss football coach, a year older than William, held back for football. William blazed past him in the last flag football game for a dramatic touchdown.

We collect William from the nurse's office and take him home. He's teary but won't talk. "What names were they calling you?" Kent asks, holding a wet washcloth to his skinned knee, but he just shakes his head.

We talk to the principal again. She wants to drop it. She says that's what William wants too. "This is just one of those things," she says.

We wonder if William needs counseling, not because this one incident is so terrible in and of itself, but because he seems so lonely in it. I want him to have someone to confide in, so he doesn't have to live with secrets and cover-ups like I did all those years. But he suggests it's the bullies, not him, who need counseling. Besides, he says, if anyone finds out he is seeing a therapist, that will only make it worse. So, we lay down arms, following the principal's advice, and let it go.

✲ ✲ ✲

Here I am, driving to Conway, Arkansas, to knock on my half-sister Susan's door. Is this a wise idea? Probably not. Susan's never heard of me, has no idea she has a half-brother. But I've decided I might as well introduce myself, as Janie isn't going to do it. That day, when I met Janie in Texas, she threatened never to see me again if I tried to contact my half-siblings. But she hasn't seen me again anyway, so why am I obeying her ban?

Conway is big compared to Oxford, with a public university and seemingly a church for every one hundred houses. Almost everything is new because the growth is recent and explosive. Yet, restaurants are dry, thanks to many churches. Susan's husband, I know from a bit of recon, is a preacher at one of them.

It's a weekday, and I arrive in Conway early-afternoon after a four-hour drive. But somehow, I can't bring myself to knock on her door without warning her first. From a gas station phone booth, I call Susan's husband at the church he leads. I explain who I am and why I'm here. "Can you help?" I ask.

"This sounds real," he says. "I think you should meet and see. Come to the house at three. I'll run home and talk to her first, prepare her."

I weave through the curving roads in her subdivision, large new houses that border a country club golf course. I pull into the driveway, wipe my sweaty palms on my pant legs, and make my way to the door.

The door opens, and my half-sister Susan stands wordlessly, taking a long hard look. Tears start streaming down her face, and she smothers them with her hands.

"Oh my," she says, muffled. "You are my brother. I'd know it if I saw you walking down the road."

I smile, wiping away tears of my own. "I always wanted a sister who's blood," I say.

She invites me in, and we sit on her overstuffed couch. "Forgive me for being shocked," she says, "but I've never heard of any of this. Might take a little getting used to." Susan smiles. "But I know it's true. You have Mother's nose, and you have her eyes and forehead. And you look a lot like my grandfather."

"That's what Janie said," I tell her.

We talk all afternoon. We talk into the night. We sleep just a few hours, then we talk all the next morning. Before I leave, she says we need to figure out what to do next.

"You mean, are we gonna tell Janie?" I ask.

"It's your call. But I do want you to meet my brother and sister." She rears back a little. "I mean, *our* brother and sister. They deserve to get to know you. Maybe you should meet them before you tell Mom."

Janie's not taking my call anyway, so what's another secret?

I knock on my brother's door.

Jimmy lives in Little Rock, near my sister-in-law. Meeting him is just as trippy and unique as meeting Susan. We seem to be opposites. Jimmy is a tax attorney, recently divorced, with smarts off the chart; he made a thirty-six on his ACT, while I made a twenty-one. He's shorter, and he calls himself an introvert. But we're wearing the same pair of leather shoes, worn to the same degree. We've got the same forehead and eyes. Seated, we cross our legs the same way.

And we both share a passion for the wet-dry combo of red wine and nicotine. We've already made a run to the convenience store for smokes, and we're several bottles in by the time Jimmy's serious girlfriend, also a lawyer, stops by to meet me. We have a blast, long-lost brothers talking about sports, family, golf, family, business, family, and alcohol. I notice he's out-drinking me two to one.

"My adopted parents didn't drink," I say. "Didn't even have it in the house. But it's in my blood. I started drinking the summer before high school."

"Sounds about right," he says. "My parents drank, but I didn't see it. They had parties and went to parties, but they didn't have booze at the dinner table or sitting around the house. But it's in my blood too."

"Definitely," I say.

"You've got the bug," he says, "but I've probably got it more than you."

We laugh and go outside for a smoke. "Love you, bro," he says, delivering a hug.

* * *

Susan and Jimmy introduce me to Tonya, my youngest sister. She's nineteen, a sophomore at the University of Arkansas, and pretty as a peach in June. We meet once, briefly, but it's not until I travel with Kent to an Ole Miss football game in Fayetteville that I get to know her.

We meet up at a Mexican restaurant downtown, and our conversation is easy, as if we've known one another for a lifetime. I order a beer, asking if she wants one. Beer was legal when I was nineteen, so it feels perfectly normal.

"I want one," she says, "but they're tight about the law in here."

"Are you sure? You're with family, so I'm not sure that counts."

"Maybe," she says.

When the waiter returns, she orders a beer.

Halfway through the meal, Tonya is walking to the bathroom, but a manager pulls her aside.

I've only gotten to know Tonya for a few hours but already I can read her face, so I make my way over to where the manager is cornering her.

"What's going on?" I ask.

"Nothing," says the manager, "as long as this young lady can prove that she's legal to order that beer. We've called the police. She needs to wait here." He turns to Tonya. "They'll want to see your ID."

"I don't have one with me," she says.

"Well, then, they'll take you downtown."

"Listen," I say, "I'm her brother. She's with me, and it was my mistake."

"She's too young to drink in here," he says, looking at me sternly.

"Yes," I say, "you're right. One hundred percent. It won't happen again."

After a few more apologies and reassurances, Tonya is free to go, and we manage to laugh later at the close call. I feel bad, though, for nearly getting her thrown in the slammer the first night we hang out. I want to make it up to her, and I want her to meet our children, so I invite Tonya to visit us in Oxford. She flies into Memphis, I pick her up at the airport, and by 6:00 p.m., we are home with a bottle of wine opened. It goes down fast.

I run to the liquor store for more wine, stopping by my convenience store near the town square. Yes, the convenience store/gas station is mine. I don't really care for the business, but when the owner moved, I couldn't let this prime location slip away, even if the building was run down and half of it was a laundromat. While I was remaking the business, the Oxford post office moved from the town center to the outskirts, and I knew folks wanted someplace easy to mail their phone bill. So I went to postmaster training, sold off the laundry machines in the far end of the building at twenty cents on the dollar, and opened Oxford's new post office. But I wasn't done. A popular downtown grocery store, long famous for its chicken salad, closed and folks lamented the loss. I contracted with the grocery store owner, adding the chicken salad, and renaming the place from Amoco to James', after the grocery. I'm oddly proud of my convenience store/gas station/post office/chicken salad shop. But having beer and nicotine available at wholesale cost spells trouble.

I dash into the store, grabbing two packs of Marlboro Lights from behind the cash register and a six-pack of beer just because it's there and I already own it. We don't need the beer, but I'm always thinking ahead.

I'm back in minutes, and it seems like minutes after that when I look at my watch, but it's 1:00 a.m. We're standing on my porch, overlooking the town cemetery. There's a full moon overhead, and the sky is so cloudless and clear that I can practically read the headstones.

"What an incredible night," I say.

The conversation, fueled by alcohol's sugar, the nicotine, and new brother-sister companionship, remains equally clear, but it's getting late. We've long since finished the wine, and we've almost finished the beer. Similarly, the second pack of cigarettes is halfway gone.

Tonya takes a long drag, drops the butt into the beer bottle that she's just emptied, and coughs.

The cough gets my attention. Tonya is only nineteen, and she's my younger sister. I look to the moon and take a deep breath, and I look back at Tonya. In her eyes, I see a reflection of my responsibility.

"I'm sorry," I say.

"For what?"

"For not being a better role model."

She politely smiles, and we call it a night.

But when I get in bed, I'm troubled, thinking Tonya might have felt the need to keep pace with my drinking and smoking when I've built up such a tolerance that I can drink two bottles of wine and not even stagger or slur. Even Kent's drinking more on weeknights, inadvertently trying to keep up with me.

I remember telling Kent on my first visits to her house that I noticed how much her parents drink. She didn't think much of it since that's the way it had always been. Her father kept the bar stocked with vodka, pouring a tall drink or two nightly to the point that her mother urged him to cut back. His father, the town doctor, was an alcoholic, successful in recovery for many years. Because she's grown up around nightly cocktail hour, she doesn't think it's strange when I instigate our own. Besides, she's now busy running her business, and I tell her she deserves to take the edge off too.

Kent had earned a degree in fashion merchandising at Ole Miss, and for ten years did nothing with it while the kids were very small. But, when a long-standing women's boutique downtown came up for sale, she purchased it and did a successful overhaul. She'd come home exhausted, make dinner, and help the children with homework. Then, she was ready to shed her work clothes, turn on some soft music, and chat over her one glass of wine. But I'd be refilling her glass, a splash here and a splash there, keeping our party of two moving. It's the drinker's best trick since the other person doesn't notice how much you are drinking as long as you keep them sipping too.

✳ ✳ ✳

William begins the sixth grade, the most exciting part of which is he can now join the school band. They even get to pick an instrument, and he chooses the trombone. He's good at it, but there's one problem: because the instruments are expensive, the director doesn't want them left overnight in the band hall, which means students must take them home. For William, who walks home, already wearing a heavy backpack, the bulky trombone case is a magnet for bullies. Some of the same bullies who dragged him away from the playground follow him for a few blocks, taunting and imitating him lugging the giant case. Just like that, his band enthusiasm withers.

I hate that he can't see himself as we do, quirky and sensitive but also a natural athlete and handsome, with a broad smile, his mother's eyes, and thick sandy-brown hair and eyebrows. He's also very, very smart. But William is determined to master middle school cool, which means losing the smart label. He succeeds. His grades are good enough since he's a quick learner, but teachers say he's unengaged at times. In seventh grade, he's still playing football, his first year in pads, but he isn't aggressive, so he sits on the bench. Still, he's got a girlfriend, Katie, one of the cutest in the grade, and he's gained some swagger and grown some inches taller. Yet, he remains anxious and fidgety, always seeking acceptance.

Katie breaks up with him, and he's upset, but that's just middle school, I tell him, though I remember how I ached and played my sad records when Ashley dumped me. What I can't say to William is that I know Katie didn't jettison him for some older guy; we've heard she's developed an eating disorder, yet it's not something we can share with our son.

Otherwise, his social life is improving. He's socializing more among classmates. One weekend, he's spending the night at a friend's house, and the parents are out at a party. The friend suggests they raid the liquor cabinet. He pours some shots, and presto, William's drinking virginity is gone. He keeps this from us, of course. When we ask if he sees drugs or alcohol around the kids at school, he says no.

William goes out for the track team. Kent was a sprinter in high school, running on the girls' 4 x 100 relay team. The coach assigns William to the hurdles, which we know is bad news. You need proportionally long legs to clear the hurdles, which William doesn't have. Apparently, the coach isn't expecting much from William, either. When we line the fence at his first meet, he's slotted to race on the C-team heat.

The gun fires, and William starts running. He clears the first hurdle, his legs coltishly unfolding beneath him, then finding purchase again. He keeps pace, clears the second hurdle, and I feel my spirits start to soar as his legs do, approaching the third. But his back knee crashes the hurdle. He sprawls hard, face planting into the dirt, almost bouncing.

Kent gasps, "William!"

The other runners have sped away by the time William pushes to his feet, brushing off his hands and knees. I think he'll limp off the track, and we'll say better luck next time, but he looks ahead and starts running, picking up speed as he goes, clearing one hurdle and another.

William finishes last, by far, the slowest time in the third heat, but he's gained an ovation from the thirty or so parents watching, and when he walks over to the fence, his friend Lindsey jogs over. She asks to see his hands, he extends them, and Lindsey takes hold, cooing and wiping away the pebbles half-embedded in his skin.

He walks to us with a grin; he lost the race but won Lindsey's heart.

"We're proud of you, Son," I say, wrapping my arm around his shoulders.

"Thanks, Dad," he says. "I'm proud of you too."

In some ways, Oxford is stunningly small for a major university town. I put less than eight thousand miles a year on my car, know many of the students, and know most everyone I see at the grocery store. But when it comes to books, our little town is enormous, with more published authors per capita than likely anywhere in the world.

Maybe it started with Faulkner and later Willie Morris, but by this point, Barry Hannah's at the university, and our longtime friend Larry Brown, a firefighter working out of Station No. 1 on North Lamar, has broken through with his southern grit novels and nonfiction. There's the bestseller novelist John Grisham, who recently moved away but still has his second home on the western outskirts of town. Our local bookstore, Square Books, is considered the best in the South, and its owner, Richard Howorth, is president of the American Booksellers Association. I understand that in Nashville your waiter really intends to be a songwriter. In Oxford, your waiter is a struggling novelist. People here read books and talk about books and write books. As a columnist at the Podunk local newspaper with less than five thousand daily subscribers, I think of myself as a small-town journalist, but I can't help dreaming about writing a book myself.

Kent says I should try. I want to because I seem to get bored with things, but I never get bored with storytelling. I decide to write a memoir. Although I don't know who I am, literally, I'll write about my adoption story and growing up as a borrowed child. I've even got the name, *A Bastard's Life*. I pitch it to a small publishing house, and they offer a contract.

It's hard to get a book deal when you are a nobody in the field—it's hard enough when you *are* somebody—so the small press offer is validating, especially for someone who always feels like an imposter. Still, I can't manage to finish it because I can't manage to give the book the perspective it needs. I recognize that in my late thirties, I'm still growing up, not yet ready for a memoir. I want it so badly, but for all the wrong reasons, like imagining Dad walking by Square Books and seeing my memoir in the window, pushing up his glasses in surprise. But who am I kidding, anyway? He'd probably buy a copy only to circle my mistakes in black marker. And I know I can't tell this story correctly if I'm writing it out of spite and blame instead of generosity and curiosity.

Like many other struggling writers before me, I pay a visit to my neighbor Richard, the owner of Square Books. I've heard he's like a one-person, tough-love MFA program, recommending books and offering advice. He's helped Grisham, he's helped Larry Brown, and most everyone else who can knit stories together in our town. There's no reason he won't help me.

I share the memoir concept.

"Too soon," he says. "That memoir is not the first book you should write. Take some time, get some practice writing something else, find some success, and close in on your story. Then you can write the memoir."

Right.

"Your newspaper columns weren't bad," he adds.

"Sure, but I was writing for the *Oxford Eagle.* I mean, yes, I enjoyed writing, but I'm no Larry Brown or John Grisham . . ."

"That's right," he says, "you aren't, so don't try to be them. Be yourself. Start with what makes you curious about the world, something you can bring insight to. Find your voice, work on your writing, reread the greats, and grow from there."

"That makes sense. Anything else you can tell me?"

"My advice?" Richard says. "Think bigger than Oxford, think bigger than the region. And don't try to define yourself as southern. Let others do that."

I nod.

"Also, think about writing something like a business book. You're good at business. You understand it, and that's a gift, one you shouldn't overlook."

It's comical, honestly, that I'm sitting in Oxford, Mississippi, getting advice to write a business book when I've never had the first byline in the *Wall Street Journal*. Yet, it makes a kind of sense; I've created successful small businesses, and I love both the risk-taking of new enterprise and the strategizing that sustaining one requires. Sometimes folks have come to me for advice when their business is struggling, and I love to analyze whatever the difficulty is, financial or personnel or marketing. Along with my work on city council, keeping mom-and-pops from going under feels like a meaningful way to contribute to my small town. And, if you believe that the hand of fate shapes our paths, you'll have no trouble believing what happens next, mere weeks after Richard's advice. A friend invites me to lunch with a CEO who's touring Mississippi because his company is opening a new plant in the state.

I've never heard of Carlos Ghosn, the new Nissan president visiting from Japan. Google reveals he's a big deal: the hard-driving globalist born in Lebanon, educated in France, who led Michelin North America to success, now charged with turning around the struggling Japanese automaker.

We dine at a restaurant on the square in Oxford, and he asks questions like the quality of job training in the state and the proximity of casinos. Ghosn is also intrigued by my diverse professional background, something I usually downplay, embarrassed. After all, how do you explain that you own a convenience store/post office/chicken salad factory, serve on the city council, own a copying center, and do contract marketing for another company, but at heart, you're a writer?

The diversity provides me a broad base of learning, he says. The writing makes me valuable, he says. Ghosn hands over his business card with direct dial to his office in Tokyo at the end of lunch.

"There's a pot of gold out there for a good speechwriter," Ghosn says.

For a few days, I consider adding "speechwriter" to my professional potpourri. I do some research, learning Ghosn is a uniquely innovative leader, breaking traditions in Japan to save Nissan. He's an emerging celebrity there, starring in comics, with crowds gathering for autographs.

Then I realize I don't want to write speeches for Ghosn. I want to write his life story.

I've found my book.

I send an email to Ghosn, explaining I want to come to Japan to study, learn, and tell his story. He responds, "Interesting. I'll be in the Detroit area soon for the auto show. Let's meet there and talk about it." I send a query to a business book agent, who loves the concept.

I land at Detroit's John Wayne Airport with a smile. I've been a small-town Mississippi boy with ideas, but maybe they've been too local: a post office here, a historical preservation ordinance there. As Richard says, I should think on a larger scale. Enter Carlos Ghosn, my ticket to the world.

In the morning, we'll be meeting for an early breakfast in the luxurious Townsend Hotel in Birmingham, Detroit's upscale neighboring city. With just twenty thousand residents, Birmingham boasts an art museum, premium shopping, and first-class restaurants and cafés that thrive off the binge spending from the auto industry. I decide I'll grab some dinner and a drink at the hotel restaurant and get to bed early, rest for conquering the most significant professional meeting of my life.

I take a seat at the hotel bar with a firm plan: one glass of wine, order food, then a nightcap glass of wine, and call it a night.

On my right sits a middle-aged man who begins telling me about the global automotive parts supply company he owns. He's smart and interesting, and I'm a sucker for a conversation that helps me learn, so I'm surprised how fast my plate is clean and my second glass of wine is empty.

"Here's your check, sir," the bartender says.

"Well," I say, placing my credit card on the bar, "this has been fun."

"Don't you have time for one more?" the man asks. "It's on me."

I look at my watch. It's not yet eight o'clock. "Sure," I say. "One more."

There's something that happens to some of us from about the third glass of wine onward that I can't explain. The first two go down fine, like with everybody else, but once that third one goes down, it's like there isn't enough wine.

It doesn't help that an interesting couple in town for the auto show has taken seats to my other side. The man introduces his wife as the ex of Lee Majors, the actor. Maybe it's true, perhaps it's not, but she's drinking and smoking like the Bionic Woman, and the rest of us are now trying to keep up. Whenever she excuses herself from the bar, we follow, lighting up smokes on the sidewalk.

It's early January, and a cold northerly wind blows down from nearby Canada, spitting intermittent snowflakes, fuel for the wet-dry fire igniting within. If I get up to leave, they wink at the bartender, and here comes another. When the smokes are nearly gone, they get another pack. I see my dream dying before my eyes, yet I don't know how to escape.

I look at my watch; it's 1:00 a.m. I'm ashamed that I've broken my plan, but I take another sip when the next drink arrives.

"What time does the bar close?" I ask.

"Two a.m.," the bartender says.

I've traveled from central time and Detroit's in eastern time, an hour later, and my meeting with Ghosn is at 8:00 a.m.

My head spins like a carousel, and I take another sip.

The Bionic Woman and her husband head back outside. "Come on," they say. "One last smoke?"

"Why not?" I say, following them into the cold.

Back inside, the bartender delivers the news. "Last call."

I look at my watch: it's 1:45 a.m.

"Ladies and gentlemen," I slur, "I'm going to bed. G'night."

I stumble through my hotel room door, stopping in the bathroom and standing in front of the mirror. My eyes are bloodshot, my hair reeks, and my heart is working too hard to keep tainted blood flowing through my body. I need an exorcism to get this much devil out, but sleep is my only reasonable option.

When the bedside alarm buzzes at 7:00 a.m., I stand up and wobble, reaching for the wall to steady. I've got a drinking problem. That's the only possible explanation for getting drunk just before my most important meeting ever.

I'll make changes, I think—if I can just get through this morning, if I can just get this deal done.

I sit on the bed and close my eyes.

"Dear Lord," I pray, "give me the strength for this meeting, and I promise to do better."

I take a deep breath and make a list of what I need: caffeine, lots of caffeine, Tylenol, lots of Tylenol, Visine, lots of Visine. And a long hot shower.

At 7:55, I'm walking out of the elevator and toward Ghosn's hotel suite.

Two hours later, I'm leaving the suite with a handshake agreement to write a book about the world's hottest executive.

Two months later, my agent lands a $200,000 advance contract with HarperCollins.

Twelve months later, I'm holding a copy of the *Harvard Business Review* magazine that calls my book a "provocative case study." It's official. I'm the author of a business book with global success, selling from Japan to France to Brazil and across the US. I'm speaking in Quebec and Japan, and they shuttle me to engagements in fancy cars with drivers.

Waiting at the airport, someone says, "Didn't I see you on TV?" And I smile, saying, "Yes, that's me appearing as a guest on CNBC, and it's not just once but regularly as a business expert. That's right; I said a business expert."

I should celebrate; I should, but I'm half-embarrassed. My book, I realize bit by bit, could have been better. I'm a novice, and I didn't give myself time to learn some slow skills. In particular, I didn't practice painstaking revision, revision, revision. I didn't understand the value, and also, I got swept up in the publisher's marketing plan and PR efforts when I should have seen nothing but the approaching deadline. Maybe that was arrogance or ignorance or both. But good writing doesn't come easy, even with a story as easy to tell as Carlos Ghosn's.

The *New York Times* rips my work in a Sunday review consuming nearly three-quarters of a broadsheet, calling it "hagiography," and they are right.

William, my sensitive boy, tunes into my pain, tucking my book under his arm at bedtime for reading.

"Dad," he says at breakfast several days later, "I finished your book. It's good."

Tears come to my eyes. "Really?"

"Yes. Really."

"William, you may be one of the few seventh-grade students in America to read a business book this week," I say. "I love you."

"I love you, too, Dad."

But among my writer friends in town, the critics that matter most, I'm ashamed because they all read the *Times* every Sunday, and I know they saw the review. I'm not worthy of being called an "Oxford writer." I'm not worthy of being called a writer at all. I've let them down; I've let myself down. When I told Dad I wanted to write books, he told me I should be a salesman. Maybe he was right. Maybe that's all I'll ever be.

I want to run away and get a fresh start, just like I did when I transferred high schools. William needs a fresh start, too, because he's still being bullied and still struggling to shed his smart boy label so they stop noticing him.

And perhaps if I escape this town, where I have tried and failed to figure out who I am, I can find myself once and for all. I can do better, he can do better, we all can do better. Let's go right now, and I'll write a new story for myself and my family, one that doesn't include Mom, Dad, Eunice, or even Janie, and especially not the worst of me.

∗ Chapter Six ∗

Family Matters

We make a run for the hills: Lookout Mountain, Tennessee, elevation 1,850 feet, population about the same. Lookout Mountain looks out on the Tennessee Valley, where Chattanooga sits, a mid-size southern metro beginning to percolate. Here, on this mountain, I am not among my people. Which is the point. My children will not grow up where I grew up, or failed to grow up.

The people here are old money. We pretend to be. We remodel a 1928 home near the mountain's west brow, leaving just enough cash left to join the country club and golf club after we pay the enormous private school tuitions. There's one school for boys only and a sister girls' school for Mary Halley. Both schools look like small colleges, with large endowments, diversity, and low student-teacher ratios.

It's late summer, but a steady breeze lifts across the plateau and collides with the mountain, lowering our temperature six to eight degrees from the valley below. It's just the cooling breath I need. I've signed another book contract, this one a biography on Ford Motor Company Chairman and CEO Bill Ford Jr., the great-grandson of company founder Henry Ford. And I'm committed to a plan: I'll drink less, considerably;

I'll be faithful, absolutely; and I'll meet or exceed the commitments of my fatherhood vow.

Nobody back home understands why we left. "Leave your beautiful home?" they asked, incredulous. "Take your kids out of school? And what about your businesses? What about historic preservation? And who will coach the soccer teams now?" I'd just smile awkwardly, then shake my head awkwardly, then smile awkwardly again. Of course, our departure would be perplexing. Wounded, troubled hearts beat out of view.

Dad cried when I visited to explain my need to move from the few square miles where I've lived my entire life. He's retired, with less leverage to entice young men to sit for photo sessions, and he's lonely now. I should feel empathy—I was lonely every day I spent in this house—but I don't. I watch him cry. "You and your family are about the only good I have left," he says between sobs. "I'm afraid you'll never come back."

"Probably not," I say.

✳ ✳ ✳

It's William's first day of eighth-grade, full-contact football practice at McCallie, the boy's school. He wants to earn a starting position and establish himself at this new school. But McCallie, with stately brick buildings and a century of tradition built upon its motto of "Honor, Truth, Duty," is a proud football school. William is faster than ever, but last year, when William was sidelined, he didn't master the game's physical aspects.

I'm waiting for William in the school parking lot after the practice. I look in the rearview mirror and see him slowly walking toward the car, head down, a Gatorade bottle in hand.

He opens the car door and plunks down on the seat.

"Hey, sweet William," I say.

Silence. William shuts the door and takes a long slug of Gatorade.

"How'd it go?"

He sniffles and chokes on the drink. "Not very well," he says, his voice cracking.

"What do you mean?"

He starts to cry.

"Take a deep breath now," I say, running my fingers through his hair, still wet with sweat. "It's OK. Just talk whenever you are ready."

"They hit me so hard," William says. "I didn't know kids could hit so hard. It hurts. I can't play football."

"What do you mean, you can't play football?"

"I'm not tough enough, that's what I mean. They pushed me all over the field. I probably have cleat marks on my back, Dad. I can't do it."

"OK, William," I say. "You are tough enough. You just don't know. We can fix this. No more getting pushed around. If you want this, you can do this, and I can help."

"What do you mean?"

"I mean, I can you teach how to hit them first."

"Really?"

"Really. Do you want it?" I ask.

"Yes," he says, meekly.

"I said, do you want it?" This time I yell it.

"Yes," he says louder.

"Do you want it?" I yell louder.

"Yes!" he yells back, breaking into a laugh.

I put my hand on his knee, leaning closer.

"OK," I say, "let's turn sweet William into a badass."

We sit in the car for an hour with the air conditioner running, and I lecture my son on the art of hitting first.

"Your speed is your biggest asset. When the ball snaps, you explode forward, driving your legs to smash into the opponents before they move. They'll get crunched, and you'll feel no pain. But if you let them hit you first, they'll blow you ten yards down the field, and you'll ride the bench."

I turn off the engine, and we walk back to the field as the sun is setting. Everyone else has gone. I lower into a four-point stance, instructing William to do the same.

"Hut," I say, firing into his shoulders and knocking him five yards away and onto his backside.

He blinks up at me.

"See the problem?" I say, pointing a finger toward his face. "Let's try it again."

"Hut," I say, repeating the scenario.

"William?" I say. "Let me ask. Do you want to play football? It's your call, really. I want you to think hard. But I need to know."

"Yes," he says. "I want to play football."

I remember that some of William's Oxford teammates had snorted when he stuck out a hand to lift a tackled opponent back on his feet. William's timidity was why his coach benched him, but I wondered if it wasn't timidity but sensitivity that made William hold back. He never wants to hurt anyone.

"You're going to have to get mad, Son. Get furious. We're gonna try this one more time, and I need you to get mad at me. Get so mad that when I say hut, you explode with strong legs into me so fast I don't know what happened. I don't care if it hurts me. Do you understand? I don't care if it hurts. I don't care what happens. Just do it."

We get into position.

"Hut."

Before I've even straightened up, I'm flying in reverse as if zapped by a lightning strike, landing hard on my backside.

"Whoa," I say, stunned. Then laughing. "That hurt."

He's smiling, circling his prey.

"Congratulations, Son," I extend a hand for him to pull me up. "You're gonna be one heckuva football player."

The next day, I watch football practice from the school parking lot, far enough away that he can't see me but close enough that with the windows down, I can hear the pads cracking amid the coach's yelps and screams. It's after five, so I've brought along a beer to sip.

I hear the coach in the distance shouting, "Magee," and William runs over. The coach squares him off in a one-on-one, winner-takes-all hitting drill. The player my son is facing is the team's bulldog, a crunching fullback a year older because he was held back for football.

The boys take positions.

"Hut," the coach yells, and William unleashes as a coiled spring, firing into the fullback and knocking him off the line. Crunching pads echo across the valley.

"Wooo, Magee," the coach yells as players cheer. "That's a wrap, men. Let's run our sprints and hit the showers."

I call Kent, bragging, proud of how our oldest child learns from me like I've got this parenthood thing figured out, just as I had vowed when he was born—greatest dad ever.

"Our boy is a beast," I say. "Do you hear me? A beast!"

I'm finishing my beer when the car door opens.

"Hey, hey, hey," I say, giving a high five. "You're the man. I am incredibly proud of you, Son. Incredibly proud."

"I'm proud of me too," he says, smiling.

The beer bottle is empty, and it sits in the console between us like a trophy. At home, we burst into the house. I head to the bar, pouring a glass of red wine, and soon another, as we recount the details about how William won the day, sending a message to both the coaches and his teammates that the newcomer Magee won't get pushed around.

He earns a starting position, and the team goes undefeated. It seems we're winning this father-son game, something Dad and I never did.

So by the next year, I'm confident our plan for the kids is working: get them into a new environment where they can thrive. William is growing more confident without the bullying. All three are involved in school activities: Mary Halley has dance. Hudson makes the middle school A-team in soccer. And William has set his sights on playing soccer for the McCallie high school team. He played in middle school, where his speed helped him, but I fear his ball-handling skills aren't at the high school level. Still, he wants to try out.

On the final day before roster selection, the coach calls him aside. "I'm not saying you can't make the JV team and maybe even get on the varsity team one day," the coach tells William. "But I feel confident that your skills level will keep you from being a key player in our soccer program."

William is visibly upset that night at dinner but doesn't want to talk about it. We clear the dishes, and I ask William to hang around a moment in the den. I pour a splash of wine and sit close on the couch, turning to face him. I put a hand on his knee.

"William," I say, "I am so sorry about this. I wish they had a spot for you."

Silence.

"But, Son, this is not your darkest day," I say. "Not even close. Today is an opportunity."

He smirks. "I get it. One door closes, another door opens."

"That's right!" I say.

The next morning, William announces that he is joining the McCallie track team.

For a moment, I hesitate. McCallie competes for the state championship in boys' track most years, and it isn't unusual for graduates to run in college. I don't know if I'm setting him up for disappointment by encouraging him, especially as he's a ninth grader. But I also can't stand to dash his hopes the way my father dashed mine every time I expressed an aspiration.

"That's great," I find myself saying. "Will you try to run distance or middle distance?"

"Neither," he says. "I am a sprinter."

Oh, brother. A sprinter. "That's great," I say, but I'm not sure he has the speed. He's fast, sure, but a sprinter?

The first month of practice is uneventful; William is an unnoticed, unassuming ninth grader working through drills. He doesn't run in the first two meets. But one day when the team is doing time trials, the coach notices his speed. He clocks William on the next round, calls him over, and offers pointers on form and pacing. The next week, at a large event hosted by the biggest public school in northwest Georgia, William is entered in the 100-meter dash.

"Dad," he asks at breakfast, "are you coming to my track meet?"

I kiss his forehead. "You bet. Wouldn't miss it for anything."

The sun is setting when I arrive, and I see William silhouetted. He's alone, stretching in the corner of the field, casting a shadow as he lifts one leg back, then another. His image grows with each step, and I'm impressed with his sturdy physique in the handsome McCallie blue uniform.

I pay to enter, walk through the gate, and take a seat in the stadium just in time; William is lining up in his heat to run. My eyes open wide, and I gasp; he's a boy among men. I hear someone in the stands whisper about a senior running back in football with 4.3 speed who's on a starting block. William looks not only very small and very young but very nervous, fidgeting with his hands on his face. I want to tell him to relax, to take a deep breath and center. But I'm not relaxed either. My knee is bouncing in the metal stands. I remember that seventh-grade meet when he ran the hurdles and crashed, finishing in last place, and want to slide over to the track, take his hand, and lead him away.

He's not flinching, however; he's taking his mark, crouching with his hand touching the ground, slotting his feet back against the angled blocks.

I say a quick prayer, and the starter fires the gun.

The crowd jumps to its feet, and so do I, my eyes Velcroed to the smallest runner bolting from the blocks.

"Let's go, William!" I shout.

I'm stunned. He's among the leaders in the eight-man field as his thighs flash down the rust-colored track, his arms pumping in form like an efficient machine, his eyes focused on the finish line.

The crowd is humming, and it's my boy delivering the charge.

"Look at that little boy run," someone yells. "Wooo, look at him go." Someone else yells, "Get 'em, boy. Get 'em."

William crosses the finish line in third place, just a half step behind the winner, the running back three grades ahead, known for so much speed. I turn and look at the digital score clock: 11.3 seconds.

I hustle down to the fence surrounding the track, where William's talking to his coach. He sees me and waves.

"Amazing!" I shout across the track.

I pull my phone from my pocket and dial Kent, who's eager for an update.

"Good news," I say. "Your firstborn is a track star."

* * *

I'm sprinting into my new field and seem to be having success, just like William. I've signed another book contract, and I'm invited to do more and more speaking gigs. CNBC, the financial TV network, keeps requesting appearances. I've become an "expert on the global automotive industry," at least according to the way they introduce me before my segment. Sometimes I travel to New York, appearing live in the studio, while other times, I'll connect via satellite from a local TV station.

I get text messages and emails from friends seeing my books in stores and my face on TV.

"You're a star," they say.

I laugh and wave that away, but I secretly enjoy feeling like a star when the TV studio sends a driver in a Town Car for me or when folks gather around me at cocktail parties, asking for unreported tidbits about the CEOs and companies I've worked with. Friends say I'm living the dream, working from home. The good part is spending so much time with Kent, from trading newspaper sections over coffee in the morning all the way to the opening of a bottle of wine early in the evening and eating dinner. The bad part is spending so much time with Kent because she's aware of my increasing anxiety as well as my increasing intake. I've gotten used to drinking a lot on the road, traveling for speaking engagements and book conferences, where there's always an open bar. And, off the road, on our old-money mountain, the cocktail hour with friends is a lifestyle. The accompanying relationships are rewarding, except that I'm behind the deadline on my latest book, the first time that's happened.

On this morning, a Monday, I've settled on the couch in the den, drinking a second cup of coffee and trying to find a writing rhythm, when I hear Kent cry out from the upstairs. Within a minute, Kent stands in front of me holding a strange object: a Gatorade bottle with a straw taped into the top.

"What's this?" she asks.

I know she knows, but I also know she's looking for confirmation.

"I'd say that's a homemade bong for smoking marijuana. Where'd you find it?"

Now, I'm looking for confirmation.

"In William's closet."

I puff out my cheeks and let out a slow breath.

"Our tenth-grade son is smoking marijuana," she says as if she needs to hear herself say it.

That hangs in the air for a minute. I say, "We'll talk to William tonight after dinner, once we clear the dishes and Hudson and Mary Halley are doing homework."

And from the way she turns on her heel, I can tell she's too upset to say another word.

I open a bottle of wine at 5:00 p.m. per our evening ritual and pour us each a glass. We've read that drinking wine, especially red, is beneficial for cholesterol. Kent is petite, and I like to remind her that the government's chart suggests that men at my weight can drink double her consumption.

Dinner is Kent's specialty, just right for a hungry family. Tonight, it's Crock-Pot roast and gravy and rice, with steamed buttered broccoli and puffy dinner rolls. After a long day of school, William and Hudson devour the food, leaving but few words between mouthfuls. Mary Halley is still young enough to pick at her food, but she makes dinner lively with chatter, and her favorite hobby is making me laugh.

Hudson and Mary Halley leave the table, off to their rooms for homework on their computers, phoning friends, or navigating this new Facebook thing. I ask William to join us in the den. I bring what's left of my wine. William plops down in an armchair, across from the one I'm in. Kent sits on the edge of the sofa, leaning forward over her crossed legs.

"William," she says. "We need to talk. I found your Gatorade bottle contraption."

His posture tenses, but he says nothing.

She continues. "I can only assume you've been smoking marijuana in your room, and I'm very, very upset to see that."

William looks at his mother but doesn't say a word.

"Well," I say, betraying a hint of agitation, "don't you have anything to say?"

I swing my glass of pinot noir to my lips, drinking deeply.

"Well," William says slowly, "when Michael spent the night last weekend after the dance, he had some marijuana and asked me if I wanted to try it. I had never done it before, so I said OK."

"You did this in our house?" I say, raising my voice. "With your brother and sister sleeping nearby? With us sleeping downstairs?"

"I guess so," he says. "It was my first time. I won't do it again."

"You say it's the first time. You want us to believe you?" I say, flinging hands in the air, including the one holding my wineglass. Kent is looking at the rug, shaking her head, to see the few blood-colored drops land.

Instinct says he's lying. Last year, we noticed our liquor bottles had been refilled with water. We spoke gravely to him then about consequences. And now he's smoking pot in the house.

"You have so much going for you, William," I say. "I don't understand your decision. Why waste your time with substances that will only bring you down, distracting you from the mission?"

"It was my first time," he asserts, "and it won't happen again."

We want to believe him. And we do, or mostly we do; we can't help it. We're programmed to be our children's greatest advocates, after all. We accept the statement, offering obligatory punishment.

"We love you, William," I say, "but we need to teach you a lesson from this. We're grounding you for two weeks. That means no car and no going anywhere but school and church and with the family."

He loves his car, a new gray Toyota 4Runner Kent's mother purchased for him, delivered with a credit card linked to her account for buying gas, and I assume the punishment will sting, that he'll argue back, but he's too smooth for that. He smiles a half-smile and accepts the penalty.

"We love you, William," Kent says.

"Love you too," he says, getting up to walk upstairs.

Grounding a child these days, as it turns out, doesn't have the same punch as in days gone by. They can't leave the house—so what?—they stay in their bedrooms, using social media to connect to friends, and if you take away their phones, they'll use their computers to connect, and you can't take their computers, as kids are quick to remind you, because they need computers for homework. They've outsmarted us. Later, we'll learn grounded kids also acquire sympathy substances, like alcohol or marijuana, from friends, used for whittling away the time during home incarceration.

We don't know any of this, of course. Because we had our kids so young, we think we're more knowledgeable than the parents of other kids in the high school, more woke to what they don't want us to know.

The truth is we don't know anything but what we see on the surface: he's thriving in school, mastering Spanish, and bringing home friends. He attends all the church youth group meetings, and he's even begun a weekly church small group with friends led by Len, a seasoned youth minister. In track, William places in state meets. It's hard to imagine he's habitually using substances, even if it wasn't the first time.

Still, the warning signs keep popping up, and William's caught with beer at one school event, and later, he's found with a bottle of whiskey on a school trip. The school's punishment for a second alcohol offense involves sending him to two Alcoholics Anonymous meetings in the community. It doesn't scare him straight, though. He doesn't relate to the participants at that meeting, all middle-age or older, smoking before and after the meeting, and slurping old coffee from Styrofoam cups.

The other warning signs we don't know about. We don't know that he passed out in the corner at a party. We don't know that he bumped a car leaving another party. We don't know that he went to a concert with friends and tried Xanax. And we don't know that he's now regularly smoking marijuana.

That's the sort of information his friends will share at his funeral.

"I'm so sorry," one said. "We didn't know he would overdose. We didn't know he had a problem. It's what everyone was doing. Though I guess it was strange that William was the only one who passed out in the corner."

Most students don't know to recognize warning signs, and even if they do, their strongest loyalty lies with protecting their friends from the trouble caused by prying parents. Thus, we are oblivious except for William's occasional slipups, which I approach with increasing frustration.

"Don't you understand how foolish this is?" I'll shout during a one-sided conversation after we find rolling papers in his car.

Maybe he needs to switch his scenery for a bit. He loves Spanish so we send him to Madrid for the summer with money in his pockets to become fluent. Hudson, also in Spanish, follows along, though he and William live in different homes. We don't know that William tries cocaine and likes it, and we don't know that he's out dancing and partying until dawn almost every night. We just hope that by giving him advantages we did not have, he will do better—what every parent wants.

Initially, we were relieved when William got a girlfriend, his first serious one; maybe this will take the pressure off of keeping up with the boys, trying to fit in with substance use. Christine was his first kiss, but soon they were doing more than kissing, and brassy Christine is leading the charge, sitting in his lap and slurping on him in public. She called and sent text messages at all hours, and when Kent looked up the phone records, she found William and Christine texted nearly six thousand times in one month.

"You cannot possibly have time for schoolwork or time with friends and family," she said, but he kept staring at the device, sending messages and waiting for a response.

"You are addicted to that phone," Kent said.

After nine months, Christine asked William to meet late on a Sunday afternoon. He zipped down the mountain in his 4Runner, eager for the unexpected date. But he arrived home just an hour later, hurrying up the stairs and slamming his bedroom door.

"William?" I called across the house.

No answer.

I walked up the stairs and knocked on his door.

"William?"

I heard muffled sobbing.

"William?"

The sobbing deepened.

I opened the door, walking gently to his side. He was curled up, with his face smashed into the pillow. I took a seat on the bed, running my hand through his hair and down his back.

"I'm so sorry, William," I said.

"I know how rejection feels," I said, and his cries intensify. "The hurt will go away eventually."

But it didn't. For days and weeks, William came home after school, ate dinner, and went into his room with the door closed. The old air vents that traverse the house amplified his sobbing like a megaphone. My visits to his side weren't helping.

"I love her," he said, his voice cracking. "Why did she do this?"

Eventually, I got over Ashley, but he struggled with healing. Kent and I grew concerned.

"Does he need to see a therapist?" Kent wondered.

None of us have seen a therapist, so I didn't know.

"Hopefully, it will soon pass," I said.

I've had enough of waking up in the morning to the stench of alcohol on my breath. I've had enough of underperforming, and I've had enough of wondering if my drinking is influencing William. I've had enough guilt and shame for trying to swallow guilt and shame. Also, my half-brother, Jimmy, sends a message that he has quit drinking, had enough of it.

"Life is better," he says.

I've got a similarly fed-up friend, and we've pondered our drinking over drinking as drinkers do.

"I can quit any time I want to," he says.

"Me too," I say.

"I can go as long as I want without a drink," he says.

"Me too," I say.

He proposes a bet: we'll both quit, and the first one to break owes the other five hundred dollars.

"Deal," I say, and we shake.

To kick off our abstinence, we meet for dinner and drinks with our wives at the country club; we'll catch one last drunk that we'll label a "buzz" because that sounds better. We slaughter one bottle of wine after another until we're full after steaks, dessert, and bold conversation.

It's time to go, but my friend wants to toast the bet, ordering a shot of cognac for each of us.

"Here's to too much of a good thing," he says, rattling my glass.

We laugh, and I send it down the hatch.

"Cognac is for sipping, not shooting," he tells me in a slur.

"Unless it's your last drink," I say.

He orders another round.

"If we wake up feeling bad, quitting will be easier," he says with a chuckle.

"Well, that's a good point," I say, and down goes the very last shot.

The strange thing is that quitting is relatively easy since I'm not physically hooked. I'm drinking enough for distraction. I'm psychologically addicted; my body does not miss it, just my mind. I know booze is the lubricant that smooths me into a cocktail party, makes me expansive, fun, and funny, the center of the storytelling circle, the guy other guys lean closer to hear. But no more. Because I quit booze, I quit people.

Come to our suite for the football game Saturday night.

Pass.

Come on the golf trip.

Pass.

Come to the hunting lodge for the weekend.

Pass.

When Kent drags me to one party, I'm standing in a corner looking at my watch. An acquaintance approaches.

"You can quit drinking," he says, "but if you don't know why and you don't know how, it's that much harder."

"I'm just trying to get a reset," I say.

"Did you eat dinner before you came to the party?" he asks.

"No."

"There are strategies you can learn that will help."

"OK, well, thank you," I say, walking away to find Kent, and leave the party.

Kent is concerned. I've effectively shut down her social life, too, and I don't have a plan or tools and coping skills. I'm edgy at 5:00 p.m. and don't like waiting for dinner, as Kent sips wine and cooks. Yet one month passes and another, and I'm sticking with no alcohol, and so is my friend in the bet. I'm ahead of the deadline on my latest book, *How Toyota Became #1*, and I'm really enjoying the writing, not just simply transferring interview notes from my notebook into chapters.

I'm also enjoying writing this book because I'm connecting with some of the philosophy that undergirds it. Before World War II, a member of the founding Toyoda family spent time in Europe, coming across the world's first prominent self-help book, *Self-Help*, by Samuel Smiles. Sakichi Toyoda was deeply influenced by Smiles's disregard for irresponsible habits and waste and brought the book back to Japan, where it became a critical part of Toyota's management strategy.

As I'm writing my book, I'm fascinated by the self-help aspect, obsessing over the table of contents and chapter headings, which seem like mantras I should adopt: Rid all that adds no value; improve quality by exposing the truth; favor long-term strategies over short-term fixes; and let failure be your teacher.

The Toyota book breaks through, selling well in multiple languages, and it also finds more critical acclaim than my other books. Finally, the approval I've so desperately wanted. I notice my success comes during my year without alcohol, and I imagine the future of everything I can achieve now. I'll show Dad, and I'll show the birth dad who's out there somewhere, and I'll show everyone. This bastard's life will finish strong.

I'm in the living room at Mom and Dad's house for a visit, smiling as I recite how well our family is doing in our new environment. Mom is in her seventies and walking with a cane. She's sitting beside me on the arm of the La-Z-Boy recliner, with a hand on my shoulder. Dad is in his early eighties and barely walking at all. He's on the couch facing me, focused on every word. Everything looks the same: the same TV

Dad bought for the family on my twelfth birthday with our first cable subscription, explaining that it was my present, and the same wallpaper Mom once picked out for Mother's Day.

Dad gently interrupts my stream of braggadocio.

"I want you to know," he says, "how proud of you I am."

I smile. "Thank you, Dad."

Eunice is out of town. She's still got the farmhouse they bought her five miles outside of Oxford, but she's spending most of her time now in Tennessee, where her birth mother lives. They met several years back, and it was love at first sight, until it wasn't, since conflict is their nature. They fight and make up, fight and make up. Mom and Dad don't seem to mind paying electricity and water for Eunice's empty house, probably because it gives them a breather. They seem easier with each other and with me. We're smiling, and they're soaking in my pride, sending affirmation right back.

Dad crosses his legs, and his pant leg rises to reveal a grotesque swollen ankle, bulging and round like a tree trunk.

"Whoa," I say. "Are you OK?"

"Yes," he says. "That's just some water retention."

But it looks more serious than that, and suddenly I'm worried.

As if he can read my face, he says, "I want you to know that I have everything worked out. You know this house is worth more than one million dollars, so even though we were just university employees, there will be a little bit of money for you and Eunice."

"OK?"

"But don't worry, I've worked everything out, so this won't be something you and Eunice have to fight over. It will all be clear and split evenly."

"OK. Are you planning to go anywhere any time soon?" I ask.

He smiles. "I'm getting older," he says.

I wrap my arms around his neck and give a tight squeeze, my cheeks rubbing across his to catch tears streaming from his face. Mom takes her cane and waddles over, wrapping an arm around each of us, and we're hugging together, as family.

"We're so proud of you, David," she says.

I drive five hours back home with a smile and the radio up loud, singing along with songs, making up words when I don't know the lyrics.

Within a week, the phone rings. "Dad's had a heart attack," Mom says.

I meet Mom and Eunice at the hospital, and for days, we scrutinize the heart rate monitor doing its work. Mom thinks he'll get better, going home soon, while Eunice believes the doctors and nurses are doing everything wrong, like there's some conspiracy to kill an otherwise healthy man. In a week, Dad's breathing has slowed precipitously, along with his heartbeat. He's calling out for his mother, who's been dead for thirty-five years, and he's talking gibberish about going to church.

"He doesn't have much longer," I say.

A nurse stops by, checking Dad's vitals, and Eunice badgers her with annoying questions like, "Does he need to be rolled over?" and "Have you checked his oxygen level?" Mom tries to smooth it over.

"I'm sure they're doing the best they can."

"Mom, you can't just let them kill him!" Eunice shouts.

"Everybody dies eventually," I say, hoping to deflect the tension.

Eunice erupts, lashing out about inequities she's suffered over the years, and I can't argue because our father is beside us taking his last breaths.

Mom walks outside, and I follow.

"David," she says, "maybe it's best if you just go. Eunice and I will sit here with him."

I draw up short, incredulous, then pivot, stalk from the hospital to my car in the parking lot, slam a fist against the hood, and drive to a bar for a drink. I've long since forgotten about the bet. I prefer to change how I feel, but I'll try to have more control. I'll have just one, maybe two. Or perhaps four and I'll walk home. Several hours later, Mom calls.

Dad has passed.

Lucky, I think.

The funeral is on a fall Saturday with a script he planned, including songs and readings. There's even a family headstone in place, chosen by Dad, our family's burial spot with room for all four, though I made it clear they don't need to be saving any space for me. The vision of our four embalmed corpses lying side by side makes me want to gouge out my eyes.

I've already made Kent promise, back in the funeral home. "Cremation only, and spread the ashes elsewhere, do you understand?"

Some of Dad's former students are here, mostly because they've been hand-selected as pallbearers. Mom called each to explain that Dad wanted them to carry the casket. So, here I am, hoisting Dad's body in a metal box from the hearse to the cemetery when I have a revelation: the other pallbearers, aside from me and Wyck, the former Ole Miss football player, never married.

After the service, a pallbearer my age, the one Dad visited in the fraternity house, turns and whispers, "Did you know?"

I look down at my shiny black leather shoes.

"Yes," I say. "I knew."

I mean, how could I not know?

But the truth is I didn't, not really. I suppose it must have been the same with Mom, though I'm not sure. Later, at the house, when visitors have left and Eunice has retreated to her room, Mom and I are sitting in the den. I wonder how she felt seeing those pallbearers.

"Can I ask a question?" I say.

"Yes, of course."

"Did you know that Dad was gay?"

She looks into her lap and sighs.

"David," she says, now looking at me, "he wasn't gay with me."

"What does that mean?"

"It means he wasn't gay with me."

She slowly stands, takes her cane, and begins hobbling from the den. I wonder how she'd walk and act and who she'd be if she hadn't been married to a closeted gay man for over fifty years. If she hadn't had to keep that secret, even from herself.

"Sleep tight," she says, heading upstairs to the bedroom that's now hers alone. "Sleep tight."

* * *

Eunice has long brown hair parted away from her face, and she's wearing cowboy boots that click on the floor as she paces across the tile in Mom's hospital room.

"Goddamn doctors are going to get their asses sued," she says, pivoting at the window to pace back. "I can't believe this shit."

Mom had put off her hip replacement while caring for Dad, but after he passed, she figured she might as well go ahead. She was ready to lose the cane. It was supposed to be routine surgery, but she's gotten a C. difficile infection from her extended stay. The doctor said her hip bone was thin, crumbling like dry clay, and she needs another procedure to make it right. I've only been to Oxford for a day, and already, my entire childhood is playing out again. Eunice asked for and received the role of Mom's healthcare power of attorney, so she's in charge, raving and vengeful, threatening to sue the doctors and the hospital. Mom can barely talk and regrets putting Eunice in charge. I, meanwhile, am indulging in a bitter and mean amusement. All these years, Mom has let Eunice have her way at everyone else's expense, but this time, Mom's the one paying. And it looks like the price might be her life. Because of Eunice's threatened lawsuits, the doctors have decided to discharge Mom tomorrow, even though she can't walk and prolific diarrhea from the C. diff infection will kill her soon.

The room smells so bad from Mom's oozing bowels that I can hardly think. Mom waves a weak hand toward Eunice.

"You've got to give us a minute," Mom says. Eunice turns and stomps out, pulling the door closed hard.

"You've got to send Eunice home," Mom tells me. "She's driving me crazy, and she's driving the doctors crazy, and they are going to let me die because they are afraid to treat me. Please help, David. Convince them we're not going to sue. You know the hospital administrator. You know the doctors. You know this town. You've got to fix this. They'll trust you."

"OK," I say. "Nobody is letting you die."

"And, David," she says, her voice weak, "there's one more thing. I need you to get my will from the black bag in my closet. Work on the hospital and a doctor first, but tonight or in the morning, get my will and bring it here."

I leave the room to work on my assignments, sending Eunice in so Mom can do the dirty work of sending her home.

My first call is to Todd, a gastroenterologist who's a lifelong friend. He's not been Mom's doctor, but he's heard about her C. diff and Eunice predicament.

"I need to get in there to clean out her colon and repair any ulcerations or perforations," he tells me. "But the only way that's going to happen is if you assure the hospital nobody is getting sued."

"Todd," I say, "how long have you known me?"

"Since dirt was new," he says.

"Have you ever known me to pick a fight? Have you ever known my mother to sue anyone? Nobody is getting sued. That's just crazy talk."

"I know," Todd says. "I hear you. I'll get this fixed, don't worry."

At Mom's house, I shuffle through her closet, finding the black bag on a top shelf in the corner. I place it on her bed, pulling out contents one by one. There's a bag of old silver dollars that Dad collected, there's a couple of life insurance policies, there's her marriage certificate, her will, and there's a tall stack of bank certificates of deposit held together by a thick rubber band.

Mom-Mom saved her money in the bank, but I never knew how much there was, didn't ask. I knew she'd given Eunice fifty thousand dollars when she'd asked for it and that she'd transferred the rest to Mom when she died. Thumbing through the CDs, I'm surprised at how many there are, with a dozen totaling fifty thousand dollars or more, and several for one hundred thousand dollars. My God, I think. Mom-Mom was rich. And now Mom is. Good for her.

I reach for the rubber band, and when I'm snapping it back on, I notice something. Mom's name is on the top CD as the owner. But she's added another name: Eunice. I flip to the next CD: also co-owned by Eunice. The next and the next. I drop the stack and lose my breath, like I've been sucker-punched. And in a way I have been. I pick up the stack again, thinking I must be crazy somehow, but I'm not the crazy one. Mom has assigned most of the cash in our family's estate to Eunice.

I feel sick about the money, yes, but it's more than that. Here in my hands is confirmation of everything I always knew: that I'm not loved as much as my sibling. Maybe not loved at all. Why else would Mom go to the trouble of adding Eunice's name to bank CDs so the funds can't possibly be split upon her death? I lower my head into my hands and squeeze like I could pop it. I've never asked for anything, even when times were hard and new business ventures uneven. Meanwhile, Eunice asked for much, and much was granted: her house, her household expenses, insurance for decades, cold hard cash.

My birth mom gave me away, and my adopted mom prefers her other child.

For dinner, I eat a six-pack of Bud Light. I don't sleep much. The next morning, I drive to the convenience store for a pack of cigarettes, hoping nicotine will help me get through.

At the hospital, I learn my doctor friend has come through, calling in favors from his team so Mom can have surgery the next day. I walk into Mom's room, where the stench remains.

"Thank you, David," she says when I appear. News of her surgery has given her some energy. "Thank you. You've saved me."

I toss her will onto the hospital bed.

She knows that I know.

"I'm sorry," Mom says. "I'm truly sorry you had to see that without warning. I felt so bad I wasn't thinking. I wish I had told you first."

"Yep."

"David," she says, "I want you to know something. Money is not equal, but neither is love. I love you more, but I want Eunice to have the money."

"Mom, you are always telling people what you think they want to hear. You're always trying to fix everything, but it's still broken."

"It's true, David. My love is not equal. As for the money, I want to give you a little bit now to help, but most of it, including the house, I'm giving to Eunice."

"You are saying that I will get a little bit, and Eunice may get nearly two million dollars once you add it all up? That's not what Dad wanted."

"I'm saying that I love you, David, and that's what I want."

"Here's what I want," I say, pointing a finger toward Mom's face. "How about you just give her *all* of that money? That's fine, and give her everything else too. I want nothing from that house of horrors. No mementos, no photos, no stick of family furniture, no nothing. I just want to be free of it all."

I'm only saying this to hurt Mom, to show her how badly I'm hurting. I say it to bring her to her senses.

Instead, she nods. "Maybe that's best," she says. "Just let this go. Let Eunice have everything."

"Let Eunice have everything," I dully repeat.

"I'm sorry," Mom says. "I hope one day you will understand."

"Lord, help me," I say. "I got adopted into the wrong family."

147

Chapter Seven

Falling Down

The dinner table feels a bit tentative with William off at college. I hesitate before I say the blessing, as if he's in the bathroom washing up, about to join us. But he's at Ole Miss, sharing a table with his new Sigma Nu brothers. Yes, he's attending my former school, pledging my fraternity house, and my pride almost compensates for my mini-me living six hours away. Though maybe William is less of a mini-me now that he's surpassing me. I used to dream of playing sports in college, but William is doing it, becoming a hurdler for one of the country's best men's track programs. I used to dream of positioning myself academically to do something special in life, but William is doing it, as an international relations major in the Honors College. It's the ultimate satisfaction for a parent to watch the first child raise the family's bar of achievement, then hurdle over it.

Hudson and William have always been close, and he, too, is feeling a bit unmoored. But Mary Halley comes up with a solution, she says, to fill the void in our home. She's in the ninth grade, our rule follower who hasn't presented a hint of trouble, and she now turns to me, tilting her head.

"Daddy, please, can we get a puppy? Please?" Her enormous hazel eyes are working their magic. "Do you really want to deny your girl a puppy?"

"When I was a child," I explain, "Dad made our dachshund Happy live in the basement with fleas, and it still makes me sad to this day." I shake my head. "Maybe we're just not dog people," I say, thinking of my exhaustion, given how much I have to travel for work.

But she's relentless. "Who wants to know," she asks over dinner the next night, "the absolutely, positively, most perfect dog for our family based on an internet questionnaire?"

"Pass the butter beans," I say, an attempt to head this off.

"A Cavalier King Charles Spaniel! Anybody want to see a picture of one?" And, my goodness, the dog's adorable, with floppy ears and eyes almost as beseeching as Mary Halley's. Score one for the youngest child.

The next night at dinner, it's "I miss William." Mary Halley sighs elaborately. "If only we had something to distract us, something that is, according to dogtime.com, 'fearless and sporting in character, yet at the same time gentle and affectionate . . .'"

No one is surprised that we're soon shopping for a Cavalier King Charles Spaniel. A police officer in the city who breeds dogs on the side has a new litter. There, we select the big girl from the lot, oversized for the breed, perhaps, but just right for us. Mary Halley names her Lady, from *Lady and the Tramp*, and for the next nine months, she chews her way through our closets and furniture and into our hearts.

In the eleventh grade, Hudson has a new girlfriend, his first serious one, called Lo, short for Logan. They met in a church Sunday school class. She's a year older and, like him, a soccer player. The family takes to her. Lady takes to her a bit too enthusiastically. Lo brings over a CD set of TV shows she got for Christmas, and Lady decides they're her new Christmas chew toy. Lo leaves her sandals on the floor, and Lady gnaws them like beef jerky.

"We need to do something about Lady," Hudson says after we find she's Scooby-snacked on the leg of an antique chair. Yes, we do, but I've always been the soccer coach who favored praise over discipline. And also, though the kids might not know the full extent of our problems, we've no time for a training regimen; we're busier than is healthy or sustainable.

When we moved to Chattanooga, buoyed by those cooling breezes that slalomed up the mountain, we played old money and bought our house and our lifestyle and, looking down over the valley, had no warning that our lofty perch was precarious. Now it's 2008, and the recession has rattled us like an earthquake. Right before things bottomed out, Kent opened a new business, a women's clothing boutique. Now, fewer women are buying high-end fashion, but she doesn't want to close and can't stand to lay off her employees, so she is working seven days a week, every week. This changes the dynamic of our home, as we're all suddenly bereft of her quiet competence in the house, her efficient hands making fast work of chores, and her low voice soothing any tensions we've carried in off the school bus or drive from the airport.

I'm writing not one, not two, but three books this year. Even I know this is impossible. There's no way I'll be able to give any of the three the attention they deserve, but I felt forced into this bad math. The publishing industry has been declining, and it fell through the trap door of the recession. The six-figure advances I'd become accustomed to—and used to sustain our family for the year—have suddenly shrunk. So now, I must write three to earn what one once earned. Alongside the loss of income is the stinging loss of stature. My commercial business books were once stacked high in bookstores across America. My publishers could barely give away my latest, *Jeff Immelt and the New GE Way*, since Jack Welch is long gone from General Electric.

We're doing what we think we should do, doubling down with extra work to keep the illusion shining and give our children everything they deserve. We could quit the country club to save money, but where would our children meet friends? (Also, how would that look?)

We could move, leaving the expensive private schools, but how would our children weather a mid-year transfer? (Also, how would that look?)

The only bit of normal we've maintained is family dinner. Somehow, Kent comes home from the dress shop and still brings us together for a nutritious meal, her tablecloth like a parachute that slows our descent. Then, we sip wine, wonder what William is doing at college, ask Hudson and Mary Halley questions about school, and double-check schedules for upcoming events. Otherwise, we hardly see each other. Everyone feels how stressed I am and is oppressed by the gloom. It's like the shades are pulled all the time in our house.

Hudson is the quiet one in the family, slow to complain, fast to see the best in others. He hasn't been in trouble, or he hasn't been in any real trouble. He has a close-knit group of friends from church and school, he's got a keyboard he plays when alone in his room, he's on the McCallie school soccer team as well as a travel soccer team ranked among the best in the South. Once, Kent finds a case of beer hidden under his bed, but when we sit him down for questions, he explains, "I was saving it for some friends." We don't like this and say so, but we also know high school kids drink beer. His grades are fine, we remind ourselves. And Hudson meets weekly with his church small group, led by Len, the youth minister.

Still, he seems to have grown beyond quiet to—well, sullen almost. But maybe this is just teenage sulkiness, hormones running the show. "Boys will be boys," says a parent, a bit blithely, when we explain that we think a bottle may be missing from our liquor cabinet and ask if anyone else thinks their son might be drinking.

"Boys will be boys" smoking pot in Peter's basement: that's what we don't know. Smoking and drinking a lot, all weekend long.

We ask if he's drinking.

"No," he says, nothing more than experimentation.

We ask if he's smoking marijuana.

"No," he says, nothing more than experimentation.

We know he drank some in Spain, with William, but we weren't sure that was so terrible. Maybe being introduced to the European way, where the drinking age is sixteen and kids learn to drink in modest amounts with their families, is better than America's forbidden fruit, where kids have their stomachs pumped on their twenty-first birthdays. We're even proud at a senior party chaperoned by parents seeing Hudson drinking beer because he doesn't seem intoxicated at all. We thought he was showing good judgment, failing to recognize the possibility that he's developed tolerance, and several beers won't make him slur or stumble.

But something is wrong, we sense this, and we know it for sure when he says he wants to quit the school soccer team his senior year.

I sit him down for a talk after dinner, reminding him how, starting when he was eleven years old, I began driving him thirty minutes each way to travel team practice. I suggest he needs to finish for himself, for his teammates and coaches, and even for me.

"Quitting makes no sense," I say, waving a half-full wineglass in my hand. "Your team is a favorite for the state championship. You may start at forward. And you want to quit?"

"I just don't want to play anymore," he says. "I'd rather hang out with my friends."

Kent and I talk later that night, making a firm decision. "You are not allowed to quit," I explain after dinner the next night. "It's not an option."

By midway through the season, the team has just one loss, and Hudson is a part-time starter, scoring goals and contributing with a state championship in sight. I attend all the games, cheering from the bleachers. Today, they've got a midweek game on the road. Although I have a looming deadline and the game is an hour-and-a-half away, I wouldn't miss it.

I arrive at the field a few minutes early, and the McCallie team is off to the side, crouching in a huddle together, saying a prayer. They break with a "Go Blue!" and the boys trot toward the sideline. I'm scanning the white jerseys for Hudson. I'm sure he's there, somewhere, because he left for school this morning, but I can't find his number sixteen.

I call Kent.

"Hudson's not at the game," I say.

It's late in the day, but Kent calls the school office. The assistant headmaster answers on his way out the door.

"Well," he says, "I noticed Hudson took a sick day today. I gather from your voice that he's not at home."

I call Lo, his girlfriend.

"This is not good," she says, "but he's not with me. I suspect you'll find him with his friends."

I'm at home, pacing in the kitchen. I call his phone for the tenth time. No answer. I send a text for the tenth time. No answer.

I call Lo again. "Maybe he'll answer if you call."

Ten minutes later, the phone rings, and it's Hudson.

"I'm with friends," he says, explaining they organized a senior skip day.

"But other seniors on the soccer team were there," I say.

"This was a skip day for just us. Me, Peter, Richard, and Dan," he says, referring to boys from the church small group.

"You have an obligation for your team. They started a tenth grader in your place."

I expect the image to fill him with envy and shame, but he says nothing.

"Well, it's time for dinner," I say. "Come on home, and we'll talk more."

I turn to Kent, who is gripping the counter as if it's keeping her from falling backward. "We spend all this money to give him the best education, and he's just skipping school? Making the team was the most important thing in his life, and now he's skipping the game? It doesn't make sense." She shakes her head and says in a low voice, "There's something else."

"Seems like it," I say.

"We need to get a drug test."

By the time I drive down the mountain to a pharmacy and return, Hudson is sitting in the den with Kent.

"We were just hanging out," he says.

"You're sure about that?"

"Yes," he says. "I just didn't want to miss the skip day with my friends."

"Were you drinking or doing drugs?"

"No, I told you, I don't do that."

I reach into the white paper bag and pull out the white drug test box.

"Will you take this?" I say.

"I don't want to," he says.

"But we need you to."

He goes into the bathroom, pees into the cup, and hands it to Kent to insert the test strip: it's positive for marijuana.

I see a pattern, first with our oldest and now with our second child, and as a parent, I'm entirely unprepared and unskilled for this dilemma. It's possible I'm overreacting; he's got just another few weeks of high school, and seniors are always cutting loose at this point. I simply don't know the difference between experimenting and a problem. And I was always the coach more suited for encouragement than counseling. Lady continued her CD-and-sandal diet, having learned early that I wasn't focused on discipline. I sense she craves more boundaries, but I'm paralyzed with inaction, hoping each plea in response—"Lady! No!"—will stop the destruction.

One reason I'm struggling is because I can't compare my own youthful indiscretions to Hudson's or William's because the cultural differences in our generations are so extreme. When or if we got high on mild marijuana, it felt transgressive, and we did it behind closed doors. Their generation celebrates inebriation in private group messages and doesn't even consider pot, often many times stronger than what we experienced, a "real" drug. We didn't have access to mental health professionals, didn't even know terms like ADD. Now, kids are tested early and frequently referred to specialists, which has helped a lot of people. But it's also normalized the taking of pills; if a doctor prescribed them to you—or to your friend or your friend's brother's roommate—what could be wrong?

I plead with Hudson nonetheless, explaining that while marijuana may have medicinal benefits if legally prescribed by a physician in some states, spending every day high, from the wake and bake to lights out, will quickly derail anyone's ambitions.

"There's no good life as a pothead. Please, Hudson, don't make that mistake."

What gives us hope that Hudson is simply acting out, that this teenage rebellion is a phase that will pass, is that William is excelling.

Perhaps my final warning to William is working, when I said I'd seen too many people over the years think they could use drugs regularly during college, sure that they could quit when it was time to graduate and move on, only to find they were hooked.

"I'm not going to let that happen, Dad," William said.

William is making straight As in the Honors College, which is more than I ever did without the honors. Because he's shy and a bit insecure, I can imagine he's not going to all the Sigma Nu mixers stone-cold sober, but clearly he's managing. He's running the 400 hurdles, considered the most challenging event in track and field because it requires an athlete to have the tremendous speed of a sprinter, the strength of an 800-meter runner, and the visual steering ability of a horizontal jumper, and, in addition, have dynamic mobility within the hips to efficiently hurdle. Of course the hardest part of track takes place out of view: the 6:00 a.m. weight workouts and sprint sessions year-round.

Another good sign is the girlfriend he finds his freshman year. Stephanie is beautiful and bright, and they go to fraternity and sorority parties together, and she visits us in Tennessee. Though we don't say it to William, Kent and I whisper to each other that we could picture them marrying one day.

But there are signs that we could have seen, that anyone could have seen if they had all the information and if they weren't looking with a parent's hopeful eye.

I know that William gets a citation from campus police his freshman year for drinking in his car in the dorm parking lot. Deep down, I suspect he is smoking something in his car when the policeman arrives. Still, he tells a convincing story, blaming the incident on the officer, and we pay a lawyer to get him out of trouble.

I know that Kent's mother purchased a house in Oxford as a second home about the time William enrolled at Ole Miss. William is her favorite grandchild, and she showers him with cash and gifts to gain affection. We beg her to limit the money and not provide him with a key to her house when she's away, but she does anyway. I show up at the house unannounced one Monday, finding vomit in a laundry hamper and a half-empty gallon of whiskey under a chair in the den.

I don't know that a friend of Stephanie's sees him snorting something at a party at the house and that Stephanie confronts him, saying she will not date anyone who snorts cocaine, and he denies, denies, denies.

"Your friend was drunk and confused," he says, recasting the blame.

I don't know that William gets kicked out of living in the Sigma Nu house late one semester for smoking marijuana and that he lived with Kent's mother for several weeks.

I don't know that William's fraternity brother doubles as a drug dealer. He makes regular runs to his Atlanta hometown to keep William and other fraternity members higher than a bat's ass, day in, day out. His specialty is the new prescription drugs flooding the college market. There's Xanax, the benzodiazepine that doctors use to treat anxiety and panic disorders, and OxyContin, the opioid pain killer with a reputation for abuse among impoverished whites in the Kentucky and West Virginia hill country.

I don't know that William and his fraternity brother are in love with how OxyContin pills mix with alcohol for a double-down affect, and I don't know that he and the fraternity brother have purchased pill scrapers to turn the OxyContin pills into a powder they can snort for a quadruple-down effect.

I don't know that William starts ingesting multiple prescription opioid pills a day.

I don't know that William, thinking he's discovered some magical pill, shares Xanax with Hudson.

"These are great," he says, dropping a handful into his younger brother's palm.

I'd given William two lofty goals when he went to college, motivation perhaps to keep him on the right side of substance excess.

"If you can get a letter in track," I explained, "and make a 3.5 GPA or higher that same year, you will make the Southeastern Conference's Academic Honor Roll. You'll have an Ole Miss letter jacket and a plaque from the SEC, and that's a big deal. Nobody will ever be able to take that away from you."

William earned his way to the SEC Outdoor Track and Field Championships his sophomore year and made the grades. He was so proud when the coach presented his letter jacket, and when he stood on the basketball court at halftime of a big game, and when they gave the academic honor to student-athletes.

"I did it, Dad," he said.

"That's something nobody in our family has done, William," I said. "We'll always remember those accomplishments."

I do wonder, though, if I should have presented those goals as just part of a bigger program of engagement and healthy habits. Because once he met those goals, he didn't have anything else to shoot for. He decided to stop running track; this was hard to be happy about, but he explained his reasoning. He wanted to focus on his international studies, and he couldn't study abroad as long as he was running track. Without the mandatory weight and sprinting practice, however, he had too much idle time.

He studies abroad in Ecuador with friends the summer before his junior year, and we hear that his Spanish is among the best in the group, which is saying something. What we don't hear is that he finds a new habit in the land known as a cocaine superhighway of South America. We just notice, back home, that he's lost his sculpted physique—quitting daily weight training overnight will do that—but he's also lost the bloom of health in his cheeks, and he has dark circles under his eyes.

I wonder if he has a problem, but I'm not sure. I talk to William, but he's adamant there's nothing wrong. Look at his record, he says, straight As, a letter in track. Worry over something else. Someone else.

And that other person I'm worrying about faces me daily in the mirror.

Surgery got Mom back on her feet, but I've lost my footing. I'm so wounded by Mom deciding to give Eunice all the family money that I can't seem to recover. I keep telling myself that we don't need it, although that's no longer exactly true. But it's not about the money. It's about how her decision confirms everything I ever feared about myself, my unlovable self.

I've started another book, yet I'm behind on the deadline, and I'm not sure I have the strength to finish it. That's a problem since I've signed another one to follow that. With my career in jeopardy and my self-worth shattered, I'm in such a low place I'm dragging the whole family down. Finally, Kent tells me I need help.

"Like a psychologist?" I ask.

"A psychologist, a psychiatrist . . . whatever it takes. But, David? Get some help because this can't go on any longer."

The look she gives me is weary. She's still that gorgeous coed in a Bugs Bunny one-piece, and still the centered counterbalance to my impulsiveness, but she seems tired. She's losing weight she doesn't need to lose. Maybe it's all the yoga she's doing. But new wrinkles, like two staples, appear between her eyebrows. I've aged her. My antics, my depression, have aged her. It's just another thing to despise myself for.

How could any doctor help me? How could I find the strength to open up and talk about the things I've never talked about? No, impossible. I'm not a suicide risk. I remember all too well the pain from Charlie's death, how it shattered family and friends so completely that, three decades later, we're still repairing cracks. Instead, I'll just keep moving through my days with the walking dead's slow crawl.

* * *

I'm in Oxford to visit William and see Mom at the nursing home she's been taken to from the hospital. The surgery that my friend Todd arranged saved her life, and now she requires rehabilitation therapy. She can't go home because she can't walk or care for herself, so Eunice has taken her to the only local nursing home Mom's Medicaid insurance will cover.

When I pull up, the place looks like some abandoned, asbestos-filled detention center. Its ceilings are low, and its rooms are dark. Mom's room smells like urine. There's too little staff, so when she rings for an assistant, she has to hope someone comes before she loses control of her bladder. It's clear that not a lot of rehab is going on here; most patients are whittling away the time until death, a sort of non-labeled hospice for the underprivileged. But the crazy thing is that Mom is privileged. I know—I've seen the CDs; sometimes I see them in my nightmares. Even if it's not covered by insurance, she shouldn't have to stay here, marinating in her own urine.

I'm standing at Mom's bedside and holding her hand. From down the hall, I hear someone's terrible hacking cough, more like a death rattle.

"Why are you here?" I ask.

"This is what Eunice has arranged," she says. "It's what the insurance pays for."

I suppose Eunice doesn't want to send Mom to a nicer place because she thinks it will eat into the huge amount of cash she'll get when Mom kicks the bucket, which, in this place, won't be long. I want to tell Mom that for once in her life she has to stand up to Eunice. I want to make Eunice come here so I can talk some sense into her, fight to get Mom better care. But I already know how that will play out. Mom will ask me to leave because I'm upsetting Eunice. I feel so agonized and powerless; I don't think I can stand it.

I walk outside with my phone and google local psychiatrists. It's time.

There's just a couple of options, and I casually know one whose office is in a building I once owned near campus. I'm sure he treats mostly students grappling with stress and peer pressure instead of middle-aged men worrying over their mothers, but I take the first available appointment.

"Have you considered suicide?" the psychiatrist asks during our appointment.

"No, not really," I say. "I mean, doesn't everyone imagine at one time or another what the world will be like without them?"

"I think so," he says. "Yes."

"I've contemplated that," I say, "but my friend Charlie put a shotgun in his mouth, and I'm not over it yet. Maybe I'm just killing myself slowly, taking on more problems with every passing day so the weight of it all ultimately crushes me."

"What's your biggest problem right now?" he asks.

I open my mouth, but how could I possibly describe the complicated history of our "family," and the current heartbreaking scenario at the center, where Mom's like a hostage with Stockholm syndrome, loving the person who keeps her trapped? No, instead, "I'm behind on a book deadline," comes out. "I can't concentrate at all. It's like I have things to do, but I've got them all swirling in a million pieces in my head, and it's too hard to put the puzzle together, so I put it off another day."

"Hmm," he says, making notes. "I've got a test that I'd like you to take."

He sits me in front of a computer, starting a program with questions and pictures, and I can't concentrate, wondering if Mom is ringing right now for a nurse that isn't coming, but I'm clicking the mouse to keep it moving until completion.

He calls me back to the office.

"I'd like to treat you for attention deficit disorder," he says. "We see a lot of that here, and you say you'd feel better if you can finish your book. Let's start you on some Adderall and see if that helps."

I arrived thinking of depression pills, but I'm leaving with speed. One hour later, I've got the prescription in hand, swallowing one down as the doctor ordered.

Within thirty minutes, I'm incandescent. I've never been so alert. It's like the world just stopped, and it's only me and what's precisely in front of me to focus upon, and I want to thank God, and raise my hands to the sky, because I know in that instant that I can not only finish my book this year, I can finish that entire freaking thing right now, right this very minute.

It's almost too good to be true.

I should have answered the doctor's questions more honestly. It wasn't the book deadline that's swallowing me up, it's the giant hole of rejection that I've had since adoption that I keep trying to fill. I didn't even bring that up. However, it probably doesn't matter because clearly Dr. Feelgood is a genius with his quickly dispensed miracle cure. By the end of the month, I've finished my book. I've also found the strength to fight for Mom's welfare, and I've moved her from that Hotel California to a good place near us in Chattanooga. Its excellent rehab facility gets her walking again. I've started a national talk radio show on twenty stations. Oh, and one day, I mowed my lawn when it didn't even need it.

Another thing different about this month is I've barely gotten buzzed from wine. That's because Adderall, in full force, overpowers alcohol, so one doesn't feel its effects at all until the Adderall wears off. That's one reason students abuse Adderall, of course. They can drink and drink and drink all night long or get smashed one night and perk up the next morning in an instant just by swallowing one of these doctor-dispensed pills.

"Best drug ever," I tell Kent.

* * *

It's early on Christmas morning, one year and six months from that day I swallowed the first prescribed pill. I find myself so utterly lost and broken that I can see my end approaching in a nightmare that frightens me awake. In the dream, my bare skeleton is lying in the corner of an alley, behind a bar. People walk around or step over my discarded bones. Mr. Nobody, ending up as he began. Somebody careless kicks my skeleton, and my bones scatter, my skull rolling into a corner like a pool ball.

It's still dark outside, but I can't get back to sleep: nightmare plus a bottle of evening wine plus the nagging pull of nicotine. I reach for my pack, light up, swing my legs off the bed, and hack out a few phlegmy coughs.

At our home, Kent and the children are soon to wake up to that rarest of things, a white Christmas. Lookout Mountain always receives more snow than the valley below. I bet six inches are on the ground there by now. I wish I were there, pouring a mug of the coffee Kent brewed, peering out the window to see the mountain glistening, snow so bright you could read by it, while our three children sleep warmly in bed. After finishing my cup of coffee, I could creep to the bedside of each, whispering in their ears that Santa has brought a special surprise this year, and they'd pretend they are too old to care, but then they'd run to the window, pull back the curtains, and gasp.

Instead, I pull on a heavy jacket and leave the basement apartment I've been renting in the suburbs alone, which is actually an improvement from the Days Inn I'd been living in until recently, renting by the week, surrounded by prostitutes and drug dealers. I'm wearing tennis shoes and slipping across the several inches of wet, icy snow that has fallen so far. I've got boots in my closet at the house, though when I packed in a rush a month ago, I forgot them. Besides, later today, I'll be in sunny Phoenix, Arizona.

I'm driving in the dark to the airport through heavy falling snow, the windshield wipers of my little Honda Insight on full power. The glove box is stuffed with overdue bills. I turn on the radio and one of Kent's favorite Christmas songs is playing. *"Well, I know there's more snow, up in Colorado, than my roof will ever see,"* sings Amy Grant, *"but a tender Tennessee Christmas is the only Christmas for me."*

The snow, if possible, gets heavier, almost blizzardy, and the radio squawks out a travel advisory for icy road conditions. My flight doesn't leave for five hours, and I'm hungry, with zero food at the apartment. Neither sleet nor snow nor Christmas Day will close down a Waffle House in the Deep South, open 24-7, 365. I'm navigating my way there at fifteen miles per hour, and I've got my window rolled down because I've lit a cigarette. I'm trying to blow smoke out the window, but the strong gales keep shoving it back into my face, and I'm reminded of that summer day, riding in the back seat on the beer run when Donna's sister shrouded my face in a smoky haze and I knew, come what may, I'd never smoke.

I still hate cigarettes, actually, but the Vyvanse—sister drug to Adderall—begs for them because the nicotine keeps the Vyvanse elevated. The doctor switched me from Adderall to Vyvanse six months ago because it's supposedly less addictive, but my cravings haven't decreased. Swallowing the pill each day is like communion with the devil. It robs my personality. Mostly what I think throughout the day is what time the Vyvanse will wear off and when I need to order a refill so I don't run out.

The bright lights of the shining yellow Waffle House guide me through the snow like a beacon. I walk through the door to cheers of "Merry Christmas" from the several waitresses wearing Santa hats. I stroll through the aroma of frying bacon and hash browns being pressed with a spatula to find an open seat at the bar. I notice a clock on the wall. It's only 5:30 a.m. I've still got time to figure out if I should get on the plane or not.

"Ho, ho, ho," the waitress says, approaching with a pitcher of coffee. "Looks like you need a cup of something warm."

"Merry Christmas," I say. "Yes, I'll have some coffee and a menu. I'm a hungry man."

"Looks like you've missed a few meals, honey," she says, flashing a smile.

I look down at my skinny frame, and she's right. My pants barely stay up around my waist, and my shirt hangs off like an oversized sack. I've lost thirty pounds and most of my muscle tone. A friend even called me aside last week, asking if I'm on drugs and need help because I'm thin with dark circles under my eyes.

"What, cocaine?" I said. "You think I'm on cocaine? I've never tried cocaine in my life; I've never even seen it up close, and I don't plan on it. I've barely done any drugs, ever. I didn't even like marijuana."

"Well," the friend said, "it appears you are on something."

I don't think that a doctor's prescription, wine sold at the grocery, nicotine sold at the convenience store, or even an affair count.

"No," I said, "not at all. I'm not on anything."

The affair started last winter when I was in Manhattan for a CNBC appearance. I was alone and hungry as usual and went early to the hotel bar for a glass of wine and dinner. My plan was two glasses of wine with food and off to my room by 7:00 p.m. so I'd be ready to catch my early departure the next morning. It's a boutique hotel, with a bar the size of a large storage stall, so when a woman in her early forties sat beside me, of course we might as well exchange pleasantries. I drank a third glass, chatting and leaning closer because the fast-beat music and the crowd coming in made it harder to hear. I drank a fourth. Two days later, I was still in New York and Rachel and I were sharing a bed. I was supposed to be home with my wife and family, and I was due on the air for live TV.

I've landed my own cable television program, *The David Magee Show*, a daily business and current events talk program "from Main Street to Wall Street." My old journalism professors would be surprised, I know. They guided me toward newspaper journalism in college because, one said, I have the face for TV but a Deep South drawl. It's true, my drawl was the kiss of death for TV hopefuls in those days. But now, it seems there's an infatuation with the South and its folksy voices, so when a small network offered me a two-hour daily slot, I said, "Sure, why not?" It's on the American Life Network, airing in markets across the country for two hours a day, in the high channels like 257 in Los Angeles or 413 in New York. It's even on in Oxford, and friends will text, surprised I'm on the TV with my very own program. I host the show with my sidekick, Sean, who books the talent, does the research, and tries to keep me motivated to get on the air. There's pain across the country from economic hardship due to the great recession. I relate to the pain because I, too, have lost so much, and I'm becoming a B-list voice for America's shattered dreams, trying to instill hope that everything will get better soon.

The show finds its audience; the very fact that I'm a novice, not a polished East Coast sophisticate with a degree from Columbia, seems to work in my favor. I've landed a top agent, who's worked with Dr. Phil, and we meet at the Beverly Wilshire Hotel in Los Angeles and talk of the next-big-thing possibilities. My network even has a promising major sponsor that will "change my life."

But my life has changed already. For starters, I'm completely broke. I had to build a studio to get on the air from small-market Chattanooga, draining already-dwindling funds. Also, I've become a daytime drinker. I need the booze to help me titrate my mood. Hardwired on prescription speed, I need to warm up and soften a bit on the air. Thus, some days with the camera rolling, I'll sip from a solo cup, hoping a red wine mustache never alerts the viewer that it's not water. So the drugs need the grapes, and the grapes need the smokes.

I've got the timing down. "We'll be right back," I say on the air, "after this break, with more news you can use from Main Street to Wall Street."

I'll glance at my watch, rip out my earpiece connecting to the producer, and run to the fire escape door in the hallway while reaching into my pocket for a lighter and smoke. It takes fifteen seconds to get there, allowing seventy seconds to inhale and exhale quickly, then twenty-five seconds to return to my post, take a sip of wine, cough several times, and replace my earpiece before the camera light comes back on.

"Welcome back to *The David Magee Show*," cohost Sean says. "David, modern America has never faced such a crisis. What do you see as the secret to people getting back on their feet?"

"Sean, I learned by studying some of the biggest and best businesses in the world that you've got to be healthy at the core. We've got to get back to the basics, rid all that adds no value, have more transparency, and stop the assembly line when there's an obvious problem. That will get Americans rolling again."

Two hours on the air feels like twenty minutes. "That's a wrap," Sean will say. "We'll see you tomorrow on *The David Magee Show*."

Sometimes, there is no tomorrow. For instance, several weeks ago, Rachel called, saying she was coming to see me, but I'm anxious, eager to get away from the bills in the glove box, from burgeoning stress at home.

"I'd rather come there," I said.

She lives in Southern California, where palm trees and sunny seventy-degree days await.

"Even better," she says, since she won't need to arrange days of babysitting for her two young children. "But are you sure your schedule allows?"

"Yes."

Within half an hour, I booked a flight, delivering the news to Sean.

"We're off the air Thursday and Friday," I exclaimed. "Call the network and ask them to run reruns."

"But, David," Sean said, "we did that once last week and twice the week before."

"Do it," I said.

The next day, I landed at LAX and turned on my phone while waiting in the taxi line, finding several messages from the same number.

"David," the voice said, "this is Virginia Riley letting you know that we are here at the club waiting on you. We'll go ahead and start eating and introduce you when you arrive."

Oh Lord. I'd done it this time. I was the featured speaker for the women's book club annual luncheon, seventy-five members. The date has been on my calendar for months.

Mrs. Riley, the president, was among my biggest fans after hearing me speak to a local civic club. She'd read my latest, *The Education of Mr. Mayfield*, a true story about racial change in the South, and planned to have me sign copies for the entire club after speaking. Instead, I stood them up, put reruns on the air, and abandoned my family to check into a hotel I can't afford, to drink wine I can't afford, with a girlfriend I can't afford. That's because I'm living a life I can't afford, and I'd like to die, but I can't afford that either since I'm bankrupt spiritually.

Kent, apparently, has had enough of my nothingness. We are doing a wrap of *The David Magee Show*, and I deliver Sean a half-hearted high five, unfasten my lapel microphone, and walk over to the table to grab a napkin and wipe off the thick stage makeup from my face. There is a knock at the studio door, and the show's producer opens it, welcoming in a sheriff's constable.

"David Magee?" he says, walking straight toward me.

"That's me," I say, looking at Sean.

"I am serving you a summons to appear in court."

I glance at the papers, and my face inflames. How did it come to this?

Vyvanse robs me daily like a stickup at the end of a deserted dirt road, and yet, I swallow each morning, doctor's orders. And now, in this waffle hut, I also know that this trip on Christmas Day isn't advisable either, but as I look around the Waffle House at strangers' faces, the thought of Christmas alone in my apartment holds no appeal. I look out the greasy window at the falling snow. Dawn is breaking, and I can see Lookout Mountain glowing in the distance, so close but yet unreachable.

"Here's your eggs and bacon, honey," the waitress says, sliding a plate before me. It feels like I'm in the opening scene of a Hallmark movie, alone at a diner on Christmas morning with snow falling, pondering my life. Somebody change the channel, quick.

"That waffle is coming up in a minute," the waitress says.

"Thank you," I say, digging in.

"I hope Santa's gonna be good to you today," she says. "Have you been a good boy?"

"Not exactly," I say.

The Christmas Day flight to Phoenix is wildly turbulent midway, causing an array of gasps from the passengers, but we land OK and now Phoenix's freeway traffic is light. I'm in a rental car with the window rolled down, and the warm climate helps take some edge off. Rachel is with her two young children at her parents' house, awaiting my arrival. I've never met her parents, but at 7:00 p.m. tonight, we'll have a holiday dinner together.

Kent must be making Christmas dinner right now: cheese grits, green beans with bacon, and a roasted turkey that's been brined just right. Although I've moved out, with divorce proceedings underway, I've never told her about Rachel. She knows, of course, but it's my denial; I'm living a double life, just like Dad. I'm a fraud, espousing on TV the virtues of transparency while doing the one thing I vowed never to do, putting my family at risk. Yet, I keep piloting down the highway, barely steering, relying on cruise control, driving the rental car of my heart closer and closer to my illicit girlfriend's parents' holiday table.

In their early seventies, her parents live down a winding road amid a one-thousand-home subdivision where one residence can be confused for another, though inside, it feels warm and familial. Rachel's dad gives me a comfortable chair on the back patio, then goes to fix me a drink.

While I'm looking at the winter garden, I overhear Rachel's mother talking about how bad my skin looks, dry and brittle, "like a statue."

"It's the Vyvanse," Rachel says.

Yes, the Vyvanse. And the alcohol, nicotine, and stress, so much stress. And I'm suddenly, frighteningly, clichéingly middle-aged and worrying over all I've done and haven't done.

"Here we are," says Rachel's father, handing me a gin and tonic and taking the recliner next to my own. "Tell me about your children. What are they getting for Christmas?"

I give a brief snapshot of each and the gifts they are getting: a Spanish dictionary for William, boots for Hudson, and tickets to a concert for Mary Halley. I don't mention Kent, or the iPad I'd purchased with money I didn't have and left for her at the home that's no longer mine.

"I can tell," he says, "that you sure do love your children."

I ask him about his children, the two sons not here for Christmas. The youngest is in New York and has to work. The oldest, however, is estranged. He's married with children, but they've barely talked in years.

"What's that about?" I ask.

"I'm not quite sure," he says, his voice thickening, and I see he's trying not to cry.

Back in the den, I watch them open family presents, and Rachel's daughters sit close to my side, searching for my approval, explaining why a certain gift is cool or how the giver is related. I'm not sure where their father is, and I'm not asking. I'm thinking of Kent and Mary Halley and Hudson and William, and I wonder if they, too, are thinking of me.

We take seats at the round dinner table, and her father surprises me, asking if I'll say grace.

"Sure," I say, gathering my thoughts.

We hold hands, and I thank God for the food, our many blessings, and our beloved family members who are not with us. We let go of our hands, picking up dishes to pass. Rachel's father pauses and looks at me.

"You like advising on improvement, with those leadership books and TV show and all," he says. "What advice would you give me to get my son back?"

I'm surprised at this sudden heavy turn. We haven't even taken our first bites. "What do you mean?"

"I mean, I love my son, and it doesn't make sense that he's not here with me. What do you recommend to get him back?"

"Well," I say, "you should just call him or go see him and tell him that you love him. Don't try to explain yourself, as it might make you defensive, might stir up the old aggravations. Just tell him you're sorry. Just say, 'I love you, and I miss you, and I'm sorry for everything, and I don't want another day to go by without you in my life because you are my son.' Then, listen. Listen to whatever he has to say, receive it with humility, and respond with, 'I love you, and I am sorry.'"

Rachel's father smiles, and my mouth hinges open dumbly. He doesn't need my advice; he's giving advice. He's leading me to the answer I'm avoiding because I'm afraid that if I reach out to my family, I'll get rejected, and I've had enough rejection.

Dinner is quiet as Rachel senses a shift, and all I can think about is my family, thanks to my girlfriend's father. Once we clear the dishes, I read Rachel's daughters a bedtime story and say goodbye to her at the door with a kiss on the cheek, driving to a nearby hotel where I sleep alone. The next morning, I take an early flight out. I'll never see Rachel again.

* * *

Mary Halley, my baby girl whom I'd do anything to protect, is no longer talking to me. My girl who laughed at all my jokes, who waltzed with her feet on my toes so I could spin and dip her like a fairy-tale princess, who charmingly manipulated me with her big hazel eyes into buying a puppy, can barely look at me. She's in high school, the only child still living at home.

Her counselor from school called Kent last month, explaining Mary Halley has developed an eating disorder. It's bulimia, the counselor said, purging after meals.

"We've got a lot going on at home," Kent says.

"I'm sorry," the counselor says. "She's also got something going on at school."

Mary Halley transferred her junior year from the girls' school to Baylor, a century-old coed school, where she began dating Matthew, the star quarterback. Some girls she once called friends don't like that fact, bullying her at school and on social media. She'd deal with this all day, then she'd return to the house where her parents were fighting. For the first time, she'd gained extra weight. She mostly stayed in her room with the door closed, playing music, trying not to hear our arguments, which the hardwood floors slid right under her doorjamb.

I want desperately to talk to Mary Halley, about the bullying, about the bulimia. I text her, and she doesn't respond. I call her, and she doesn't call back. When I left the house, checking into a prolonged stay at the Days Inn, I ran out on her mother, and I ran out on her. She's alone with Kent, who she's worried about. Kent is much too thin, her skin stretched tight over her collarbones and ribs. She subsides on baked potatoes topped with sautéed kale from the garden while working long hours and practicing yoga, sometimes twice a day.

But it's not only Mary Halley and Kent who are floundering. I randomly saw Lo's parents when I was seated at a restaurant bar, alone, eating dinner and drinking wine. When they passed me on their way to a table, we exchanged pleasantries, and I commented that I'm sad Hudson and Lo are no longer dating.

At the mention of Hudson's name, Lo's parents exchange a glance. Lo's mother takes a step closer to my stool. "We're concerned about Hudson," she says. "I don't think he's doing too well."

"What do you mean?"

"I mean, he's not doing well."

He's now a freshman at Ole Miss, having followed William's and my footsteps to pledge Sigma Nu, and I got to pin him at the initiation. William is more than a brother and a fraternity brother to Hudson; he's a best friend. I've felt comfort in thinking of them together, having each other's backs. But what if them being together means they're dragging each other further into booze and drugs?

My beautiful family of five: all breaking, one by one. I desperately want to help, but I, their father, am broken. For so many years, my duties to my children helped me keep myself from going overboard. Now, my children are mostly gone, and the Vyvanse has taken charge. My average daily drink quantity has doubled, tripled, because I can barely feel the first few, the prescription speed batting them away like mosquitoes. Thus, on the occasional binge night, quantity doubles in accord. But the Vyvanse only lasts eight hours, max. Once it wears off, I'm like Superman without his cape, and the alcohol is kryptonite.

That's why I'm stumbling toward my friend's car with his arm around my shoulders to steer me. We've been at a party. I can see his car in the distance, parked alone in a field since the others have long left. Kent was there, and she begged me to leave hours ago, but I said no, the blowout is still going. It was quite a bash, with hundreds of guests under a big-top tent, starting with a seated dinner followed by dancing with a live band. One could buy a decent house for what this bash cost.

"I need to stop," I say to my friend, falling to my knees, the car another football field–distance away. "I'm too tired to get there."

I look down at my shirt, seeing something red spilled across the front. Wine? Or vomit? I'm too exhausted to decide.

"Come on, buddy," my friend says, pulling me to my feet. "Let's get you home."

Home, he said.

"OK," I mumble.

It's just, I'm not sure where that is.

Chapter Eight

Humility

I'm running away. I'm so sick of me that I want to get far, far away. Southern California might not be far enough to fix what's wrong with me, but it will have to do. There's a TV studio there that's invited me out to work, sharing costs for producing my TV show, so I'm headed to Carlsbad, a city I've never seen, to live among people I don't know, which sounds perfect. The drive will take three or four days, allowing just a week and a half to find a place to live and get situated since the network demands I'm back on the air within two weeks.

William has asked to come with me. "You've only got room for a backpack or small bag," I tell him on the phone, the day before departure. "The only space you have to put anything is the floorboard around your feet."

"Do you even want me to go?" he asks, sensing my hesitancy.

Truth is, I don't want him to go. The highway to California is the long plank I'm walking for my misdeeds. When I jump off, I want to be alone. I'll sink or swim. My plan is to swim, though I'm not quite sure how.

But Kent asked William to invite himself along for the road trip. Even though we're divorced, she's worried I won't make it to California alive traveling alone. What's amazing is that she doesn't want me to die, even though she thinks I'm running off to California to be with Rachel. That's the kind of woman I was once married to.

But she's wrong. I'm not there for Rachel, or any other woman. I don't have the energy. I can barely get my bags packed.

"My dear William," I tell my son, "I want time with you more than I want anything in the world."

"I'd like to come along, but only if you want me."

"It's just that I don't know what to expect. I'm driving into the unknown. I don't have a place to live there yet, and I don't have much money."

"That's OK, Dad. We'll figure it out."

"Also, I know you're leaving in a few weeks." William was about to embark on a study abroad semester in Argentina before his senior year. "So if you decide you don't have time, of course, I'll understand."

No dice. He's coming. "I'll share the driving. We'll talk," he says, "and I'll make sure you don't get lost."

"Too late for that," I say.

It's early Monday morning when I squeeze the last bit of TV studio equipment, wrapped in a sweater, into the Insight and ease the hatchback closed so it latches without breaking the tripod. Then we're off, my twenty-one-year-old son at my side for a thirty-two-hour drive west. The only open room in the car is the center console, where our elbows touch. We're holding jackets on our laps, since cold and snow is forecasted for the road ahead. I take the first shift, fueled by coffee and the morning's Vyvanse. William tries to recline his car seat back; it won't budge.

"Great," he says, trying and failing to shove away some cargo behind the seat.

"Can't say I didn't warn you."

He puts on sunglasses and earphones, making a pillow with his coat against the window. "I'm going to sleep until it's time to drive, if that's OK," he says.

"Did you just get up?" I ask, to no response.

During a bathroom stop, William wakes, saying little, and he wakes during a lunch stop, eating little; otherwise, he mostly sleeps until midafternoon. We're in western Arkansas, and temperatures have quickly dropped, turning drizzle into freezing rain.

"Hey," I say, jiggling his knee, "if you're going to drive, you should take your turn now. This weather is only going to get worse. And I'm getting sleepy. My morning pill is wearing off."

"OK," he says, sitting upright. "Let's stop first. I need to run to the bathroom."

I exit into Love's travel stop along Interstate 40, busy with cars jockeying for an open pump to fill up before the forecasted snow. William takes his backpack into the station with him.

"Be right back," he says.

I fill the tank, pumping slow in the high demand, go inside the bustling store, get a coffee, stand in line, and pay for it, and William is nowhere in sight. I glance toward the bathroom. There's no line. I get back to the car and pull up to the front of the convenience store, waiting. I get out, stretch my legs, and take the passenger seat, catching up on messages and waiting. Finally, William approaches. I glance at my watch; he's taken twenty minutes. The car door swings open with a quick pull.

"What are you waiting on, Daddio?"

I smile awkwardly. "Just you. Just waiting for you. What took so long?"

"What do you mean what took so long?" he says, with a hint of defensiveness. "Don't you know there are two kinds of going to the bathroom? One takes longer than the other."

William jabs the key into the ignition. He starts the car, pulls the gearshift into reverse, and jabs the accelerator with his foot. A car is moving behind us. "Whoa!" I say as he slams the brakes. "Not so fast."

Safely on the interstate, William turns up the radio and starts talking about the weather, the band on the radio, and that he's never been to Oklahoma, which is less than an hour away. Typically the quieter one, William is talking so much I can barely keep up—now it's about Hudson and Mary Halley, Ole Miss sports, and his girlfriend, Stephanie. I want to bash my head against the dash. My son, at the wheel, is high as a kite on an upper—cocaine, perhaps—that he snorted in the gas station bathroom. I should grab his backpack and throw it out the window, but that's his job, not mine. He needs to be the one who decides he needs to stop. My despair and powerlessness make me want to cry, though the one hundred milligrams of Vyvanse I've swallowed won't let me. Speed freaks don't cry.

"The temperature has dropped to twenty-seven degrees," William says, pointing to the car thermometer. "We should stop for some beers and call it a day."

My brow furrows. I've never shared a beer with William and don't want to start. I check my phone; the National Weather Service has issued a blizzard warning for Oklahoma, projecting historic snowfall accompanied by gusting winds. We don't have a hotel reservation; we plan to drive each day until we can't go any farther. At the moment, we're surrounded by rural oil fields and ranches in every direction. I want to continue, hoping we can reach Oklahoma City for a decent hotel and dinner, where we can talk face-to-face about the bathroom stop.

"Keep driving," I say.

The conditions deteriorate quickly, with heavy, blowing snow limiting visibility. Even fast semitrucks drive slowly in tracks with hazard lights on. We pull to the road shoulder and change places, allowing me to navigate worsening conditions. We've turned the music down, and William is talking less, watching me struggle to keep the car in the tracks, to follow the red taillights ahead of me, the only thing I can see.

"I'm not sure the Honda Insight was made for this," William says.

I push the gas pedal, and we barely gain speed. The windshield wipers swish back and forth at maximum speed, yet the pie wedge of view is instantly whited-out. The car thermometer reads twenty-one degrees, and the gas tank shows near empty. It occurs to me we could be in real trouble out here.

"Sleeping in the car isn't an option," I say. Kent is going to kill me if I let her son freeze to death. William is searching on his phone for somewhere to stop. There's an exit fifteen miles ahead with a couple of hotels, he says. We count the minutes of the next hour, slowly making our way with few words and too many heartbeats.

"I see the exit!" he says, noting lights ahead.

I'm not sure the Honda can cross the snow pile at the exit. Abandoned cars and trucks already line both sides, but I've got to try. We hold our breath and *swoosh*, the car slams into a wall of white, coming to a stop.

"Good Lord," I say. "We're stuck." There's just one option, and it's not a good one: leave my possessions in the car and leave my car in the middle of the interstate exit for the night. We pull on our jackets, entirely too lightweight for the storm, though they're a nice match for our tennis shoes. William gets his backpack, and I grab my Vyvanse prescription bottle from the console: the essentials.

"Ready?" I ask.

"Yep," he says.

And we run clumsily, slipping and catching each other, slipping and falling, until we're inside the lobby of a warm Holiday Inn Express, hugging and cheering and high-fiving as if we've won an Olympic relay race.

"We've gotta tell your mom," I say. "She'll never believe it."

William asks the attendant if there's a nearby bar open.

"No, honey. Everything's closed. We've never had snow like this. It's just you and that bed tonight."

In the room, we take hot showers, turn the TV on to a *Family Guy* rerun, lean into fluffy pillows on the bed, wonder if the car is hit yet, and we talk—about the atmosphere and oil wells, about how long hybrid engines like the Insight's will last before it's all electric. We move on to meaningless trivia.

"Do you know what kind of car Peter drives?" I ask William, referring to the TV show.

"A big red one?" he says.

"Yes, but it's a Ford LTD wagon, just like we had when I was ten years old, but ours was blue."

"Did y'all take family trips in it?" William asks.

"Yep. We went to Dogpatch USA one summer in northwest Arkansas. Stayed at a Days Inn. Eunice hated it, but I loved it, and I'd imagine I was Li'l Abner and that Daisy Mae was my girlfriend."

William laughs. "Who's Li'l Abner?"

We're connecting like we once did, when the cookie cutter was our special play.

"It's funny," he says. "This trip is a disaster, but it's also amazing."

I want to ask about his ignited mood in the car, but I don't want to kill the moment.

"Perhaps that's the thing about life," I say. "What seems awful might put us on the road to something good."

$$* * *$$

The next morning, the first day of February, I peek through the blinds. It's sunny out, and flakes swirl in the air, although the sky is all blue. Everything else is white, alien, sparkling. I turn on the local TV news quietly. We have survived one of the heaviest snowfalls in Oklahoma history, nearly a foot and a half. I'm in a chair beside my bed, sipping coffee and watching William sleep. I study his strong brow line, his dark lashes, his face both a man's and a child's, and still the toddler's innocence with his knees curled up high by his waist. He didn't have to come on this decidedly unglamorous trip. He could be with his friends, where he wouldn't have to hide his drug use. But he wanted to look out for me. Because I'm fragile. His boy-man face grows wavery as I blink back tears.

My mind is clear, and I'm looking at my son, but seeing myself in better focus. I want to be a positive, an influential father, not a negative, a father under the influence. How can I hope to get my son clean when I'm addicted myself? Why do I keep drawing a line between my doctor-prescribed drug use and his illegal one if both of us are being cored with the same sharp knife?

These feelings that I'm having—feelings strong enough to tug tears to my ducts—are what this drug prevents. I want access to the me that feels feelings.

I walk into the bathroom, take the top off my prescription bottle, and dump the remaining month's supply of Vyvanse, some twenty-five pills, into the toilet. I flush—*swoosh*—and the pills make a loud exit. They're gone. I exhale and whisper a thank-you to myself for the courage. I'm a bit nervous about repercussions, but I'm giddy at the instant freedom. I bound over to William's bed.

"Get up, get up! The sun is up," I sing, giving his shoulder a tap. "We've got new frontiers to conquer."

An hour later, we're beside the Honda, watching a man who lives nearby move vehicles from the roadway with his John Deere tractor.

"That's a little car for this big tractor," he shouts our way, his version of a liability release form.

"It doesn't matter," I shout back. "Whatever it takes."

We get in, and I shift the gear to neutral and take the steering wheel. The tractor crunches into the front bumper but gives the Honda its push back toward the interstate, and we gain enough traction to resume the journey, driving slowly in a single lane of traffic through North Texas with hopes of making Albuquerque, New Mexico, by bedtime. The skies are rich powder blue without a cloud in sight, but the temperature is alarming, hovering near zero and dropping.

"I've only been in zero degrees a few times," William says, picking up on last night's conversation. "It's supposed to be the coldest night tonight on record in the region where we're traveling."

Once the weather topic is exhausted, we're talking humanity, pondering what makes us happy, and I strike upon the opportunity to father my son.

"What really matters, William, is not whether or not you mess up, because everyone messes up. What matters is what comes next. The world will provide you plenty of excuses, so the easy thing is to blame circumstances and other people. But as long as one is seeking elsewhere to cast blame, there's no hope for improvement. Only when we take responsibility can we learn to respect ourselves and find peace."

It's not lost on me that I'm talking to William but lecturing myself, and he must understand that too, because he's listening intently, without the first snide remark. In the silence that fills the car after I've said my piece, I begin drafting a personal action plan that takes on more shape with every mile traveled. I'm thinking about the lessons and principles in all those books I wrote over eight years. I can see it now. I've felt stuck, but I've got the answers. I need to take responsibility because if I accept responsibility for everything and do my best to fix what's possible, I can begin to respect myself.

I think about Mom and Dad, and the four decades I've spent blaming them for how messed up I am. Our family was troubled, sure, yet no family escapes trouble. I was an orphan at three months of age and needed a home. Mom and Dad gave me that.

And while I've really struggled with Mom's decision to give Eunice the majority of family money, she's doing it for the right reasons. "I believe people are happiest when they can earn their way," she told me. "Eunice needs our help, but you don't. You're strong enough to do it on your own."

In my perspective, Mom was taking something from me. In her view, she was giving me a path to sustainable happiness. And when I look at it that way, I'm able to stop resenting Eunice. And giving up that cherished resentment, the story I tell myself in which I'm a victim, is the truly liberating gift.

Even with Dad, I feel empathy. The world had no conventional place for Dad, so he hid his true self. It wasn't easy for him, just as it wasn't easy for any of us. I'm not even sure he was entirely in touch with his actions outside of marriage, perhaps locking them away in some inaccessible attic corner in his mind, the same way Janie locked away having a baby and giving it up for adoption: forget about it; that never happened. I do know that Dad was a kind person at heart, the kindest. I'll no longer judge him for making mistakes when I've made so many.

Dad's gone, but Janie's still here. When we stop for gas, I send her a text message, the first I've texted her this year. "Just wanted to say thank you for teaching me patience. And I love you." I had wanted a fairy-tale reunion with my birth mother, instantaneous acceptance, radical love. But there was so much thatched pain within her soul, within her family, that a wrenching opening of her heart was more than she could handle. It took years for her to safely pry herself open. And maybe that was best for me, he who's never been good at waiting.

Perhaps this long apprenticeship of learning how to be a better human will leave me better prepared to do something meaningful with my life. For so long, I'd felt called to do something more impactful than running a convenience store, or even singing America to sleep with my main-street-lullaby cable show. But, despite my desire, I was always so consumed with the immediate present that I couldn't raise my gaze to the horizon.

"Well, thank you!" Janie texts back within fifteen minutes. "I love you too. Melts my heart."

I'm thinking about Kent, too, and my responsibility, not just to her but also to myself. I remember, when we first started dating, introducing her to a fellow classmate.

"Figures Magee would snatch up the perfect girl at the opening party," the classmate later told a friend.

Yes, I did snatch up the perfect girl, yet here I am, on the lam from that relationship, busy explaining to a child that we created together why he should build a code of ethics based on honesty and responsibility. I left her, not because she stopped being perfect for me, but because I felt unworthy of her love due to my shame and guilt. Lord, I want to embrace her now. This very minute, I want to pull her sharp shoulders into my chest and never let them go. Still, the car keeps moving due west.

"I love your mother," I say, looking at William with a smile and placing a hand on his knee.

"I know, Dad," he says, placing a hand on top of my hand.

We're into the higher altitudes of northern New Mexico, and the sun set an hour ago. The night shimmers from vivid starlight, brightened by the dry, crisp air. The temperature is dropping, already the lowest we've ever witnessed in our lives: sixteen degrees below zero. I'm worried about my Honda's hybrid battery, but with no hotels near, we press on.

"It feels like we're traveling in space," I say with a chuckle, "whatever that feels like."

William smiles. "Well," he says, "we should stop and run around outside for a minute to see what it feels like."

"That sounds fun," I say, "but here's an update: it's now eighteen below zero, according to the car. The wind chill factor is probably thirty below."

"Well, Daddio," he says, "you only live once."

I slow the car onto the shoulder, shift into park, and leave the engine running, sure it would not restart. We pull on jackets, look at one another, and grin.

"Let's go!" I say. We fling the car doors open and bolt into the frigid night air.

"Ahhh," William says, laughing, "my lungs are burning."

I'm sprinting into outer space with my son, laughing clouds of crystals, my eyes smarting with happy tears, mucus in my nose freezing. We curve in wide parabolas, running fast, fast, faster, then meet behind the car, away from the headlights. We're panting, bending over, hands on our hips, grinning like deranged escapees. Then, I pass my arm through his, and we lean our heads back and lock arms as we gaze into the starry night.

"We're in the center of the universe," I say. "It's never been so cold at this spot at this moment, and we are here for it."

"Woohooooo!" William shouts into the night. "Wooooooo!"

I look up at the stars. I've never seen so many, and I'm sure they've never shined so bright. The vastness, the beauty, the reality—for the first time, that logical part of my brain that works to keep faith at arm's length, away from my soul, gives way. I have an insight, and I don't mean the car before us. I am but a man traversing a universe so much larger than myself, a universe managed by a higher power. And I must trust because I, just a man, am powerless, and my life has become unmanageable.

I cup my hands around my mouth and shout into the night, "Thank you, Lord."

"Woooooooo," William shouts. "Thank you, Lord."

$$* * *$$

When we arrive in Southern California two days later, I find a carriage house apartment in a gated Carlsbad suburb through an online listing, and I don't have to sign a lease since the homeowner is in default on the mortgage and can't sell the house for what he has in it due to the ongoing recession.

"Don't know how long we'll be here," he says. But that's OK since I'm day-to-day as well. William helps me unload the car, asking if we should leave the studio equipment—no sense moving it twice, first into my place and from there to the TV studio.

"No," I say, "let's move it in. I'm not sure about TV."

"Really?" he asks. "You're not gonna do your show?"

I shrug and lift a box out of the hatchback. Mostly, I want to sleep. For the past year and a half, the Adderall and Vyvanse have torched my adrenal glands, provoking unnatural stimulation. Now, I've extinguished the torch with a flush of the toilet, and I'm crashing hard. William is planning to stay for two more weeks, but that won't work. I'm exhausted and need to rest.

"I need to book your flight home," I say.

"Are you sure? I'm not leaving for Argentina for two more weeks."

"I'm sure," I say. "I'll miss you so much. But I need time alone."

I drive William to the airport, thumbing away a tear as we pull up. I'll worry about him in Argentina; I'm worried about me in California; I'm worried about Hudson at Ole Miss; I'm worried about Kent and Mary Halley in Chattanooga. Oh, and I'm worried that he's worried about me, worried about leaving his emotional, soon-to-be-jobless father alone in an apartment without a lease in a house that's in foreclosure in a city that's not his.

"Are you gonna be OK, Dad?" he asks, looking me eye to eye. "If you aren't going to do TV, what will you do?"

"I'm not sure," I say. "But don't you worry. I will be fine."

The next month is mostly a slumber. When I failed to get back on the air, the American Life Network dropped my show. I sold the studio equipment on eBay for cash to buy some time, and my days throughout February play out like this: sleep until seven, coffee, a walk along the beach, rest, lunch, a nap, coffee, reading, a walk, dinner, reading, and back to sleep. There's no alcohol, no nicotine, no Vyvanse, and no Rachel. It's just me and my thoughts and the emotions that I've gone years without feeling. I'm slowly healing, but it undoubtedly looks like I'm sick. Even my landlord asks if I'm OK.

"Never been better," I say. That's the truth since, despite fatigue and fragility, I found freedom along my journey west.

I'm not just sleeping; I'm reflecting, hard, about work and life. How often I've let my ego drive my choices. The happy human is a humble human, I surmise. So, I call Kent. To my surprise, she answers. I tell her about Rachel, every detail. She already knew most of it, of course, but not from me. I apologize for letting substances disrupt everything good we had. The doctor made the prescription, but that was me swallowing the pills each day.

A week later, I visit a tattoo parlor in Oceanside, Carlsbad's unsavory neighbor to the north. I tell the artist I'd like to permanently remember this date, on which I vow that drunkenness and infidelity are mistakes of the past. I want the ink to look like an inmate's number, which is a reminder that shame and substances keep me imprisoned. The needle stings, blotting ink across the back of my left shoulder, but no pain has ever felt so good.

"There you go, all done," the artist says. He holds up a mirror so I can see. The reflection is clear: 03082011. Walking out the door, I call Kent.

"Well," I say, "I got a tattoo."

She's silent, and I can sense her eye roll through the phone. "A tattoo of what?"

"Today's date. I know that doesn't sound like much, but it's a permanent reminder that everything has changed. From now on, I'll treat you with respect, and I will respect myself."

Two weeks later, I pick up Kent at the Carlsbad airport. I've talked her into a four-day visit. We walk along the beach, holding hands. We listen to the gulls cry and feel the salt spray on our cheeks, and I pull her sharp shoulders to my chest, and we kiss as we did in college, except it's also better, deeper, more historied, this beautiful woman with whom I've made three humans. Not that it's all sea spray and smooches, however. She's skittish and smarting, distrustful, and every so often, she lets me have it. When she does that, I take it, absorb it, listen, and love her. Several weeks later, I'm driving home to Chattanooga, leaving California, to sleep at her side and try and figure out where or how to restart.

I can't just pick up where we left off because there's not much left. I've thrown away a career, and bills are piling up. I need a job immediately, but what? I've done unconventional work for the past decade that makes good cocktail party conversation, but it's not much for the resumé. I've got hope with a contact at the *Wall Street Journal*, but journalism has changed completely; he says it's now a digital world, and the last time I worked full-time at a newspaper, there was no internet.

I see an ad for a startup digital business publication in New York that looks promising. However, when I look up the *International Business Times* online, it looks dodgy, more of a clickbait tabloid than real reporting. Still, I apply since there's nothing else. I get no response. Three days later, incensed that a flimsy, wannabe global business online newspaper won't respond to me, I write an email to the publisher.

Subject: "Are you kidding me?"

"Mr. Smith, you must have missed my message. I recently sent a resumé to your company for the open position of Companies Editor. I'm surprised I have not heard back since your company needs help, and I'm the best one for the job. For the past decade, I've written top-selling business books. I've worked closely with companies, including Ford, John Deere, General Electric, and Nissan and regularly appeared on CNBC. I'm willing to move to New York immediately and get this done for you."

Ten minutes later, Mr. Smith responds. Three days later, he's offered me a job, starting the next week in Manhattan. The pay is so low, even Kent bristles.

"You can't afford to live in a New York closet for that!" She's right, though I've thrown away my ego. I need to start somewhere so I can begin maneuvering to somewhere better.

I leave Tennessee for New York, my second move in six months. I'm forty-five, but it's like I'm a recent college graduate, departing home for entry-level pay at a questionable company.

Kent loans me $1,500 to get started, and I sign a monthly lease at the only place I can afford that's a reasonable commute to Manhattan's financial district: a boardinghouse in Weehawken, New Jersey. New York experiences record highs the summer I move, with temperatures above one hundred degrees, and my boardinghouse lacks air-conditioning. I'm eating SpaghettiOs for dinner since that's all I can afford, sweating through my T-shirt. Folks at work say things like, "You must be used to this since you're from the South," and I smile. But no, not at all; in the South, we have seersucker suits, not searing concrete. I can't sleep because the backfiring cars and sirens from the street keep waking me, but I can't close the windows because I'll immolate.

In my first week, the company misses payroll, and in my second week, a writer publishes a farce story that gets published with little concern, but in the third month, the company gives me a raise. Mr. Smith says that I'm a natural at getting readers clicking on digital stories. Previous me would have been embarrassed by this compliment, this job. But I'm proud. I'm clear-minded, and I'm working up from the bottom, seven days every week. I enjoy purely one aspect of the job: recruiting top journalism graduates from around the country who are William's age and teaching them digital techniques. I know they won't be with me long, but I know this job can be the springboard they need to move up. I'll be reading them in the *Wall Street Journal* one day.

Kent visits once a month, and I've moved from the boardinghouse to a studio apartment with West Elm lamps, on East 12th Street in the Village. On weekends she visits, I ease off my seven-day work ritual, and we walk miles throughout the city, see independent movies, and enjoy early, relaxed dinners before the crowds crush at Momofuku Noodle Bar, Union Square Café, and Gramercy Tavern. At Christmas, she's determined to bring the family together, driving Mary Halley, Hudson, William, and Lady up from Chattanooga, all stuffed into her black Toyota Prius for the thirteen-hour drive. We stroll along the High Line, taking a family photo that cannot hide our tired eyes and pale faces, but we're together. We take Communion together on Christmas Eve at First Presbyterian Church on Fifth Avenue. We watch a matinee together on Christmas Day, sharing popcorn. Afterward, we stroll through Washington Square Park together, walking Lady on a leash.

We'll have to make it together, because individually, we're still afflicted. Hudson is uncharacteristically pale and flabby, and recently, he had a trip to the emergency room, needing stitches in his head after blacking out and falling after taking a deep inhale from "a cigarette." Hudson said he's OK, that he made a mistake and didn't have a problem, and we left him in school on a sort of probation: one more strike and you're out. But now, he tells me on our walk that he'd like to "get healthier." And seeing as this is his suggestion, not mine, I think he might do it.

Mary Halley is still in treatment for bulimia. She hasn't purged in a year, and she's seeing a therapist and a nutritionist. She knows she'll be working through her eating disorder for a long time to come.

Of all of us, William seems the most in jeopardy. Something happened to him in Argentina, though we're not sure what. He mumbled something to us about how he and a friend should never have gone into that house one night, and we assumed they got into a fight, then it was over. Yet, he's still hiding something. He spends too much time in the bathroom, emerging flushed, a bit disoriented for a moment, and he has continual excuses to leave on his own. In the city with Mary Halley, he tries to convince her she should smoke marijuana.

"No," she says.

"Why not?"

"Look at what it's doing to you."

When I hear about it, I'm angry, and I challenge William.

"Really? You want to encourage your sister to use substances?" I say.

"Dad," he says, "there's nothing wrong with it."

There's no way out of the woods yet, but we're beginning to knit together and become stronger. Even our laughter is a healthy sign. And I'm healthier now than I was before, and they see that and take comfort and courage from it. We'll get through. It seems the worst is over, and there is hope, real hope, that we are getting a second chance.

* * *

I'm sitting at a long conference table, trying to nudge us closer to becoming a real newspaper. I'm aware that the longer we spend drinking coffee and passing around a box of pastel macarons, our improvement is less likely. Around the table are journalists I handpicked to turn around the chump news aggregator. So far, the work being done by my team is still more about collecting from everybody else's stories about the Amy Winehouse tragedy than actual analysis of rising bond yields or Japan's lingering recession.

The other set of folks around the table is from IT because, in addition to our content problem, we have a technology problem that's linked to a money problem. The owners have momentarily missed payroll twice since my arrival, so shelling out for a new website is unlikely.

"Our stories aren't as easily searchable as the *New York Times*," I say, bringing the chatter that filled in during my absence back to the business at hand. "Google prefers them for legitimacy."

I take a sip of coffee that isn't hot enough anymore. I am the kind of person who wants to be sitting at a table at the *New York Times*, not around this table of pretenders, but now I've got to pretend, or I'm not getting paid. Besides, I'm good at finding the right headline and story angle with search engine optimization and publishing it fast before other papers.

Headline: "It's 7/11 Slurpee Day: What's Your Favorite Flavor?"

Headline: "Hurricane Irene Path: New York Dodges Bullet, Damage Light"

Headline: "How Did Amy Winehouse Die? Overdose Likely Cause of Death"

I turn to the head of IT.

"What do we need to do to fix our tech problems?"

"An entirely new website that may cost five hundred grand," he says, and that's nowhere near our budget. My boss, who never worked in the journalism industry before becoming my boss, doesn't care about increasing our proportion of good journalism in the short term as long as we get the clicks to appease the owners.

"We got to fake it till we make it," he says.

But I'm determined to use the talent of these new journalists I've recruited and increase the percentage of real reporting.

"I think it's time we make it," I say, smiling. I'm weary of faking it, having learned that fraud is a ticket to emptiness.

When the meeting is over, I walk back to my office overlooking the East River and pick up my phone, where I left it to prevent continually checking the time. Kent has called me six times, left several voicemails, and a long string of text messages, most of which scream, "Where are you????" Then I read this one: "Call me now! It's Hudson. It's an emergency!"

I think car accident. That's the phone call every parent dreads from the moment their child gets a license. I call Kent, and she answers on the first ring.

"It's Hudson," she says, her voice loud and breaking at the same time. "He arrived at the hospital dead. He's on life support now. They don't think he's going to make it."

I grab the desk, feeling faint. "Not going to make it? As in, he might die?" The blood in my body rushes to the floor. I must be standing in a pool of it. "What kind of accident?"

"Hudson's fraternity pledge brothers found him this morning, outside in a hammock at the fraternity house," she says. "They tried to wake him up, but his face was blue. He wasn't breathing. He had thrown up, maybe choked on it. I don't know."

"Dear God."

"He's on a ventilator," she says. "His heart wasn't beating, but the ER doctor got it going. He says to hurry up, David. He's going to try to keep Hudson alive until we can get there."

Kent is halfway to Oxford from Chattanooga, where she still runs her business. I've got much farther to go to get to Oxford, and the doctor said Hudson might not live long, so I run from my office without slowing to explain. On the street, I hail a taxi.

"I've got an emergency at home," I tell the driver. "Get me to LaGuardia, fast."

Inside the cab, I imagine Hudson in a hospital bed. Did Kent say he was brain dead? I can't remember the words she used. His heart stopped, but it was beating again. And ventilator. She said that word. Many people don't get off a ventilator; it's the one machine in the hospital you don't want when you are sick, a slow, mechanized, breathy march to death, the machine doing the work for you until someone decides to stop the flow of electricity. I can't believe this is happening, and I'd like it to stop.

At the airport, I buy a nonstop ticket to Memphis at the counter and look at the time. With thirty minutes to boarding, I'm staring hard at the bar near the gate, dreaming of buying several beers and slugging them down fast, but I'd sworn off drunkenness the year before. For distraction, I need to tell someone what's happened to Hudson, someone who might help me cope. I search the name Janie in my contacts and compose a text that's the most real thing I can say.

"I'm afraid we're going to lose our boy, Hudson."

"What?" she texts back.

"Hudson. He might die."

"Oh, no," she responds. "What happened?"

Janie says she's sorry and asks for updates, and I'm comforted by her support, just as I'm comforted by Mom's. When I call her, she answers on the first ring.

"David," she says, "I've already heard. I'm so sorry." Mom says she's heading to the hospital and will meet me there. She invites me to stay at the house, but I decline. I've come a long way in appreciation for my family, but I'm not sleeping there, in that house, no matter how much reckoning I've done with the past.

William and his girlfriend, Stephanie, are waiting for me at the curb outside the Memphis airport in William's SUV, and she is driving. Stephanie is kind and competent, in Honors College with William. They're seniors, having dated since their freshman year. Kent and I are sure they're going to marry. I can see them living in a big city, both lawyers, with two sweet children wearing glasses. I open the back door and throw my duffel bag in ahead of me. She and William both turn toward me from the front seats.

William's skin is pale gray, and his eyes are the dullest I've ever seen them.

"Dad, I don't know what to say," William murmurs. I can barely hear him.

Stephanie pulls from the curb, and I look out the window at tall, leafy trees as we speed down the highway. I'm a long way from New York City and feel suspended in time like I'm not anywhere.

"So, what happened?" If anyone knows what happened to Hudson, it's William.

"Accidental overdose," William says, staring straight out the windshield. I can barely hear him. I bore holes into the back of William's head, but he doesn't turn around. It's like he's paralyzed. A cold feeling washes over me.

"I just don't understand," I said. "When I was in college, we drank a few light beers, and some people smoked pot. We didn't overdose."

William sits silent.

"Why would Hudson drink so much or do so many drugs that he choked on his vomit?"

"Maybe he couldn't help it," William murmurs.

"What?" I'm frustrated by William's mumbling.

"Maybe he didn't realize what he was doing," he says, louder but still not looking at me.

I lean back and rub my eyes. "Right," I say, on an exhale. "Maybe he didn't realize what he was doing."

Finally, we round the drive at Baptist Hospital in Oxford. I'm not sure I'm up to this, but I have no choice since my boy Hudson is in there somewhere, fighting for his life. I hop from the car before it's fully stopped and run through sliding glass doors, into an elevator, and into the intensive care unit. The waiting room is filled with people, so many beautiful young people with distraught faces.

"Where's Hudson?" I say to the entire room.

A tall boy, one of Hudson's fraternity brothers, hugs me while directing me. "Intensive care, down the hall."

Kent and Mary Halley are standing beside the hospital bed, watching the ventilator keep him alive. They reach for me, and we hug each other, our three sobs flowing into one. I move to Hudson's bedside and touch his arm. He doesn't respond. The rasp of the ventilator pushing air into his lungs fills the room. His chest falls, and it rasps full again. He's intubated, with thick tape covering the skin around his mouth. His eyes are closed, but he doesn't look like he's sleeping. He looks like he's being kept alive. He looks like he's as good as dead.

I hold Kent to my chest, and I remember that we are divorced, but it doesn't matter since something so monstrous has happened that makes everything else in the world—good or bad—mean nothing at all. That's the thing about tragedy I've never understood. My son is dying, yet everything else keeps moving; stories are published, taxicabs swerve to curbs, elevators open and close.

The doctor comes in to talk with us. Kent and I sit down on the chairs without being asked, as if our bodies know we'll need to be sitting. Our son's prognosis hasn't changed. Eventually, we'll have to decide when to pull life support, ending the ventilator's rhythmic work. Hudson has no brain activity, so the doctor is sure he'll never be able to breathe on his own. How long would we like to keep our son on the ventilator? I don't know—maybe five days? It seems too cruel that parents have to decide this. I can't look at Kent because I remember that day Hudson was born, so precious that we trembled when the pediatrician suggested, at Hudson's post-labor checkup, that he might have a hole in his heart. I remember our bone-rattling gratitude when we learned a few days later that the gap had closed.

Now I'll have a hole in my heart, and it will never close.

Hours pass without my knowledge. Kent and I go back to the waiting room to see Mary Halley, William, and his girlfriend. I'm surprised to see that Hudson's friends and some faculty and staff from Ole Miss are still there too. It's late at night, and it feels like days since I left New York, but it hasn't even been twenty-four hours. I keep my eyes on Mary Halley, trying to keep count on how many visits she makes to the bathroom and her demeanor immediately after.

I talk with Hudson's fraternity brothers, including the one who discovered Hudson in the hammock by the pool. I'd already learned from Kent that someone called an ambulance, but two fraternity brothers thought better. They carried Hudson, unconscious, laying him in the back of a pickup truck, then drove like bats out of hell to the hospital.

"Thank you," I say, looking at each of the boys.

"That's what we brothers do for one another," one says.

But his words hit me wrong. Was there pride in his voice? I belonged to the same fraternity twenty-some years ago. Cocaine showed up here and there, but I never actually saw it. Going to the hospital wasn't a thing, except for that time it snowed a few inches, a rare treat in North Mississippi, and some boys got aggressive sledding and broke bones. Hard drugs and overdosing were for the jetset, for rock stars and skinny New York models. Now your fraternity brothers will drive you to the hospital after you choke on your own vomit.

A couple of Hudson's other close friends pull me aside.

"Hey, um, Mr. Magee," says Peter. "If Hudson does wake up, he's going to need some attention. He's been on something for a while now."

"On drugs?"

"Yes."

"What kind?"

"Several kinds."

Who else knew? Why didn't they tell us? Isn't that what brothers are supposed to do, look out for one another? They knew he was struggling but merely watched? I turn to look at my family nearby, and my daughter, Mary Halley, turns away from my gaze, literally biting her lip. I recognize a theme—a code of the road among youth—to keep everything from the parents, no matter what.

The next day, back in Hudson's room, I put my arm around Kent. "Is this real?" We watch his chest get inflated. "I can't stand watching him on this machine," I say. "And I can't be the person to stop it." I want to look him in the eyes, run my hand along the back of his neck, remind him how much I love him. But I also want to punch him in the chest and yell, "This was so selfish."

The day wears on, and the waiting room gets less crowded. Students have classes, and Hudson is lying in limbo. Kent and I sit numbly, wondering if we'll get to talk to Hudson again. William moves closer to us. He still looks like he needs a doctor's care himself. He's hunched in the chair next to mine, staring at the carpet.

"I made a deal with God," he says softly.

"What?"

"I made a deal with God," he says. "I told God if Hudson lives, I'll never do drugs again."

I softly grasp William's arm. "Oh, my dear William, I'm not sure God makes deals like that. Maybe, I don't know. But we're going to hope and pray that you do walk away from drugs."

"I feel responsible," he says. "I may be responsible. For so long, we were just having fun, just brothers hanging out, having fun . . ."

I put my hand on William's knee and look into his eyes. I've got to impress upon him that he can't take on responsibility for Hudson's death; it would kill him. Before I can speak, a small miracle unfolds. In this strange suspended moment, the very familiar face of Len Teague, the boys' youth group pastor from Chattanooga, walks through the waiting room door. I almost don't grasp who he is for a moment, sur-prised at first, then not at all, to see him here. Thank God, I say to myself.

"Well, look here, William," I say. "Look who's come to pay a visit."

The three of us stand to embrace Len.

"I had to come when I heard about Hudson," Len says. "I was just wandering around my front yard, picking up sticks, thinking, how am I going to get to Oxford? That's when a friend was driving by and stopped. He asked me if everything was OK, and I told him, no, not at all. I told him what had happened, and he said he could have his plane ready in an hour. God never so literally gave me wings to fly."

I look at William, who can't stop the tears running down his cheeks.

"We are just so glad you're here, Len," Kent says.

For the next several hours, Len leads prayers in the waiting room while we all take turns visiting Hudson in his ICU room. When Len is with Hudson, I look in on them from the door, listening to Len give him news of his high school friends. He talks about what Hudson will do next once he's out of the hospital, something I can't yet comprehend. I start to lose track of how long we've been at the hospital. The waiting room crowd has dwindled. Hudson's condition isn't changing, and all I know is we don't have much more time with him.

Len announces it's time for him to go. I watch him walk down the hall to say goodbye to Hudson, and it feels like the first step toward the end we all know is coming. I move about the waiting room, restless, finally taking a seat next to Kent. Then, we hear Len's voice call out from down the hall, clear like he's singing.

"He's awake!" he cries. "Hudson is awake!"

"What?" I leap to my feet.

"Hudson is awake!"

My heart is pumping, and I believe. Len runs to tell us.

"I was saying goodbye," he said, eyes glistening behind the lens of his glasses. "I said, 'Hudson, I love you.' And Hudson raised his right hand, pointing it at me. He made two signs with his fingers—U 2—as in, 'I love you too!'"

I exhale and look to the ceiling with my arms raised, as the medical staff rushes into the ICU to attend to my son.

"Bless you," I say to Len. Kent wraps her arms around me, digging her face into my neck. I feel the vibration of her muffled cries and the flow of her tears.

"Thank God," I say, my head falling into her shoulders. It doesn't seem possible, but it's true: Hudson is alive. I'm exhilarated and exhausted and need to sit down. I walk to a vacant corner of the waiting room and ease into a chair, leaning my head back against the wall and closing my eyes. A moment passes, and there's a hand on my knee.

"Dad?" Mary Halley says.

"Yes," I say, opening my eyes.

"Do you know?" she asks.

"Do I know what, dear?"

"How did we get so broken?"

Chapter Nine

Movement

It's day three of Hudson's resurrection, and we're sitting at his bedside, celebrating. He's out of the ICU, alert, and speaking in complete sentences. He doesn't have brain damage. The doctor comes in to announce, "Your son is a miracle."

We nod, happily.

"A recovery like this rarely happens."

Another happy nod.

"If there's a next time, Hudson won't be so lucky. He'll have to change his life," the doctor says, and we nod, a little less happily. "Hudson had Xanax, marijuana, and cocaine in his system, as you know. But there's something else. The tests we've run show he's got some liver damage. To have liver damage at age twenty means he's been drinking a lot, and for a long time." The doctor turns from us to Hudson. "That has to stop now."

Kent and I exchange startled glances; we've barely seen Hudson drink. Both Hudson and the doctor register our surprise.

"I'm sorry," Hudson says. "I'm so sorry. But listen to me, OK? It should have been William, not me. William is the one in trouble."

I rub my eyes. "OK, Hudson, I hear you, but you just arrived at the emergency room dead. *Dead.* There's more to this story than William."

"I know it looks like I'm just trying to change the subject, deflect negative attention. But I'm not. William has a huge problem, much bigger than me. He needs help now, or he's going to die."

Hudson's eyes are clear, his concern genuine. We leave Hudson's hospital room and join William in the waiting room, asking him to take a break from the hospital and take a drive with us. I turn the car into a city park and pull up under the knitted shade of a stand of live oaks, their tiny leaves shuddering in the breeze. It's peaceful. Kent and I unbuckle our seat belts and turn toward William in the back seat. I reach through the space between the front seats and softly grasp his knee.

"We love you," I say. "We are here for you. Tell us where you are."

He looks down at his hands in his lap. "I guess I've been struggling with drugs."

"What does that mean? Are you addicted to anything?" I'm trying to stay calm, but my nerves rattle my voice.

"No. I'm not addicted to any one substance."

"Oh, well, that's good," I say, not hearing the truth behind the statement. I am afraid to dig too deeply. I glance at Kent for a cue. She's good at gauging these kinds of things, and she doesn't take her eyes off William.

"But I see now it's a problem," William continues. "I'm going to take care of it. Like I told you, I made that deal with God. I'm going to quit."

"It's not something you can do alone," Kent says, her voice warm but firm. "You are going to need *professional* help."

"I know," he says. "I will go. I just need to focus on my senior thesis right now. A few more weeks, that's all I've got left until graduation. I promise I'm not going to do drugs anymore."

He looks at both of us. His eyes are just as pleading as Hudson's were when he told us his brother needs help. I take a deep breath and sigh. William's on the verge of becoming an Honors College graduate.

If we take him out of school now, not only will he miss graduation with his friends, but it's possible he may never return, never finish his thesis, never graduate at all, which could set him back emotionally and make a recovery that much harder.

"They gave me extra time to finish my thesis," he says. "I'll go to treatment after I've got it done. A few more weeks isn't going to hurt."

As we've seen with Hudson, it could hurt everything, yet we want to believe our children. Kent and I agree that he can stay, merely to finish his thesis and graduate, but he has to live with her mother in her second home not far from campus. Kent returns to Chattanooga with Hudson to get him started in treatment and to manage her business and see Mary Halley through her junior year in high school, and I return to New York, keeping the click meter rolling. William and I talk daily on the phone, and it's evident after one week that he is in over his head. I urge him to visit student health services, and he agrees, but he leaves the place with a pamphlet.

Nonetheless, "I can get through this," William says. The semester ends, and he earns his bachelor's degree, following in our footsteps as a graduate of Ole Miss, but he's unable to finish the thesis. "I can't concentrate," he says. His girlfriend, Stephanie, breaks up with him, in part because we encouraged it. "He needs consequences," we say.

William sobbed, "She was the only good in my life."

I pleaded, "If you get sober, you'll likely have her and so much more that's good in your life."

A couple of weeks later, the phone rings. It's William, trying to explain something that already sounds bad because his voice has the familiar tone of a cover-up.

"I wanted ice cream, so I drove to Sonic, got a milkshake, and was driving home. I stupidly looked down at my phone, swerved off the road right near the house, and hit a telephone pole. I'm totally fine, but the car is totaled." There are few Oxford streets that I know better than that one, and I had never heard of or seen a wreck there.

"Were you on something?" I ask.

"Nope," he says. "Not at all. The police came and asked me a few questions, then they let me go," he says.

"William, tell me if this story is a little more accurate. You were at the house, watching TV or playing video games, got a craving for drugs, drove to get some, used them on the way home, got disoriented, and swerved into a telephone pole driving too fast."

"Nope," he says, though I can hear he's agitated. "Remember, the police came."

"Right. They came, asked you a few questions, and let you go."

I think, but don't say, *they didn't even know to check you*. Even high, William would have pulled it together for the officers, a clean-cut, good-looking kid, all full of "Yes, sirs." And even if they had doubts, there are no breathalyzers for opiates.

✳ ✳ ✳

I can't attend Hudson's family day for his intensive outpatient therapy because I've used my only five vacation days at the *International Business Times* during his OD. Still, Kent takes mental notes of what she terms the most excruciating and rewarding days of her life. She says Hudson talked about idolizing William and described the student alcohol and drug culture he got trapped in that began in high school, in which habitual pot smoking and alcohol bingeing were practically an expectation.

"That must have been hard to hear," I tell Kent. "I wish I was with you."

"Actually, he told a story about you," Kent says.

I brace for it, expecting the worst.

"He talked about something that happened on a beach trip. Do you remember the trip we took with my sister and her kids? Grayton Beach? When Mary Halley asked you for money so William could drive the kids to get ice cream?"

"I remember," I say. "We were standing in the dining room of that house on the lagoon."

"Yes," Kent says. "Hudson said everyone was standing around, and you took out your wallet and gave them twenty dollars, but because you'd been drinking, when you tried to put your wallet back, you missed your back pocket."

Hudson's recollection surprises me since, as I recall, Kent's brother-in-law was drinking more that day. He'd taken margaritas to the beach late in the afternoon, and I'd passed on a cup since I'm not fond of tequila and was never much for daytime drinking. For dinner, I'd had several glasses of wine, and yes, I remember missing my pocket with the wallet, and yes, the wine made me do it, but I was too busy judging her brother-in-law's tipsiness to consider my reflection. However, Hudson considered it. I embarrassed my son, and I remember how I felt when my father embarrassed me.

The good news is that Hudson is doing the hard work in thinking how drinking and drugs affect relationships. It's hard to get sober at twenty, when almost every friend you have drinks or gets high or both. Giving up substances feels like giving up friends, giving up living. Yet, he's planning for a future that will allow him fewer temptations and more resilience. He's not merely trying to resume his previous lifestyle with new habits; he's forging a new lifestyle.

Hudson has gotten a part-time job making pizzas, notifying coworkers about his situation, thus eliminating offers for after-work socialization. He's meeting weekly with Len, his former youth minister, and exploring faith on his own to find strength from a higher power. He's spending the most time with friends who are both strong in faith and willpower regarding substances. He's gotten a dog, a husky named Waker—the name refers to "someone who rouses others from sleep"—and he's rock climbing nature's most challenging walls in the Tennessee Valley.

What Hudson's not doing is attending twelve-step narcotics anonymous meetings. "They are older and different than I am, and they chain-smoke, and I can't relate," he says. We'd like him in the meetings, but he says not to worry; he's knitting together support between relationships and activities. His plan appears to be working, and he seems to have come on his own to the biggest tenets of those programs—faith in a higher power, admitting wrongness and shortcomings, a network of support, and keeping busy with work and activity. We decide to trust that Hudson, who desperately wants a new life, will find the way.

* * *

I've quit my job in New York for no good professional reason. I'd recently acquired a headhunter who's taken me to interviews for high-paying jobs at more reputable media companies, and I'm a finalist for two. Still, I miss Kent, and I miss my family. We've survived one close call, but I'm not sure we can survive another. William seems shaky, and I know he can use my support in the way I needed him on that drive to California. And if I've got any chance of winning back Kent, it likely won't happen long distance. That's why I accepted a job at the newspaper in Jackson, Mississippi, a shrinking daily that's now a shadow of its Pulitzer Prize days. The circulation isn't the only thing that's shrinking: my paycheck is 30 percent less, my responsibility is two rungs down. But I'm getting the family together at last.

I rent a house in an old neighborhood near downtown that was once genteel but now barely hangs on amid rising crime and the giant potholes. It's my third long-distance move in eighteen months, but this time, Kent joins me, leaving her successful business to an inexperienced manager because she wants to concentrate on our do-over. William is living with us, pretending to finish his thesis, but he's still struggling. He denies drug use, but we see more signs. Kent finds a pill scraper under his mattress. He leaves for a short dinner with friends and stays out all night. We leave town another night, finding vomit in the outside trash can upon return. Still, he denies it because that's the addict's default.

"Fine," Kent says, handing William a box from the drugstore. "Take this drug test, and let's see."

Result: positive for marijuana and cocaine.

We enroll William in an outpatient treatment program that conducts weekly testing of its clients, but we suspect he's duping the results, using fake urine or other tricks easily found on the internet. Several weeks later, two forged checks pass through Kent's checking account. Kent hands William another at-home test; it's also positive for marijuana and cocaine.

She's heartbroken that her son—once the sweetest, a dream child, really—would stoop to lying and stealing from his own mother.

"It hurts," she says. "It hurts."

"It's not him, dear," I say. "It's the disease."

"I know that," she says. "I just want my son back."

As William exits Ole Miss as a graduating senior, Mary Halley enters as a freshman. We're surprised because the university is small enough that most everyone knows one another, and it was just months before when Hudson's OD and William's visible decline were quite the scandal. But she grew up wearing an Ole Miss cheerleading uniform, and her boyfriend from high school enrolls there as well, which is more a coincidence than a plan, but nobody's complaining.

Mary Halley doesn't much care for alcohol. She'll hold a longneck draft beer at a fraternity party until it gets warm, but she doesn't thirst for it after she's seen the damage it can do. She's more making notes in her Bible and praying for us all than thinking about the weekend's party plan. Yet we remain observant of her for other reasons. When she's home, we notice residue in the toilet that looks like vomit, and we ask if she's OK, and she's all, "Yes, sure, I'm fine." Mary Halley has never wanted to be the family distraction, and she sees lines grooving into our faces due to concern over her brothers. She sees her mother struggling to trust in our revived relationship when painful memories surface. "I'm fine," Mary Halley says, and I close my eyes and remember how when I was growing up, and Dad and Eunice kept our family in a stir, that was my favorite line. When Coach stopped me in the halls to ask about my failing grades, that's what I told him. "I'm fine." Except I wasn't.

Parents want so much good for their children that we're practically sure we can see their rewarding future, and we'll push, consciously or subconsciously, for the path that aligns with our vision. Thus, Mary Halley goes to college without a treatment plan or support for bulimia because she convinced us everything is fine, even though I've seen the toilet. But she's my girl, and I don't want her feeling different from her friends from the start, limited, judged by those who fault her for her disease. Somehow, I think when she gets to Ole Miss, away from our problems, things will be less stressful for her. She'll be in a sorority with friends, going to parties with her boyfriend, doing as we did, and she'll thrive. It was a good story, I told myself. The real story was this: When she goes off to college, Mary Halley carries all the stress and worry of our house with her like a backpack. She avoids her sorority house because it serves three impressive meals a day, and she's petrified about overeating. When she goes to parties, she can't stand to see people cutting loose because she can't help but think of her brothers. It's worse with her boyfriend since he's in the Honors College just like William. She knows she's being irrational, so she doesn't explain her fears to anyone. But while she's smiling at these parties, the stress and anxiety build and build, bubble in her stomach, until nothing but a purge will take the pain away.

Kent tries to consult with her, knowing Mary Halley needs some friends, urging her to visit the sorority house more often for meals and peer support.

"Maybe go for breakfast to get a good start, then stop by for a salad at lunch," she suggests.

"I don't know," Mary Halley says, code for "no."

A friend in another sorority who Mary Halley has confided in invites her to hear a speaker, a young woman who graduated from Ole

Miss a decade before, talk about her eating disorder battle. McCall Dempsey is two years out of treatment after fifteen years of obsessing over numbers—her weight, the calories in a cookie, the number of miles she'd have to run after eating an Oreo. Onstage, she smashes a scale, urging the audience to do the same in a mental exercise.

"My energy was spent either counting calories or pretending everything was 'just fine.' That is not living," she says.

That night, Mary Halley calls home, asking for both Kent and me on the phone at once.

"I'm not doing well," she says, surprising us with her directness. "I need to get help before it's that much harder." I know she's talking about William, who dug such a deep hole beginning in high school that he's having difficulty getting out. "McCall said the sooner, the better, and I don't want to fight this the rest of my life."

I can see it now, how Mary Halley's struggle is as real and excruciating as William's and Hudson's. Like her brothers, she's hanging on, barely. Without help, she could lose her grip, just like that. But I'm hopeful. McCall graduated from Ole Miss eight years before Mary Halley's arrival, but she connected in a way that we haven't been able to as parents. Maybe that's the flip side of the code-of-the-road among teens, where they'll protect each other at all costs. They also can reach each other. Peer-to-peer testimony has a unique power. I can feel it working on Mary Halley, who is detailing her plan of support, which includes a counselor and nutritionist, as well as a fundamental lifestyle change: she's also stepping away from the sorority and transferring to another school.

It's a sunny Friday afternoon, and the town is buzzing, but our house is so still and quiet and dark that all we sense is tightening knots in our stomachs. Kent is holding the positive drug test high and facing William, awaiting his reply. He knows what it means, and so do we; we're just waiting for his confirmation.

"I guess I need to go to treatment," he says.

We exhale, relieved that he's stopped fighting us, at last. Kent makes some phone calls. A treatment center in the Nashville area has a thirty-day spot. We help pack his bag, assuming he'll be back before the cold starts around Thanksgiving. On the drive up, William keeps his eyes mostly closed and moves little in the back seat, and we suspect one last binge. Still, we're exhausted and can't talk about it, discussing the changing leaves along the interstate instead. We get William situated at the center and say goodbye. Then we drive home, and though we must still be tired, we don't feel like it. We talk of all the things we'll be able to do at home, now that we're not in surveillance mode.

We'll ride bikes at a state park, go for a run at the lake, visit Hudson in Chattanooga and see friends, free from the vortex of negative energy—not our son, but his disease.

"Should we feel guilty?" Kent asks. "No, absolutely not," she answers herself.

It's just the two of us at home for the first time since we were young and naïve, dreaming of our family. Kent was but a girl when we met, standing alongside the fraternity swimming pool while the speakers blasted "When Doves Cry." She was but a girl when we said our vows in her hometown church, and I clutched her smooth, trembling hand. But she's a woman now with well-earned marks from holding on so tightly, and I've never wanted her more. Our son is struggling, but it's our son, together, and we must get through this, together.

✳ ✳ ✳

I'm home early on a Thursday afternoon, the sort of fall day that's worth one hundred bad days. The temperature is cool and a light wind blows, ruffling colorful leaves. Kent has been away in Chattanooga organizing her business, not just re-stacking the jeans but cleaning the windows and pressure washing the walls, the jobs only an owner sees. She's also taking yoga teacher training classes. She knows yoga has helped her find calm in difficult days, and she's heard that it's good addiction therapy. Now she wishes to design classes for those who battle addiction, offering them yoga's slow medicine to employ alongside their other tools. That's another way our children's struggles have changed us. We're more aware of the suffering of others and more motivated to help them.

I find Kent in the kitchen, and I walk up behind her, gently wrapping my arms around her waist.

"How did teacher training go today?" I ask.

"Good," she says, leaning her head back on my chest. "Hard, but good."

"I'm proud of you, and I love you," I say.

"I love you too."

"Will you marry me?"

She turns, facing me, smiling. "What?"

"Will you marry me? Today. Right now."

She kisses my lips. "Yes," she says.

Within an hour, we're standing in front of the county courthouse holding our marriage license. It's official, we're husband and wife again, but this time, she has David 2.0, more appreciative, more self-aware, and more at peace.

"He won't let you down," I say.

"I know," she says.

We eat an early dinner at a local steakhouse, holding hands across the table; she sips a glass of wine, and I'm halfway through my second Diet Coke.

"When we get through this," Kent says, "I want you to get your career back on track and do whatever you are supposed to do. I want you to have fulfilling work."

"I want to do something that matters," I say. What, I don't know. "Just something that matters."

Downtown, the annual state fair is underway, perfect for a spontaneous honeymoon. We're walking along slowly, taking turns nibbling on a candy apple for dessert. I point to a Tilt-A-Whirl with a suggestive look.

"You know I don't like rides that make me dizzy," she says. A few steps later, she nods toward the Ferris wheel ahead, towering over the fair as if a beacon, calling for us. "Want to?" she asks.

We wait in a short line, arm in arm since the night air is cooling, and soon, we're strapped in and on our way, seated snuggly side by side. The wheel turns slowly, loading more passengers, though eventually, we're at the top. I swear I can see all the way north to Oxford, where we started together in a small apartment more than two decades before, when we were focused on nothing but our love for one another.

"The good old days," I say.

"No matter what happens," Kent says, "we can never lose that again."

"Deal," I say, squeezing her hand.

And the Ferris wheel moves, stops, moves, and stops until we're back at the bottom again. We've come full circle.

$* * *$

Two weeks later, we're in Nashville, visiting William for family day. His improvement is striking, physically at least, though his words feel like a recitation of form letters. His obligatory language suggests, "I'm doing this," and "I'm doing that," rather than delivering a heart-wrenching out-pouring that says, "I compulsively seek drugs every moment I am alone."

"How's it going?" his counselor asks us during a break, giving me a pat on the back.

"Well," I say, "you tell me."

He lifts his hands. "I'll tell you like I told William. He's got to do the hard work, or he's gonna die. That's the only way this can go. We either beat it, or we die."

I grab the chair for balance. I've seen Hudson on life support, so I understand it's about life and death, but we came here hoping William might go home the next week, after thirty days. From the way the counselor is talking, William hasn't even begun his hard work. I've been daydreaming about William opening presents with us Christmas morning and stuffing in an extra piece of cherry pie that evening at dinner, with the family laughing together, five of us. But now I'm facing reality: if William doesn't get better soon, he may die.

The treatment center recommends thirty more days at another facility, and William agrees.

"Coming home is not a good plan," he says.

Kent arranges for a center in Colorado, sending out winter clothes. The facility includes mountain biking and outdoor activities, which sounds perfect for the former athlete, who now doesn't work out or take as much as a slight jog. Maybe he will rediscover that joy again of racing his body along a path, beating his own shadow.

The Colorado treatment month seems to be going well, until we get a phone call. The boys were downtown walking around with some free time, the counselor says. William had a little money, and he went into a drugstore, bought a bottle of cough syrup, and drank it.

"What?" Kent says, incredulous. We've never heard of this. "He drank cough medicine to get high?"

"You'd be surprised what they'll do before they get better," the man says, explaining that William must find another facility because he's kicked out as of tomorrow morning.

Admissions get more complicated once a client gets kicked out of another facility. Still, Kent negotiates another thirty-day stay for William, and it goes well for a couple of weeks until William and another young man in treatment who lives in the area concoct a scheme to obtain one fentanyl pill each. The young man's friend has his wisdom teeth removed, and William remembers the card number and expiration date of his grandmother's Visa, resulting in a special delivery. When Kent gets the call, we don't quite understand because we've not heard of fentanyl, but the counselor explains that one pill made William so high, the nearby cows in a pasture likely noticed, and they're sending him packing. They'll drop him at the Salvation Army with his bag of clothes and twenty dollars, and we should leave him there, the counselor says, homeless and on his own—no more bailouts.

"Homeless?" Kent says.

"Yes, ma'am. That's what we recommend."

We know the counselor is right, but it's late December, three days before Christmas, and cold. More to the point: It's our baby. Our William. Homeless? We can't do it, instructing the center to send William to Nashville instead. We'll pick him up there from the airport and determine a plan, and by nightfall, we've got a room at a cozy Hampton Inn. An hour later, the three of us—Kent, me, and William—are eating hot, buttery rib eye steaks at a Ruth's Chris Steak House, giddy at every bite that's seasoned with laughter and catching up, all swearing it's the best dinner we've ever had. William's eyes are clear, and I can see deep into his soul, and I know our precious son is up for the fight.

"I love y'all," he says, looking us eye to eye. "Thank you for being here."

"We've never loved you so much," I say, placing a hand upon his.

"I'm ready to do this," he says.

The next four months are a gift. William graduates from residential treatment to outpatient, living in a sober house in midtown Nashville with other young men. He can't have a car, so we give him a bike for his twenty-third birthday, and he's riding it to the neighborhood grocery store, coffee shop, and gym for workouts. He also says he can bike to the nearby Apple Store, where he plans to apply for a job.

"You feel like you're ready to work?" I ask.

"For sure," he says. "I feel good, and I'll feel better to start earning my way."

He's got a plan. He'll work for a year, in which he'll continue to focus on his sobriety and study for his LSATs and save some money. Then, he wants to go to law school.

"I think the computer store will hire me," he says, noting that others in the sober living house applied but didn't get hired since they didn't graduate from college. "Some of them didn't finish high school. One lost most of his teeth because his parents let him go homeless when he turned eighteen, and he lived on the street for a couple of years."

William is correct. He gets the job, and within a month, he gets a raise and promotion as the company trainer. They pay him an hourly wage with a bonus for sales, and William calls and texts with daily updates about the money earned and the people tutored.

"I'm good at this," he says, brimming with confidence, just like when he learned to fire off the snap to hit the opponent first in football. "I think I can pay my rent, buy food, and still save ten thousand dollars to help with law school."

Self-sufficiency is among the addict's most effective tools. Still, overconfidence is dangerous, and I'm both marveling at William's progress and afraid that he's feeling so strong that his recent rock bottom will seem to have occurred in a different lifetime, to a different person.

And so, I quit my job. My son needs me. Besides, there's no compelling future for me at the Jackson newspaper, owned by a large corporation that's more into shrinkage than growth, with more layoffs every six months. I've got a book I'd researched and never finished that I can write to stay busy, so I'm back to Chattanooga with Kent. It's my fourth move in less than three years, but it's closer to William, and it's where Hudson and Mary Halley now live. They're both in school at the University of Chattanooga. Kent manages her business and training as a yoga teacher, and I'm trying to write *The Greatest Fight Ever*, a book I'd signed before the first Adderall prescription. It was a passion project that came with a small advance, spent in five trips to the grocery store, and odds are long that I'll sell enough copies to make any real money, but the hope is all I've got right now.

"How will we pay the bills?" Kent wonders, uneasy with so much pressure on her business.

"I don't know," I say, "but being near William and being together is the right thing to do, and if we're doing the right thing, we have to trust it will work out. We'll find a way."

The way includes swapping our four-bedroom home for a two-bedroom condominium near the river in downtown Chattanooga. Mary Halley lives with us. Hudson is selling craft popsicles downtown from a cart to make money, and he's purchased a starter home, paying the note with rent collected from a roommate. William visits, and he'll sit with Hudson while he sells popsicles, and we all sit for dinner together, with Lady foraging at our feet for dropped crumbs. It's the first time in too many years to count that we're together, with each one of us focused on one another without distraction, elevating the simplicity of Kent's Crock-Pot roast with carrots and potatoes by enormous proportions. There's no illusion that the future will be an easy, steady climb. I know there will be setbacks. That's why I'm visiting William every other weekend in Nashville. We take runs together through downtown, eat chicken with hot sauce, and talk like we did on the drive to California.

"You were right," William says. "Drugs aren't a toy. You can't just play with them and put them down. I went too far." I ask about Stephanie, and he says they're talking, but she's not yet ready to meet face-to-face, which frustrates him. "You got Mom back," he says.

"That's true, but not immediately. It took time."

He blows the air from his mouth, impatient.

I'm visiting William again two weeks later, early on a Saturday morning for breakfast, William's favorite. It's late April, and tender green leaves color the trees, and dogwoods are toasting us with their white cups. I'm humming a song of renewal, but William is melancholy, like winter.

"Anything wrong?" I ask.

"No," he says. "I'm just tired."

I order an omelet with bacon, tomatoes, and ham with wheat toast, and William orders a waffle covered in strawberry jelly. As he eats, it's more about the jelly with a waffle on the side. He's always had a sweet tooth, and we'd chuckle about him devouring all the filling from a doughnut, but I've not seen him spooning up jelly. Researching opioids, I've learned they can cause sugar cravings, and my worry increases throughout the meal to the point I can't eat my toast with even a little jelly.

"William," I say, looking into his eyes, "are you doing OK?"

"Yeah," he says. "I'm all right. Promise."

Driving home, he seems remorseful. "I shouldn't have done that."

"What?"

"Order a waffle with jelly. Next time, I'll get an omelet."

The next time. I take it for granted, nodding in accord. Yes, the next time.

In the afternoon, we're playful, jogging together across the Cumberland River pedestrian bridge in an exercise that's reminiscent of our offense-defense football games in the front yard so many years before when it was more about the closeness than the athletic result. Resting on a bench afterward, William is contemplative as we catch our breath.

"I'm figuring out how to help myself," he says, "and then I'd like to help other people one day. But I'm not there yet."

"One day," I say.

On Sunday morning, I leave William and drive back home, thinking of the next time I'll see him and what I'll say. But it was a fool who left William there because the next time became the following week when he didn't answer his messages, and he didn't show up for work, and I learned our precious, tenderhearted boy was gone.

* * *

I'm in the parking lot, outside the McCallie School chapel, watching the crowd file in. There are high school classmates, teachers, coaches, family, friends of the family. Even at a distance, I can see the most profound sorrow on everyone's face for the loss of our child, the loss of a young man with so much potential. And I can see in everyone's face the pity they feel for our family. How could we possibly survive this?

Uncharacteristically, I'm not speaking at the service because Len, the preacher, tells me Hudson has notes prepared for the eulogy just in case he's needed.

"Really?" I asked.

"Yes," Len said. "He says he can do it."

"Well, I have no doubt."

When the boys were students at McCallie, we urged them to sign up for the chapel talks seniors give, but they both declined due to shyness and anxiety, characteristics that fueled substance use disorder. That's why I'm moved to tears when our twenty-one-year-old son steps onto the stage before this packed chapel of friends, teachers, relatives, and strangers.

I'm in the front row, holding Kent's hand, mourning the son I've lost while beaming with pride for the one who's becoming a man before our eyes. There's a second in which he stands and looks at us, his cheeks slightly flushed, wearing his navy suit. Then he clears his throat and begins.

"William and I grew up side by side, and for two brothers so close in age, we got along very well. When we were younger, friends would talk about how much they argued and fought with their siblings, but with William and me, that was not the case. We rarely fought. The one fight I can remember is after William and I were little, and we had gotten our prized possessions for Christmas: remote control cars. After William and a friend broke mine, I retaliated and broke his. To this day, it's the maddest he ever got at me. William gave me a look that let me know it was time to run, and I ran as fast as I could. You know how fast William was, so imagine my terror to see him inching ever closer as I whipped around the house, until Mom and Dad stopped him and I lived another day."

Hudson is in beautiful control, his voice calm and calming. He recalls for the audience our days of playing offense-defense touch football, including William's famous cookie cutter and Hudson's desire to emulate it. It is sweet that those days mean as much to Hudson as they have to me; he even recalls the feeling of my prickly facial hair close against his face, whispering the play so William couldn't hear.

Hudson talks about emulating William in their youth, yet he doesn't blame William for his addiction problems, but he does address what happened.

"Last year on March 28th, William watched me suffer an accident that doctors told him had taken my life. William watched alone as the doctors pounded on my chest, attempting to bring me back. I miraculously woke up after doctors said I was not going to make it. William later revealed that while witnessing this, he made a deal with God; he offered his life in sobriety and devotion to God if he would let me live, and I firmly believe that William saved my life that day."

Hudson shares that in their last text message exchange, William told Hudson how proud he was of everything Hudson had overcome; he was proud of Hudson for his sobriety.

"My daily prayer for William over the last few months," Hudson concluded, "has been that the Lord fills him with his love, fills him so much that he radiates with it. I prayed this every day with the hope of changing William's life, freeing him from the disease, and that he could help change and heal others around him. My brother is gone, but I believe his life and his story will endure and make a difference. Let us mourn in our great loss but also celebrate the healing to come."

* * *

Keep moving. That's what we've got to do, Kent says. It's the day after the funeral, and she's made a pot of coffee and pours me a to-go cup while I'm still wondering if I have the strength to get out of bed. I was asleep when she called me from the kitchen to get up, out of bed, for a walk with her and Lady across the Walnut Street Bridge. It's still dark outside, but Lady has to go outside now, she says.

"Do you want her to go on the floor?"

"Of course not," I say.

I reluctantly get dressed in shorts and a T-shirt with tennis shoes, grab the coffee, and Kent leashes up Lady, our thirty-two-pound, tri-color Cavalier King Charles Spaniel. We like to say she's got big bones, but the vet says Lady needs to lose weight. Her breed averages half that weight, but we've been so busy and distracted by our problems that we've allowed too much food in the bowl, maybe giving her one too many treats just to see her tail wag joyfully as she scarfed it down. So, we must walk her each morning. At a half-mile, the Walnut Street Bridge is one of America's longest walking bridges, a former car path converted to pedestrians only. It spans the Tennessee River, and it's near the entrance to our condo.

It's early in May and chilly out before the sun has risen. Lady leads the way along the lighted bridge, lunging ahead, trying to catch pigeons, and we walk in silence, admiring her efforts and sipping the jostling coffee. We look down at the flowing river gently moving underneath. It's dawn, and the hints of first light accent the ripples. Kent's fixated on the water, watching its passage, followed by more on the way, and when I look at her face, I see tears streaming from her eyes, flowing so abundantly her hand remains spread across her cheekbones to collect them. We make a turn at the end, repeating our journey back across the bridge, and now, the sun shows a bit of itself splendidly, like a radiant child who's peeking around a corner.

"Look at that," I say, pointing to the eastern sky.

Kent wipes her nose and looks at me.

"Darkness into the light," she says softly.

Keep moving. That's what I've got to do. Staring at a computer to write a book about an event that's more than a century old won't work. I don't have the heart for it, and it makes no sense to dedicate myself to a passion project I feel no passion for. Which means one thing: moving, again. I've been offered a job in Birmingham, two hours away. It's now the sixth time I've changed zip codes in less than three years, but it's a growth opportunity at a media company. Kent will stay in Chattanooga, run her business and teach yoga, and visit Hudson and Mary Halley nearby. We'll take turns traveling on weekends. It's not ideal. But grieving on the job is better than idly mourning into a professional crisis. And I'm following Mom's advice, earning my way.

As she did that first morning after William's funeral, Kent leashes up Lady every morning, walking her across the Walnut Street Bridge and back, beginning in darkness and ending in light, wiping away tears. We do that now: We walk and we cry. We don't even stop walking to cry. Sometimes, Mary Halley joins Kent and Lady. But each morning, Kent and Lady walk, through a summer downpour, fall's first frost, eight inches of snow with flakes the size of a child's hand, spring pollen that goldens the girders. Lady, initially a misfit because we were so lost trying to find ourselves that we could barely look after her, is done chewing up the house. She's gotten her figure and spry prance back, fulfilling the companionship role for which we got her when William left for college. Some days are harder to walk than others, but we have each other, and we have faith, which helps.

Mary Halley is a counselor at Camp Desoto, the same camp she attended for a month each summer in her girlhood. She's anxious the first week, feeling awkward in a different role. She calls home on a break, and I can tell that what she's crying about is not what she says she's crying about. Our huge loss makes us vulnerable to little losses, makes us feel them more sharply. I know her stress is dangerous since it's a major trigger for an eating disorder.

"I'm sorry, dear," I say. "But you've got the tools to manage this. You can get through it."

"I know," she says.

Two weeks later, a letter arrives from Mary Halley, the first time we've heard from her since that phone call. We read with smiles, savoring details, about how early in her second week, Mary Halley encountered a timid third-grade camper in the dining hall. Kitty looked around at the crowded, raucous tables with fear in her big blue eyes when Mary Halley invited her to sit. It turned out that Kitty's older sisters usually helped her make meal choices or served her portions, but they were seated at other camp tables. So, Mary Halley filled that role, and they continued to share meals, and gradually, they both felt a little better, a little bit braver. Their friendship, Mary Halley writes, is one of the highlights of her summer.

Hudson, counting sobriety in years, had lost his girlfriend, Lo, at his lowest, when she couldn't bear to see him hurting himself. Now, healed and healing, she's returned, and they marry alongside the Tennessee River on a chilly spring day. Stephanie, William's former girlfriend who's become a family friend, is a bridesmaid. A few months later, we are all together again in Hudson's front yard, planting a ginkgo biloba we anoint as William's tree. We remember his laughter, love for family, friends, and different cultures, and we give thanks for our miracle survivor, Hudson, who's become my role model and closest friend. If at the same social event, it's his company I seek. If heading out to the golf course, he's the partner I want on the back nine. And in him, I can hear a hint of William's voice and see a glint of William's eyes, easing my fear that time will erode the memory of my firstborn.

I immerse myself in work, determined to get my career back on track. The company wants one billion page views on its website? Done. The company needs to nudge its one-hundred-plus journalists away from a print mentality to a digital one? Done. The biggest challenge is I want more—more responsibility, more of a chance to make a real difference. It's like I've woken after a long slumber, full of energy, burning with the desire to be useful, to do something for others. I'm aware of time passing. None of us lives forever. And I can't quit thinking about my last conversation with William.

"I want to help others one day," he said.

"We will," I assured him, but now I wonder. Will "one day" ever come? We've purchased a 1928 home in an old Birmingham neighborhood,

Kent has sold her business, and we're living together full-time again. Mary Halley enrolls in nursing school at Samford University, living in an apartment five blocks over, and two or three nights a week, we're eating dinner together. The joy has returned incrementally, like a steady, approaching drumbeat that has found us. Kent says if we could freeze the moment, she would.

* * *

Blood drips from my right nipple. I'm sitting on the edge of my bed, and I grab my white T-shirt to blot my chest.

"I could nurse a baby vampire," I tell Kent.

She's not amused. "This is serious," she says.

I pull the shirt away and study the flower of blood blooming there. My nipple continues to drip.

It's the second time it's happened. The previous month, I'd convinced myself I bumped into a wall getting dressed, but this time, I know I hadn't bumped into anything. I feel around my breast, and my fingertips suss out a lump, hard, like a marble. I look up at Kent's worried eyes.

"Here, feel this," I say, and she does. "Do men get breast cancer?"

A doctor performs a biopsy, and when he shares the results, he takes words right from Kent's mouth.

"This is serious," he says. A flurry of appointments is scheduled, a bouquet of brochures handed to me.

Yet, on the drive home, Kent notices I'm calm. "Aren't you afraid?"

"I'm not afraid of dying," I explain. "I'm afraid of dying before the work is done."

The surgeon removes my right breast with an incision stretching from my breastbone to under my arm. "Looks like we got good margins," he says. "You've got a 95 percent chance of survival." An oncologist echoes the sentiment, though he's obligated to prescribe preventive aftercare. It would ensure I'm not part of that unlucky 5 percent, but it would rob my energy and motivation for years to come.

For the first time since diagnosis, my anxiety pulsates.

"I can't do it. I can't take that risk."

"This is standard care," he says.

"But I've got work to do," I say, smiling. "I wasted too much time already, and I need all the energy I've got. A 95 percent chance of survival?" I shrug. "I'll take it."

"Well," the oncologist says, pushing his glasses from his nose to his hair and maybe really looking at me for the first time, "I guess I can understand that. Go and have a good life. I don't expect we'll see you back here."

And they don't.

✳ ✳ ✳

Six months later, the phone rings. I don't answer. Someone leaves a message. I stay in my chair, listening. The caller offers me a job in Oxford, and not a very good one: the publisher position of the small daily newspaper where I first worked in college. It's got sixteen employees, five thousand print subscribers, and a smaller digital audience than many personal blogs.

Although we've only been married two years (the second time), Kent knows me well enough to yell from the kitchen, "Don't even think about it."

But I am thinking about it. Sure, the job will end my advancing media career, but it feels right. To be back in the place where it all started—where I started, where Hudson arrived at the hospital not breathing, where William descended into a pit he couldn't escape. Has the time come? Is this the path?

"I think we're supposed to go home," I say to Kent later. "This is where we'll do our work."

Her dismay is logical. She doesn't want to leave Mary Halley and doesn't want me to quit a good job. She's also concerned I'm chasing a dream without a plan, reminiscent of David 1.0.

"What does that mean, 'we'll do our work'?" Kent says. "What work? We want to help others, but we don't yet know what that means."

"We'll figure it out once we get there," I say, and she turns away. "It's meant to be."

I leave for the office, and the subject doesn't come up that night over dinner, but the next morning over coffee, Kent wants to talk.

"It doesn't make sense," she says, fiddling with the handle of her mug, "this move. You've worked hard to get your career back. But"—she blows the air from her mouth—"if this is where you feel compelled to be, we need to go."

Two months later, we're sitting on the couch in our living room, blocks away from the town square and university campus that was my playground as a child. It's a quiet Sunday morning, weeks before the community overflows with visitors for the first football game, but more than twenty thousand students have arrived for the start of a new semester, and classes begin on Monday. Kent's reading over the newspaper column I've just drafted, which is why I'm pacing, waiting for her opinion. Part of me wants her to say, "No, tear it, burn it, delete it, but don't publish this."

In the column, I write to Ole Miss freshmen. I tell them about William. I tell them our hard truths: "I warned William that drug dealers can't be trusted, that drug dealers know tricks, like mixing heroin with cocaine to make it doubly addictive before a user knows what hit them. And it is easier to succumb when the dealer is a fraternity brother or the guy down the hall at the dorm who looks a lot like you."

I watch Kent read and flip the page to keep reading. It's been three-and-a-half years since William died. It would be possible to move back to this town and not talk about William, not relive the painful memories. Sure, everyone would know anyway, but they'd whisper about it and not feel free to discuss it openly, having read my writing about it. But talking about William truthfully is the beginning of reaching others.

"We don't want other students to suffer as he did, or other families to suffer as we have," I write. "That's why I wish I could reach out and touch every freshman to tell them William's story, to say to them that alcohol and drug bingeing and abuse aren't a collegiate rite of passage or a contextual excuse. It can be a dangerous, if not a deadly, path that is hard to escape."

Kent looks up from reading the draft. "Do it," she says and puts the paper down to squeeze my hands.

I go back to the computer, my finger hesitating over the "publish" button, then I hit it. I dig the heel of my hands into my eyes and wait. I close my eyes, trying to draw a breath down to the bottom of my lungs. I exhale slowly and open my eyes, and the meter counting online reads spins like I've won the giant jackpot; it's number 479, number 775.

"Kent?" I call her. By the time she walks around to face my computer, 1,500 people have read it. No, 1,833; 5,087; 9,931. My phone buzzes. My phone rings. My email chirps. She swivels her gaze to mine, and by the time we look back at the screen, ten thousand people are reading my column at that very moment. By the time it's been online for thirty minutes, one hundred thousand people have read it. It's been shared and forwarded everywhere; it's gone viral, as they say, and our quiet Sunday morning becomes dizzying, with calls and emails and messages from students and parents and strangers from the Carolinas to California and everywhere in between.

By the end of the day, more than one million people have read the column. And even more remarkable is the local response. Suddenly, there's a movement among Ole Miss students and staff, pledging to help raise awareness about substance use on campus and provide support and education for those who need it. The caring vibration is powerful, like a rumbling train loaded with supplies required. Before my eyes, the university and its community are coming together for the cause, and I've never been so proud because it's my university and my community; it's home.

I'm back on the couch in the living room, energized by the possibility and joyously exhausted from the day. I lean back and close my eyes, go to that place that's like dreaming, but it's remembering. This is where I go: New Mexico, with my son. It is night. It is cold, the coldest that place has ever seen. Our arms are linked, and we're shivering in the darkness. We lean our heads back, look up at the stars, and I've never seen so many, and they've never shined so bright. I cup my hands around my mouth and shout into the night, "Thank you, Lord."

"Wooooooooo," William shouts. "Thank you, Lord."

✳ *Chapter Ten* ✳

Revelation

I straighten and look in the mirror, wiping my mouth with the hand towel. A small glass vial pinched between Kent's finger and thumb wags in front of my face.

"Spit," she says.

There's no need for a DNA test, I'm thinking. I know the man looking back at me inside and out, where he's been and where he's going, and that's enough.

"Do it," she says. "Spit."

"I'm so happy. Every day is a good day, even if it's a not-so-good day. I don't need more."

We live near the old house where I grew up. Now, when I pass it, I see a beautiful home with manicured shrubs, accented shutters, and an inviting, wraparound porch. Nothing more. No house of horrors. It's good to be unburdened by the pain and resentment I was clinging to. I can simply feel appreciative of the people that gave me a home.

Mom died earlier this year, and it was time. I didn't see her much for the last eight years because she lived with Eunice. Mom believed her destiny as a mother was to allow Eunice to care for her in the end, and she was probably right; it was good for both of them. But every so often, when Eunice was out, Mom would call me.

"David," she'd forcefully say during those rare conversations, "I love you." And that was enough, for I loved her too.

My family is growing, extending its branches. Hudson and Lo have moved to Oxford. They're our neighbors now and have given us almost unbearable joy through their child, a boy named William Wilder. When I watch him, I see Hudson at that age, the eyes and agility. When I hold him, I feel William, my tenderhearted firstborn. Yes, I am a grandfather now. I, who felt impoverished, am now rich with family.

Mary Halley worked for a summer at Alpine, the boys camp where William and Hudson used to go, as a nanny to Mr. O's grandchildren. There, she met Luke, a head counselor, and soon they were both smitten but hesitant to be the focus of camp gossip. So they wrote letters back and forth across the camp, hoping to keep their growing relationship a secret. But Mr. O, the camp's founder, still observant as ever, picked up on some clue, and in the middle of dinner in the mess hall, said, "Mary Halley? Are you and my head counselor an item?" She got over her blush in time to marry Luke at our church in Oxford two-and-a-half years later. Among the guests was Tim Lindsey, a camp doctor at Alpine.

When Mary Halley was dreadfully sick with a virus, feverish and vomiting, Dr. Lindsey had gently held back her hair as she hugged a toilet. Mary Halley realized that his daughter is Kitty, the young lady she'd befriended at mealtime at neighboring Camp Desoto that summer, and because she was so attached to both father and daughter, she invited them to the wedding. We marveled that January Saturday when Dr. Tim Lindsey and his wife showed up from five hours away in Louisiana, with all six of their children. What sweet people my daughter had managed to find in her life.

Kent, losing her patience, is now butting my lip with the small vile. "Just do it!"

When I began my search for birth parents nearly three decades before, there was no such thing as DNA testing or websites like ancestry. com. There wasn't even the internet in the mainstream. It took me years to find Janie. And I wasn't searching for my birth father; she'd made it clear that she'd never tell me about him, saying that it was not her place.

"We were young," she said, "just having fun. And it happened. They told me to forget about it, which was very painful, but look at you and your family. A happy result." I want to leave it at that, but here's Kent with this vial.

"Spit into this, please," she says. "You'll be glad."

I fill the vial with spit, and she mails it away, and that's that, until three months later when the results are in. I log into ancestry.com, finding useful information, like my descent is 40 percent from Scotland, but nothing definitive. That's the thing about DNA sites: revelations come from matches, but matches come only once another biological family member has submitted their vial. I see third cousins and fourth cousins in my tree, providing hints, but further digging produces nothing identifiable.

A year passes. It's early May, the sixth anniversary of William's death. Hudson and Lo are over for dinner, and I'm telling Lo the story of finding Janie, which she's never heard in full.

"It's so interesting," she says. "Don't you want to know about your father?"

I shake my head. "At this point, I think I'm good."

Kent's in the kitchen, cooking and listening. She rounds the corner holding her laptop.

"Here," she says. "It's all right here if you can get him to log in." I roll my eyes and follow the prompt. My ancestry DNA report opens, but it looks different. There's someone new in my tree. No picture, just a name, but we share enough DNA to qualify as siblings.

"Ruthie Lindsey," Kent says.

"Ruthie Lindsey!" Lo shouts. "What?"

I don't understand.

"Ruthie Lindsey?" Lo says. "You know who that is, right? I follow her on Instagram. She's known for overcoming debilitating pain and addiction to painkillers left from a horrible accident."

"No, I don't."

"Well," she says, "you know who her brother is, all right! Remember that friendly Dr. Tim Lindsey who works at Alpine Camp who came to Mary Halley's wedding with his wife and six children? That's her brother."

"You're suggesting my brother was at my daughter's wedding, but we didn't know he was my brother?"

I laugh at the foolishness.

"Listen," I explain. "There's bound to be a lot of Ruthie Lindseys in the world. I doubt that one's my sister. Let's not jump to conclusions."

Kent, meanwhile, has pulled up Ruthie's website. "She's from Louisiana!"

"OK, but we still don't know for certain."

"Wait, look," Kent says. "Here's a video that shows a picture of her father. Take a look at that, David. Can't you see it? The face, the shoulders. It's your father."

I message Janie, even though my question might make her angry. "Did you know Lloyd Lindsey?"

"Yes," she texts back. "Yes, I did."

My mind is spinning, trying to make sense of it all. It means that, yes, my half-brother Tim came to my daughter's wedding with his wife and six children, but we didn't know he was my brother. It means that Kitty, his daughter, is my niece—the young camper Mary Halley wrote letters home about that summer, but we had no idea.

It means my life began at a whiskey-fueled college party in 1965. Location: the Sigma Alpha Epsilon house on the Louisiana State University campus in Baton Rouge. SAE had a reputation for the rowdiest parties on campus, with alcohol and loud music flowing, and Lloyd

Lindsey, my birth father, was a sophomore standing six-foot-four, full of hops and charisma. He liked holding court at parties—fraternity brothers called him "the Senator"—telling stories to a group, getting a laugh.

Janie was a petite, button-nosed high school senior with a blonde flip hairstyle and a bubbly personality, on a spring weekend visit to LSU. The first in her family to seriously consider college, she didn't know if her parents would agree to LSU, but she was eager to check it out. She'd been invited to a party at the SAE house on a blind date with Lindsey. She was staying in the girls' dorm with a sophomore from Monroe, her hometown. The weather was unexpectedly cold, and she didn't have a coat, but the girl in the dorm loaned her one. It was long, flaring at the bottom, and made of white nubby material.

"It was so beautiful," she says.

Although I now know my father's identity, I was not able to meet him because he died in 2009 after a fall. Janie had not told Lloyd she was pregnant. Several months after that spring party, her mother noticed the pregnancy, taking her to the family doctor in Monroe who recommended Sellers, the home for unwed mothers in New Orleans. There were rumors, of course, but in those days, a girl could disappear beneath the chatter, reemerging with a new story; it never happened.

Lloyd was the superintendent of West Feliciana Parish Schools in St. Francisville, Louisiana, when he died. His family and friends say we had a lot in common, including mannerisms like holding court with storytelling and coaching acquaintances who may be struggling with self-improvement tips.

"You are your father's son," says Marsha, Lloyd's widow and the mother of Lile, Tim, and Ruthie, my half-brothers and sister. Marsha welcomed me as her own, consistently sharing, "He would have loved you so." Lloyd's father, my grandfather, was a superintendent himself. Known in college by the nickname "Shongaloo," he was the standout basketball player at LSU on the Tigers' only national championship team of 1935. My aunt, Nancy, Lloyd's sister, hands me a picture of my grandfather wearing his LSU uniform.

Lloyd's friends from college called to share stories, explaining how he was the life of the party until Vietnam. No one really knows what happened to him over there. They know only that he was an officer in the Marines, on the front lines. And they know he got interested in Vietnamese culture, took the time to study, for example, how they farmed with a mule and plow. Back home, he simply never talked about the war. But his sister, my aunt, Nancy, shared with me something that gave her insight into his war years.

In the early 1970s, she and her brother were in a New Orleans bar when a man walked up to order a drink. The man turned his head, saw Lloyd, and began to hyperventilate, a full-blown panic attack. Lloyd gave the man a bear hug and pulled him off to the side to talk. Later, Aunt Nancy says the man apologized for his strange behavior, explaining that Lloyd Lindsey saved his life in Vietnam. He'd suffered a chest wound, and Lloyd, his officer, charged into gunfire, scooping the man into his arms and whisking him to a nearby helicopter for medical evacuation.

A decade after Lloyd's death, I'm standing in his house, now owned by his son Tim, my half-brother. My brother Lile is there, along with Ruthie, my sister, and nieces and nephews who dote on me and I adore in return as if we've known one another for a lifetime. Hudson and Lo have come with William Wilder, and Mary Halley is here for the party too. I'm standing by Hudson in the center of the room, which is bustling like it's Christmas morning, though it's a midsummer's eve. I reach my glass, filled with Diet Coke, toward Hudson's, filled with water.

"Here's to family," I say, and he dings his glass with mine, delivering a broad smile at the abundance.

Three months later, I'm standing on a stage on the Ole Miss campus wearing a blue suit and a red tie. We're opening the William Magee Center for Wellness Education, dedicated to providing alcohol and other drugs (AOD) support for students. William wanted to help people, and now through this center, he will. Looking into the audience, I see brothers and sisters from both sides of my biological family who've come together in a show of support, including my brother Jimmy, in his thirteenth year of sobriety. Kent smiles at me, sitting in the front row with my children and grandchildren.

All I can think about is, what if?

What if, when William wanted to ride to California with me and I was uncomfortable, I had said, "No, don't come"? What if I had taken one more Vyvanse pill instead of flushing them down the toilet? What if, when it got so bad, I had given up completely? What if Kent had not taken me back? What if I was not adopted into a college town? What if I had not forgiven everything and everyone, especially myself? What if? Life for me had not genuinely begun until it nearly ended. That's why we can't give up. That's why resilience is the salvaged soul's most generous friend. That's why I'm standing on a stage at the podium, surrounded by friends and family, dedicating a university center named for my late son that has the chance to save other people's lives.

"Three summers ago, my wife, Kent, and I were walking around town and through the campus, wondering if a center on campus named after our late son is meant to be," I explain to the audience. "We're wondering if we have the strength and courage to pull it off.

"In town, she found a quarter and picked it up, carrying it along clutched in her hand. Once on campus, we stopped outside the chapel, where we sat and quietly talked over some of the difficulties we'd have to face. We then saw the fountain in the nearby quadrangle and walked over.

"Kent looked at her hand and closed her eyes. 'If it's meant to be,' she said, tossing the quarter into the fountain. Precisely when it hit the water, bells from the chapel rang out in cascading symphony. We looked at each other, both of us with chill bumps and tears, and we knew. We walked back home, hand in hand, and the next day, we began our work."

Author's Note

My son encouraged me to write this book about our family's greatest fight before he died of an accidental drug overdose because he wanted to help others one day. I wish he could see how far we've come in that effort since that "one day" has arrived. The center his name represents has already changed, if not saved, lives on the Ole Miss campus, and the work has only begun; there's now development of an institute underway to help students beyond campus.

That's because few American problems are more prominent than substance misuse, which touches every family and every demographic, inflicting emotional distress, education and job disruptions, and suffering, including economic hardship and legal problems. No one place or segment owns this problem; everyone does. However, with a core mission of changing and improving lives through education, research, and support related to alcohol and other drugs (AOD), we're building **the William Magee Institute for Student Wellbeing** at the University of Mississippi to do something about it.

Overseeing a collaborative approach to student well-being on campus while seeking to provide national leadership to understand and mitigate the effects of AOD use, the William Magee Institute includes the William Magee Center and other centers on the campus dedicated to changing, and even saving, lives. The institute aims to give students and families their best chance for success, both on campus and far and wide.

I'm donating a portion of the author's profit from sales of this memoir to the William Magee Institute for Student Wellbeing. Therefore, by reading and recommending the book to others, you have helped this cause—thank you! If you'd like to make an additional donation, please visit magee.olemiss.edu or send a check to The William Magee Institute, 406 University Ave., Oxford, MS 38655.

Acknowledgments

Behind this book is a story involving people who believe we can and should do more to help others with addiction and substance misuse and who believe in me, providing valuable care and guidance to bring it to fruition.

There's Beth Ann Fennelly, the author, professor, and poet laureate of Mississippi (bethannfennelly.com), who edited the manuscript and provided valuable counsel, prompting for more detail while reminding me chapter after chapter of the story's importance. Beth Ann was my dream editor because she's one of the world's best writers, with a rare knack for wordplay. She also has a passion for understanding how "literature helps people think more clearly and prepares them to live their most fulfilling lives spiritually, intellectually, and creatively."

Beth Ann is so busy as a mother, professor, and a writer of renown, with multiple award-winning works published by W.W. Norton, including *Great with Child: Letters to a Young Mother* and *Heating and Cooling: 52 Micro-Memoirs*, she usually wouldn't have time for another's project. But my approach coincided with a pandemic calendar of cancellation and her passion for the cause. It's not a coincidence, either, that Beth Ann's husband, the author Tom Franklin (*Crooked Letter, Crooked Letter; Hell at the Breech*; and more), another of the best writers I know, encouraged me to take up writing again.

I was emceeing a book launch event in Alabama for Harper Lee's *Go Set a Watchman,* and Beth Ann and Tom were on a panel along with Books-A-Million CEO Terry Finley. We'd been friends for many years, but considerable time had passed since our last acquaintance, and Tom asked as we visited after the event why I had quit writing; *The Education of Mr. Mayfield* was my most recent book, published in 2009.

"I realized I'm not good enough," I said. "I can write a book, but I'm not sure I'm a real writer."

"You are a real writer, David," Tom said. "You have to keep writing and working at it. It isn't easy for any of us."

It was the way he said "us," and the way he complimented me, invoking his late best friend, the talented writer William Gay, who also became a friend of mine. I'd met William, the novelist from Hohenwald, Tennessee, at a writer's conference, which led to other meetings. His writing and storytelling captivated me, and I was honored that when we sat and talked, he asked me questions about my life and story.

"William really liked you," Tom said, and I remembered that William once suggested I write stories about growing up in small-town Oxford.

After Tom's encouragement, I decided to write again once I had something useful to say. Four years later, I began working on this book, finishing it with Beth Ann's guidance. To them both, I offer the sincerest thank-you, from my heart and from the hearts of any individuals and families this book may reach and help.

There's also Matt Holt, publisher of Matt Holt Books at BenBella. When he decided to acquire this book, I knew in that moment it was right. That's because Matt is a part of this larger story. Our relationship began in 2002 when I signed the book *Ford Tough: Bill Ford and the Battle to Rebuild America's Automaker* with Wiley. Matt was the editor who acquired the book, and he worked to get me a substantial advance and needed support for success. He also acquired my next book, *The John Deere Way*, and while the book was OK and served an audience, I wrote it in a year in which alcohol distracted me from complete focus, and it should have been much better.

However, we developed a friendship that remained over the years, sharing a bond forged in the New York blackout of 2003. It was mid-August, and the city of concrete characteristically baked in the late summer sun. I had a lunch date with Matt in Hoboken, New Jersey, to talk about the Ford book's forthcoming publication, but I was more than an hour late, moving slowly after too many drinks the night before. He waited patiently, and eventually, we dined on memorable Cuban fare, including rice, beans, and plantains. The workday was over by the time we finished, so we got on a subway that ran for two minutes before it stopped when the power went out. The doors opened, and we could see the power was out everywhere. We hailed a taxi and got in, but it never moved, as traffic logjammed.

I needed to reach a Manhattan hotel, and he needed to get to his Brooklyn apartment, and walking was our only option. He went with me into the Financial District, which had an apocalyptic feel with so many sweaty nomads moving along, until we had to go separate ways. I arrived at my boutique hotel an hour and a half later, taking a seat at the hotel bar where I drank wine with an eclectic mix of guests in candlelight until it was gone—every single bottle. Matt messaged me the next day, and I read with a dry mouth and aching head how it took him four hours to walk home, and I wished that my hotel could have been four hours away so I could have kept walking and moving instead of sitting and drowning.

We never did another book together, but we maintained contact. I was not surprised by Matt's professional ascension to senior vice president and executive editor at Wiley, and proud to see him get his imprint at BenBella. I had been working on this manuscript for more than a year when I saw that news, having started over completely multiple times in fits of revision by an implosion, and I wondered if we might one day work together again.

My agent, Esmond Harmsworth at Aevitas Creative Management, made it happen. Esmond believed that a book based upon a story that became a grassroots movement to build a university institute to help others with substance misuse might match well with a publisher known for its grassroots distribution. I knew instantly that the fit was right, a subtext to this larger story of relationships and second chances. Matt still believed in me, and I wanted to show him the kind of focused work a clear mind can deliver.

As for Esmond, he, too, stuck with me despite the hard years, even though I quit writing altogether for a decade. I'd helped craft a winning proposal for a client of his in 2006, and he'd become my agent; he represented me on *Playing to Win: Jerry Jones and the Dallas Cowboys* (Triumph). We'd never done anything substantial together, yet Esmond maintained contact and was immediately responsive when I began to think through this memoir concept in 2019. I didn't quite have it framed, and I was initially so close to it that I lacked the needed context and detail to tell the story appropriately. However, he kept listening and offering feedback. Eventually, I began to see from the guidance that I must reach deep into my gut and memory to have any chance of telling a story about addiction and family, love and loss, failure and redemption, and finding purpose, that others are willing to read.

Books have a unique role in our culture of learning and self-exploration, and it's meaningful to me to have partners who care about that very thing. To both Esmond and Matt, thank you for believing in me and believing in my story. I won't let you down.

I should also mention Margaret Riley King, a renowned literary agent who was not involved in this book via representation, yet she as a friend provided valuable help early in the process. A powerhouse known for her work with Glennon Doyle and notable authors, she took a look when I was stuck, unsure of the shaping, offering direct and honest insight that helped me forge a new and better path. As my sister Ruthie Lindsey says, Margaret Riley King is a boss, and that's so very true. She's also one of the brightest, most caring humans one can meet. Thank you, MRK.

Others who have played vital roles in this book are Katie Dickman, senior editor at Matt Holt Books/BenBella who read the proposal for this project in one sitting and never took her eyes from it, carefully shepherding it with loving care; and Brigid Pearson, designer at Ben-Bella. Additionally, I am thankful to Annie Brunholzl, a writer and editor who helped shape the proposal, stepping in when I was too close to the project to frame and organize the story.

I'm also thankful for Dr. Brandi Hephner LaBanc, the vice chancellor for student affairs and campus life at UMass Amherst. She shepherded the William Magee Center for Wellness Education's initial vision when she was at the University of Mississippi and encouraged me to expand upon my storytelling.

Many at the University of Mississippi have played an essential role in the Magee Center, which serves students on campus, and the Magee Institute, with a mission beyond campus, and they have made all the difference. They include Noel Wilkin, Alice Clark, Charlotte Parks, Brett Barefoot, Natasha Jeter, and Erin Cromeans.

A very special thank-you goes to members of the Triplett family, who love this cause and helping others so very much. Without them, we couldn't have achieved opening the center and building the institute, and I will be forever grateful. They include Diane Triplett Holloway, Suzy Triplett Fuller, Liz Triplett Walker, Lou Ann Triplett Woidtke, and Chip Triplett.

Finally, I am thankful for my wife, Kent, for courageously supporting this book's publication. Living it was excruciating, and reliving it was not easy. Yet, because there is a potential benefit to helping others, she encouraged me to go deeper, regardless of complicated or embarrassing details, which is the result.

About the Author

Author photograph by Lo Magee

David Magee is the author of award-winning books including *How Toyota Became #1* and *The Education of Mr. Mayfield*, and an inspirational TEDx speaker on addiction, recovery, and family. He helped create the William Magee Institute for Student Wellbeing at the University of Mississippi, named after his late son, and serves as the Director of Institute Advancement at the university. Learn more at daviddmagee.com.